Rain of Fire

Air War, 1969-1973

The Vietnam Experience

Rain of Fire

Air War, 1969-1973

by John Morrocco
and the editors of Boston Publishing Company

Boston Publishing Company/Boston, MA

Boston Publishing Company

President and Publisher: Robert J. George
Vice President: Richard S. Perkins, Jr.
Editor-in-Chief: Robert Manning
Managing Editor: Paul Dreyfus

Senior Writers:
Clark Dougan, Edward Doyle, David Fulghum, Samuel Lipsman, Terrence Maitland, Stephen Weiss
Senior Picture Editor: Julene Fischer

Researchers:
Jonathan Elwitt, Sandra W. Jacobs, Michael Ludwig, Anthony Maybury-Lewis, Carole Rulnick, Nicole van Ackere, Robert Yarbrough

Picture Editors:
Wendy Johnson, Lanng Tamura
Assistant Picture Editor: Kathleen A. Reidy
Picture Researchers:
Nancy Katz Colman, Robert Ebbs, Tracey Rogers, Nana Elisabeth Stern, Shirley L. Green (Washington, D.C.), Kate Lewin (Paris)
Archivist: Kathryn J. Steeves
Picture Department Assistant:
Suzanne M. Spencer

Historical Consultants:
Vincent Demma, Lee Ewing, John F. Guilmartin, Jr.
Picture Consultant: Ngo Vinh Long

Production Editor: Kerstin Gorham
Editorial Production:
Sarah E. Burns, Karen E. English, Pamela George, Dalia Lipkin, Elizabeth Campbell Peters, Theresa M. Slomkowski, Amy P. Wilson

Design: Designworks, Sally Bindari
Design Assistants: Sherry Fatla, David Vergara

Marketing Director: Jeanne C. Gibson
Business Staff: Amy Pelletier

Special Contributor to this volume: Janice Hanover (research)

About the editors and authors

Editor-in-Chief *Robert Manning*, a long-time journalist, has previously been editor-in-chief of the *Atlantic Monthly* magazine and its press. He served as assistant secretary of state for public affairs under Presidents John F. Kennedy and Lyndon B. Johnson. He has also been a fellow at the Institute of Politics at the John F. Kennedy School of Government at Harvard University.

Author: *John Morrocco*, formerly a writer with the *U.S. News and World Report* Book Division, has researched and written extensively on the air war in Vietnam. Author of *Thunder From Above*, the volume in THE VIETNAM EXPERIENCE covering the first half of the air war, Mr. Morrocco is a graduate of Boston College and has an M.A. from the London School of Economics and Political Science.

Historical Consultants: *Vincent H. Demma*, a historian with the U.S. Army Center of Military History, is currently working on the center's history of the Vietnam conflict. *Lee Ewing*, editor of *Army Times*, served two years in Vietnam as a combat intelligence officer with the U.S. Military Assistance Command, Vietnam (MACV) and the 101st Airborne Division. *John F. Guilmartin, Jr.*, adjunct professor of history at Rice University and director of NASA's Space Shuttle History Project, served two tours of duty in Vietnam as a USAF rescue helicopter pilot. He has published extensively in the field of military and naval history.

Picture Consultant: *Ngo Vinh Long* is a social historian specializing in China and Vietnam. Born in Vietnam, he returned there most recently in 1980.

Cover Photo:

A B-52 Stratofortress drops its 54,000-pound load of bombs over South Vietnam. Also used extensively over Cambodia and during the climactic Christmas 1972 bombing of Hanoi, the B-52 became symbolic of America's awesome aerial might, especially during the Vietnam War's latter years.

Library of Congress Catalog Card Number: 84-73511

ISBN: 0-939526-14-X

10 9 8 7 6
5 4 3 2 1

Contents

New Strategy, Same War

Captain Gerald J. Greven was sitting outside his hootch at the Special Forces camp outside An Loc one night early in May of 1969, when he saw three rotating beacons pass by overhead heading west toward the Cambodian border, only a few miles away. Minutes later, "large flashes appeared on the horizon," he recalled, "followed by a rolling thunder which shook the ground." Greven immediately knew they had to be B-52s. Since 1965, B-52s of the Strategic Air Command had been flying "Arc Light" bombing missions over South Vietnam.

But Greven could not understand why the B-52s were bombing to the west of An Loc that night. One of two forward air controllers (FACs) assigned to identify VC targets for tactical fighter-bombers, Greven knew of no current targets in the area. The next day he flew over the area to find a string of craters that extended from the west bank of the Cham River for a mile into Cambodian territory. Greven was bewildered.

TAXIWAY

According to the rules of engagement, U.S. pilots were strictly prohibited from bombing targets in neutral Cambodia or within a two-kilometer zone east of the Cham River boundary line.

He reported the incident to his squadron commander, who said he had no knowledge of the strike. When he questioned his regional commander, Greven got the same answer. Finally, he approached the senior commander at Bien Hoa. "I was told, with a slight smile," he said, "that obviously my 'maps were in error.'" Greven knew that meant he "did not have a need to know." He stopped asking questions. Three years would pass before Greven's curiosity was satisfied. In July 1972, he testified before a Senate investigating committee that had uncovered numerous instances of unauthorized B-52 strikes in Cambodia beginning in March 1969. The investigators traced the bits and pieces of evidence through a Byzantine set of machinations that eventually led to the White House itself.

A failed campaign

Four days after Lyndon Johnson announced the cessation of bombing operations against North Vietnam on November 1, 1968, Richard M. Nixon defeated Vice President Hubert Humphrey for the presidency. Although well known as a hard-line anti-Communist, Nixon had campaigned on a platform of peace, claiming he had a "secret plan" to end the war. One of the first things he did upon assuming office was to order his national security adviser, Henry A. Kissinger, to conduct a survey of American involvement in Vietnam. The resulting study, National Security Study Memorandum-1, noted the "emphatic differences" that existed among the various agencies. None was more striking than the disagreement over American bombing strategy.

Johnson's decision to halt unconditionally the Rolling Thunder campaign against North Vietnam had been a bitter blow to the military and advocates of air power in particular. In their eyes the United States had given up its most potent offensive

Preceding page. *Giant B-52 Stratofortresses at Andersen Air Force Base, Guam, bombs loaded, are bound for Vietnam.*

weapon. The 1968 Tet offensive had clearly shown that the Communists maintained the initiative in the ground war in South Vietnam despite General Westmoreland's search and destroy strategy. While the Communists kept the Americans on the defensive in the South, the United States controlled the pace of the air war over the North. But instead of maintaining a sustained, relentless application of force, the offensive might of American air power had frittered away in sporadic spasms.

Johnson's strategy involved the use of selective increments of force balanced against the twin goals of pressuring Hanoi to accept a negotiated settlement that would ensure the continued existence of an independent South Vietnam while avoiding the risks of Soviet or Chinese intervention. To achieve these goals, he instituted a gradually escalating bombing campaign against a highly restricted list of targets while publicly declaring the U.S. had no intention of obliterating North Vietnam. Military men argued that this policy of limited bombing had little effect on a determined enemy and gradual escalation had merely given North Vietnam time to build its air defense

system into one of the most formidable in the world.

A great number of pilots and air commanders in the field blamed the politicians in Washington for the failure of Rolling Thunder. They were embittered by the restrictions placed on them and felt they had been asked to risk their lives fighting a war they were not allowed to win. Many were convinced that unrestricted bombing against strategic targets in Hanoi and Haiphong, which the Joint Chiefs had recommended from the beginning, would have eventually destroyed North Vietnam's ability and will to continue the war.

Civilian officials, however, continued to maintain that the military's claims had already been discredited. During the Rolling Thunder campaign American aircraft had dropped nearly a million (850,000) tons of bombs on North Vietnam. But according to their statistics, the bombing had failed to reduce substantially the flow of men, arms, and ammunition to the battlefield in the South. Nor had it weakened Hanoi's resolve. In fact, their studies indicated the reverse was true. They argued that the bombing had been the chief stumbling block to any political settlement,

pointing out that until President Johnson unconditionally halted the bombing north of the twentieth parallel in March, the North Vietnamese had exhibited little interest in negotiations.

Since NSSM-1 only confirmed the bitter divisions that lingered between government bureaucrats and their uniformed counterparts over the bombing and the general conduct of the war, the new president felt free to act without deference to the Vietnam specialists who could not seem to agree on anything. But eventually Nixon would find himself embroiled in this same debate once again as his attempts to reach a negotiated peace through diplomacy and subtle military pressure failed to achieve results. He too felt obliged to resort to American air power to influence the course of the war.

Charting a new course

Nixon's options were limited by two major constraints. The first was a growing war weariness at home. After years of involvement in Vietnam, the American people were growing frustrated by the ever-spiraling costs in money and men for a war that seemed to be unwinnable. The president could not ignore the rising level of domestic discontent without risking serious political repercussions.

But neither could he repudiate America's long-standing commitment to the defense of South Vietnam. To him, American prestige and the reliability of Washington's commitments abroad were at stake. His goal remained basically the same as that of previous administrations: the continued existence of an independent, anti-Communist South Vietnam. Nixon held little hope for any breakthrough in the formal negotiations in Paris entered into by the Johnson administration, however. After six months the negotiators had managed to agree on little more than a mutually acceptable seating plan. As Hanoi stalled at the negotiating table in the hope that growing antiwar sentiment in the United States would eventually force the Americans to withdraw from Vietnam, Nixon sought ways to strengthen America's bargaining position.

Left. *B-52 Arc Light strikes like this one in the Ia Drang Valley in 1965 increased dramatically after 1968.*

First, he expanded the process, begun by the Johnson administration, of training and equipping the South Vietnamese armed forces to fight their own war. In conjunction with this "Vietnamization" program, he gradually began withdrawing American combat troops. By doing so he hoped to appease critics in Congress and undercut the antiwar movement at home, challenging Hanoi to match his move at de-escalation.

Second, Nixon continued the search for peace through negotiations, but with a new twist. He moved Vietnam to center stage in U.S. foreign policy. By playing on Sino-Soviet rivalries and both Moscow and Peking's desire for détente with the United States, Nixon hoped the two countries would exert a moderating influence on Hanoi. He knew that the Soviets wanted to expand their trade links with the U.S. and were anxious to negotiate an agreement on limiting strategic arms. Nixon used this as leverage, making any concessions conditional on Moscow's assistance in getting Hanoi to agree to a "fair" settlement. The Russians were pouring billions of dollars in military and economic aid into North Vietnam every year; a negotiated settlement offered them a face-saving way out of underwriting what appeared to be an endless commitment.

To underscore further his determination to achieve a favorable negotiated settlement, President Nixon resorted to military threats and pressure to convince the Hanoi government and its allies that he was serious. Although the same strategy had been unsuccessfully employed by President Johnson, Nixon believed the persuasive power of military force had failed before because Johnson had employed it in a limited and indecisive manner. He would follow the example of President Eisenhower, who brought a successful conclusion to the Korean conflict by hinting that if the Communists did not negotiate in good faith he would resort to "massive retaliation."

He told presidential adviser H. R. Haldeman that he wanted the North Vietnamese to believe he had reached the point where he might do anything to stop the war. "We'll just slip the word to them that, 'for God's sake, you know Nixon's obsessed about Communism. We can't restrain him when he's angry—and he has his hand on the nuclear button.'—and Ho Chi Minh himself will be in Paris in two days begging for peace," Nixon explained to Haldeman. This "madman theory," as Nixon liked to call it, was to be tempered by his aggressive efforts to undermine Hanoi's external support. While Johnson kept the possibility of a wider war with the Soviet Union or China to a minimum by carefully limiting U.S. military actions in Vietnam, Nixon believed he could do so through diplomacy.

Nixon's first priority was to signal Hanoi that he meant business. Within weeks of his inauguration, he ordered Henry Kissinger to canvass the Pentagon for a list of possible military moves. Although the Joint Chiefs of Staff immediately tried to sell the president on the idea of resuming the bombing of North Vietnam, Nixon felt such a

course could trigger a political backlash at home and rejected it. Next, the JCS forwarded to Kissinger a plan for bombing Communist sanctuaries in Cambodia, a step they had been urging for years.

Nixon's secret menu

Although Prince Norodom Sihanouk had maintained his country's neutrality through a precarious diplomatic balancing act, the Communists had been using Cambodia as a safe haven from which they could assemble and launch their attacks in South Vietnam. Since May 1967, MACV's Special Operations Group had been running Special Forces teams into Cambodia on secret "Daniel Boone" reconnaissance missions. They brought back startling evidence of the extent of Communist activities across the border. "There were hard-surface roads [and] concrete reinforced bunkers," recalled Lieutenant Randolph Harrison, a Daniel Boone team leader. "I personally found some abandoned base camps that were acres in size."

Further enticement was offered by General Creighton W. Abrams, who in June 1968 had succeeded General William Westmoreland as commander of U.S. forces in Vietnam. On February 9, he informed the JCS that he had identified the location of the Central Office for South Vietnam (COSVN), the headquarters for all Communist military and political activities in the South. COSVN had been the target of unsuccessful U.S. military sweeps in the past, but this time Abrams believed his intelligence sources had accurately located the elusive headquarters complex in an area known as the "Fish Hook," where Cambodia jutted into South Vietnam. Abrams sent two aides to Washington to argue his case for a "short duration, concentrated B-52 attack" against the suspected site.

During an early morning breakfast meeting at the Pentagon, the two MACV staffers presented Abrams's plan to Secretary of Defense Melvin Laird; chairman of the JCS, General Earle Wheeler; and Lieutenant General John Vogt, the assistant deputy chief of staff for plans and operations for the air force. Ellsworth Bunker, the U.S. ambassador in Saigon, had already voiced his approval and Wheeler now added the backing of the Joint Chiefs. The plan also won the enthusiastic support of Colonel Alexander M. Haig, Kissinger's chief military aide, whose hardline views on the war, unquestioning loyalty to the president, and "can do" attitude were standing him well in the Nixon administration. An intensely ambitious man, Haig eventually became an influential player in National Security Council policy making.

When the Communists launched a nationwide offensive on February 22, during the Tet holidays, Nixon decided to act. Although the attacks were on a far smaller scale than the offensive of 1968, he saw them as a test of his new administration and Abrams's plan provided the perfect type of unexpected military action he was looking for.

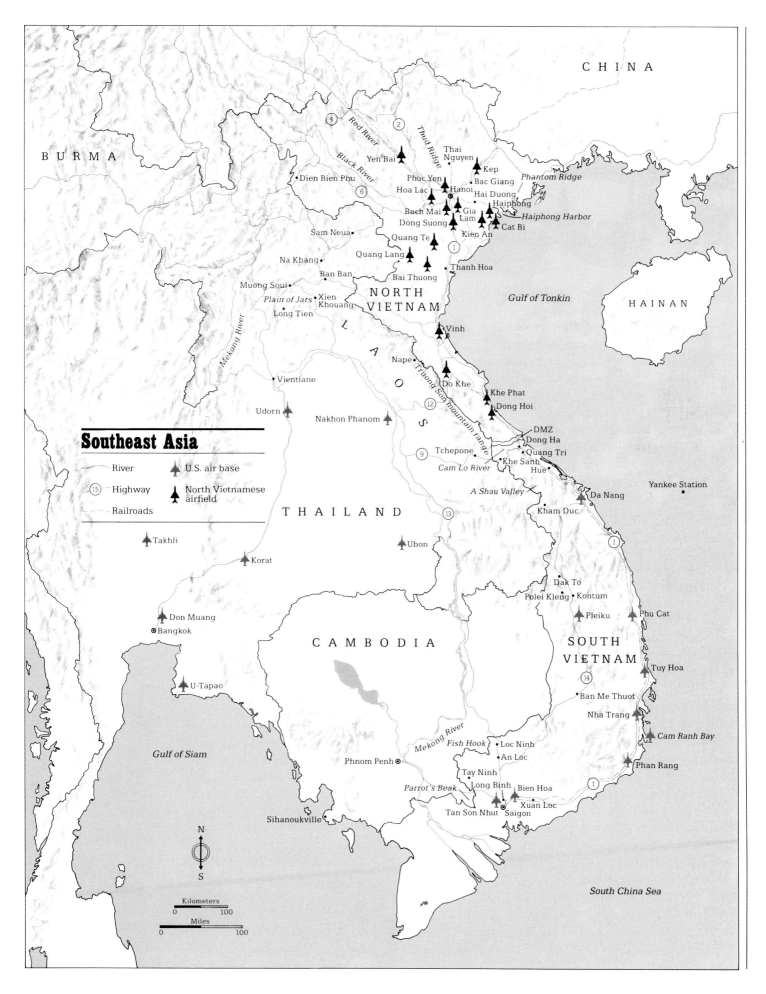

Southeast Asia

⎯⎯ River	✈	U.S. air base
⑮ Highway	▲	North Vietnamese airfield
⎯⎯ Railroads		

CHINA

BURMA

Red River

Black River

Thud Ridge

Yen Bai

Dien Bien Phu

Phuc Yen

Hoa Lac

Thai Nguyen

Kep

Bac Giang

Hanoi

Hai Duong

Haiphong

Phantom Ridge

Haiphong Harbor

Bach Mai

Gia Lam

Dong Suong

Kien An

Cat Bi

Quang Te

Sam Neua

Quang Lang

Na Khang

Ban Ban

Bai Thuong

Thanh Hoa

Muong Soui

Plain of Jars

Xien Khouang

Long Tien

NORTH VIETNAM

Gulf of Tonkin

HAINAN

Mekong River

L A O S

Vientiane

Vinh

Nape

Truong Son mountain range

Do Khe

Khe Phat

Dong Hoi

Udorn

Nakhon Phanom

⑫

DMZ

Dong Ha

⑨

Tchepone

Quang Tri

Khe Sanh

Cam Lo River

Hue

A Shau Valley

Da Nang

Yankee Station

THAILAND

⑬

Kham Duc

Takhli

Ubon

Korat

Dak To

Polei Kleng

Kontum

Phu Cat

Don Muang

◉Bangkok

Pleiku

CAMBODIA

SOUTH VIETNAM

Tuy Hoa

U-Tapao

⑭

Ban Me Thuot

Nha Trang

Cam Ranh Bay

Gulf of Siam

Mekong River

Fish Hook

Loc Ninh

An Loc

Phan Rang

Phnom Penh ◉

Tay Ninh

Long Binh

Bien Hoa

Parrot's Beak

Tan Son Nhut

Xuan Loc

Saigon ◉

Sihanoukville

South China Sea

N

S

Kilometers
0   100

Miles
0   100

A B-52 looms behind an islander's vegetable garden outside Kadena AFB, Okinawa, in 1969. The military refused to admit that the planes were based on the island or that they were secretly bombing targets in neutral Cambodia.

Secrecy was of vital importance to both Nixon and Kissinger, who were determined to keep the bombings out of the newspapers. Kissinger insisted all information be kept on a strict "need to know" basis. The B-52 strikes were to be conducted outside the Strategic Air Command's normal command and control system. Kissinger even suggested that crewmen aboard the high-flying bombers be kept in the dark as to their target assignments. Air force Colonel Ray B. Sitton, a SAC officer on the JCS staff, pointed out that the pilots and navigators would eventually figure out that they were bombing in Cambodia and rumors would spread.

Sitton devised an operational plan that would insure the secrecy so greatly desired, using Arc Light strikes in South Vietnam as cover. A number of B-52 crews scheduled to fly routine missions would be taken aside after their normal briefing and told that they would be receiving new target instructions from ground radar stations while they were airborne. Using computerized bombing techniques, the radar controllers would guide the bombers to targets across the Cambodian border and indicate the precise moment to drop their bombs. Afterwards, the radar operators and B-52 crews would file their official poststrike reports using the coordinates of the original targets in South Vietnam. The real information would be passed on via top secret back channels to a small circle of military and civilian officials.

Besides the B-52 crews and radar controllers, only Gen. Abrams and key personnel at MACV headquarters in Saigon were to know the true nature of the missions. Even at the Pentagon, knowledge was restricted to the secretary of defense, the Joint Chiefs, Col. Sitton, his two immediate superiors at SAC headquarters, and a small number of JCS staff members.

On March 15, Nixon authorized Gen. Wheeler to schedule the first mission for the eighteenth. It was code named "Breakfast," after the occasion of the Pentagon meeting where it had first been discussed. The following day Nixon convened a meeting of the National Security Council to obtain the final approval of his top advisers.

Only Secretary of State William P. Rogers, fearful of the diplomatic consequences of violating Cambodian neutrality, was opposed to the plan. Although he approved of the bombings, Secretary of Defense Laird was concerned about the president's insistence on secrecy. A former Republican congressman from Wisconsin, Laird knew that

Congress would eventually find out and that political repercussions would inevitably follow. He urged the president to go public from the start, justifying the bombings by providing evidence of Hanoi's activities in Cambodia.

President Nixon was unwilling to provoke a confrontation with antiwar critics which might further limit his options in Vietnam. Obsessed with what he perceived to be a hostile media, Nixon wanted to prevent the kind of information leaks to the press that he felt had plagued the Johnson administration. He found a natural ally in Kissinger, who shared this penchant for secrecy. Although Kissinger may have had his doubts about the wisdom of the bombing, he kept them to himself. Over the objections of Laird and Rogers, Nixon secured the NSC's backing for a decision he had already made.

The meeting set the tone that was to characterize the administration's decision-making process regarding the Vietnam War for the next four years. Unlike Lyndon Johnson, who continually sought to achieve a consensus among his advisers, Nixon was willing to act on his own instincts. Those who dissented would be isolated from the policy-making process, so gradually Nixon relied more and more on a small circle of loyal and trusted advisers who shared his views.

On March 18, Operation Breakfast began. Sixty B-52s thundered off the runway at Andersen Air Force Base in Guam and headed west toward assigned targets in South Vietnam. At the last minute, forty-eight of the planes were diverted across the Cambodian border. They dropped twenty-four tons of bombs over the area that MACV intelligence sources believed to shelter COSVN headquarters. Following on their heels, a helicopter ferried a Daniel Boone reconnaissance team of two American Green Berets and eleven South Vietnamese into the still-smoking site in hopes of capturing prisoners stunned by the effects of the bombing. Within minutes of landing the team was hit by a withering crossfire from the nearby tree line.

"This is Bullet," came a frantic radio call. "We've got four wounded and are taking hits from all directions. We don't . . . Oh God! I'm hit!" Braving heavy automatic-weapons fire, the chopper circled back to rescue the besieged team. Three of the Vietnamese soldiers scrambled aboard. One of the crewmen jumped out and managed to rescue the team leader, Captain Bill Orthman, who had crawled into a bomb crater after being wounded in the stomach and the leg. The radio operator, Barry Murphy, and the eight other Vietnamese were never heard from again. When MACV headquarters ordered another reconnaissance team into the area later that afternoon, the Green Berets refused to go.

At the White House, Kissinger was elated by reports of seventy-three secondary explosions as a result of the bombing. The B-52s had apparently hit a fuel or ammo dump. But the ambush of the Daniel Boone recon team cast some doubts on the air force's boasts of the destructive power of their B-52s. Within a few weeks it was apparent that COSVN, or what passed for it, had emerged unscathed from the ferocious bombing assault. It was not the massive headquarters complex that some U.S. military men had envisioned, but rather a mobile command unit that changed its location every ten days.

Emboldened by Prince Sihanouk's apparent unwillingness to protest the raid, and wishing to leave no doubt in Hanoi's mind about his own willingness to use force, Nixon ordered the bombings continued despite the inauspicious start. Gen. Abrams provided a list of fifteen more known base camps along the Cambodian border, and Operation Breakfast was soon followed by Operations Lunch, Dinner, Snack, Supper, and Dessert. During the next fourteen months, SAC B-52s flew 3,630 sorties against these targets, dropping more than 100,000 tons of bombs, in what collectively came to be known as Operation Menu. Only a handful of American civilian officials and senior officers were aware of the raids. Secretary of the air force Robert Seamans and even General John Ryan, who succeeded General John McConnell as air force chief of staff, were kept in the dark.

The ingenious dual reporting system devised by Col.

Signs such as this one, posted by islanders, protest the presence of B-52 bombers on Okinawa.

Sitton kept all details of the missions from ever being entered into the Department of Defense's normal reporting system, which, for logistical and budgetary purposes, maintained a meticulous record of hours flown and fuel and ordnance expended during every mission undertaken by U.S. aircraft. The system was described in detail by Major Hal Knight, who served as supervisor of the "Skyspot" radar site at Bien Hoa which controlled radar-directed bombing operations in III Corps.

Every afternoon before a Menu operation, a special courier plane would be sent to Bien Hoa from the Strategic Air Command's Advanced Echelon office (SACADVON) at Tan Son Nhut. Knight was handed a plain manila envelope containing the revised target coordinates for the next morning's raid, which had been planned in advance by MACV intelligence officers and senior SAC commanders and approved by the Joint Chiefs. He locked these in his desk drawer until the evening crew came on duty. After Knight briefed the radar operators on the new targets they fed the information into their computers, which calculated their range and bearing. The new coordinates were passed on to the B-52 crews when they arrived on station later that evening. Guiding the planes by a pencil-thin radar beam, the ground controllers led the B-52s to the target and provided a countdown with the exact time of bomb release.

Once the bombs were released, the B-52s' radio operators called back to their bases in Guam, Okinawa, or Thailand reporting the mission accomplished. Without knowing the planes had received new target instructions over South Vietnam, intelligence officers at the base logged the original coordinates on the poststrike report. After landing, the crews merely reported whether they saw any secondary explosions to the debriefing officers, who had no idea of the change in target. There was little evidence to suggest any diversion since the crew's target assignments in South Vietnam were carefully selected within a few miles of the Cambodian border. Discrepancies in fuel consumption and miles logged were virtually imperceptible.

Meanwhile, Knight gathered up all papers and computer tapes of the night's mission and proceeded to burn them in an incinerator behind his hut. Then he called a special telephone number in Saigon with the code words: "The ball game is over." Separate poststrike reports were filled out with the coordinates of the original targets in South Vietnam and sent through normal channels. According to the Pentagon's own classified records, the real strikes never occurred.

Special efforts were made to keep any word of the raids from leaking to the press. All personnel involved in the missions were warned not to discuss the subject with any "unauthorized individuals." In reply to any inquiries from reporters, MACV press officials were instructed to "neither confirm nor deny" any reports of bombings in Cambodia. If evidence was produced of Cambodian civilian casualties or damage, the press officials were to tell reporters that the bombings had been accidental and that proper apologies and compensation would be offered by the U.S. government.

Despite all the precautions, the story was leaked to the press. A sketchy article in the *New York Times* by William Beecher on May 9 caused little public stir, but Nixon was furious. He ordered Kissinger to have FBI Director J. Edgar Hoover investigate the source of the leak. Suspicion centered on NSC staffer Morton Halperin, a former official in the Johnson administration known for his dovish views on the war. When Hoover informed Kissinger of his suspicions, Kissinger agreed that Halperin's phone be tapped.

This was to be the first in a series of phone taps and surveillance operations authorized by the president in the name of national security interests. In the following years, as criticism of his Vietnam policies mounted so did his obsession for secrecy. But in early 1970, the president still had some political room for maneuver.

Planning for Armageddon

Having signaled Hanoi of his resolve with the B-52 raids in Cambodia, Nixon initiated phase two of his grand strategy. On May 14, he announced a "comprehensive peace plan." The plan proposed a mutual withdrawal of North Vietnamese and American troops, the release of all POWs, and an internationally supervised cease-fire followed by a general election according to the guidelines set down by the 1954 Geneva accords. At the same time, Kissinger privately hinted to Moscow that the U.S. was willing to discuss arms control and trade concessions, but only after some sort of agreement had been reached with North Vietnam.

A month later, Nixon announced his decision to begin the gradual, phased withdrawal of American troops from South Vietnam. The first contingent of 25,000 GIs would leave in July. Along with the stepped-up Vietnamization program, it marked the first stages in the new "Nixon doctrine." America would continue to honor its commitments in Southeast Asia, but it expected its ally to shoulder more of the burden. "We shall furnish military and economic assistance when requested and as appropriate," Nixon would later remark. "But we shall look to the nation directly threatened to assume the primary responsibility of providing the manpower for its defense."

Hanoi remained unimpressed. North Vietnamese leaders insisted that the United States must agree to a total and unconditional withdrawal of American troops and allow the National Liberation Front, now renamed the Provisional Revolutionary Government, to participate in a coalition government. Dismissing Nixon's offer as a "farce," they vowed to sit in Paris "until the chairs rot" before accepting anything less. Still recovering from the heavy losses sustained during the failed Tet offensive in 1968, North Vietnam had returned to its protracted war strategy. The government in Hanoi was willing to bide its time, waging a war of attrition in the South while recovering from the bombing in the North, waiting for the day when it could mount a final, decisive offensive.

Having failed to alter the situation through diplomatic gestures and arm-twisting, reinforced by a show of force in Cambodia, the president decided to "go for broke." In his memoirs, Nixon wrote that both he and Kissinger agreed it was time "to end the war one way or the other—either by a negotiated agreement or by an increased use of force."

On July 15, Nixon sent a secret message to Ho Chi Minh warning that if progress toward a peaceful settlement of the war was not forthcoming by November 1, he would have no choice but to resort to "measures of great consequence and force." As President Johnson had done before him, Nixon turned to American aerial might to achieve his ends. But unlike his predecessor, Nixon would impose few restrictions or limitations in carrying out his threat. In conversations with Kissinger he envisioned a series of "savage, punishing blows" against North Vietnam to leave no doubt about his determination to end the war by whatever means were necessary.

Once again, official channels were bypassed. Kissinger ordered Alexander Haig and navy Captain Rembrant C. Robinson to begin top-secret studies in accordance with the president's wishes. The two military aides worked closely with the chief of naval operations, Admiral Thomas H. Moorer, who instructed his staff to assist on the study without Secretary Laird's knowledge. On July 20, the results were forwarded to Kissinger. The plan, code named Duck Hook, included everything the military had been clamoring for during the Johnson years. It called for air strikes against strategic targets in the Red River Delta area, the mining of Haiphong Harbor and other ports in North Vietnam, and even the possible use of tactical nuclear weapons in certain "controlled" situations.

The stage was now set and Nixon and Kissinger began putting the squeeze on Hanoi and its allies. On August 4, Kissinger met secretly with North Vietnamese representatives in Paris, warning them again of the president's November 1 ultimatum. Operation Menu was stepped up to ten missions a day bringing the total number of B-52 strikes in Cambodia to 376 in the month of August. When Ho Chi Minh died on September 3, Nixon ordered a three-day cease-fire and extended the suspension of B-52 raids on Communist forces in the South for another thirty-six hours in hopes of some sign of give on Hanoi's part.

Nixon also went to work on the Russians, staging a phone call to Kissinger while Kissinger was meeting with Soviet Ambassador Anatoly Dobrynin. Hanging up the phone, Kissinger turned to Dobrynin and said: "The President has told me in that call that as far as Vietnam is con-cerned, the train has just left the station and is now headed down the track."

But as the November 1 deadline approached, it became apparent that the president's threats had failed to intimidate either Hanoi or Moscow. A series of secret meetings between Kissinger and North Vietnamese representatives in Paris proved as fruitless as the formal talks a few blocks away. Although the Soviets had seemed willing enough to put pressure on Hanoi to negotiate, their influence was apparently less than the Americans had hoped it would be.

Nixon now faced the alternatives of a major escalation of the war or an embarrassing diplomatic defeat. His instincts told him to strike back, but he found little support for the plan among his advisers. Although Laird and Rogers had not been briefed on Operation Duck Hook, they learned of the president's intentions late in September after he purposely told a group of Republican senators that he was considering mining Haiphong Harbor. Both men were adamant in their opposition. Many of Kissinger's own subordinates on the NSC staff were equally critical of the plan. Like their colleagues in the Johnson administration, they were doubtful whether intensive bombing would in itself be able to break Hanoi's will and noted that the sustained public support necessary for such a course of action was just not there. William Watts, Kissinger's staff secretary, warned of the possibility of widespread domestic unrest, which the administration would be forced to handle "as brutally as it administered the November plan." These concerns were reinforced on October 15, when 250,000 Americans converged on Washington to protest the war. Unlike previous protests, this one attracted a broad spectrum of American society. Nixon's brief "honeymoon" period with the war critics was over.

Faced with this formidable opposition from within and without, Nixon reluctantly agreed to shelve the Duck Hook plan, at least for the time being. But he refused to back down in Vietnam. In a televised speech to the nation on November 3, he underlined the dire consequences of a U.S. sellout in South Vietnam and called upon the "silent majority" of Americans to support him in honoring America's commitment to an honorable settlement of the war. He was willing to play North Vietnam's waiting game, gambling that he could ride out the gathering storm of antiwar sentiment at home and convince Hanoi's leaders that they could not force their terms on the U.S.

For the next four years, Nixon's overall strategy in Vietnam continued to rely on aggressive negotiating efforts supplemented by military pressures. Some actions, such as the bombings in Cambodia, were hidden from public view. Others were more dramatic. In all, air power played a major role. Bombing and bargaining were the key elements of U.S. strategy in Vietnam as Nixon openly threatened aerial retaliation against North Vietnam for any escalation of the war on the ground.

During the fall of 1969, the vocal dissent of increasing numbers of Americans of all ages and even members of his own cabinet dissuaded President Nixon from resuming large-scale bombing of North Vietnam.

Right. *Marchers in New York call for peace during the nationwide October 15 antiwar moratorium. Insets. Secretary of Defense Melvin Laird (left) and Secretary of State William P. Rogers, dissenters from Nixon's proposed Operation Duck Hook bombing of the North.*

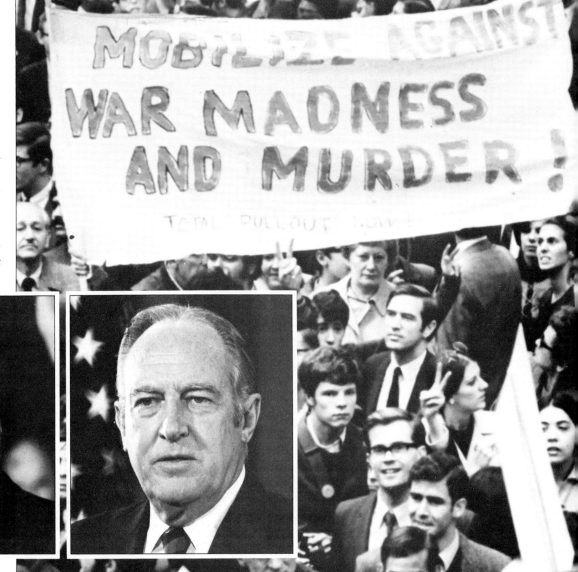

At the same time, the U.S. persisted in its efforts to mold the South Vietnamese armed forces into a self-sustaining force capable of fighting the Communists on equal terms. American troops continued to be phased out, fast enough to placate public opinion at home but not so fast as to jeopardize the battlefield situation in South Vietnam. In the process the air force supplanted the army as the prime military arm in the war.

American aircraft were assigned to fight a rear-guard, delaying action, covering the withdrawal of U.S. ground forces and buying time for the Vietnamization program. Air power was to be a substitute for ground troops within South Vietnam, as had been the case in 1965 when it was used as an alternative to committing combat forces. Gradually the U.S. military would return to the programs of the Kennedy years, providing advice and training to the South Vietnamese. It was a pattern that brought U.S. air power's involvement in Vietnam full circle, only this time its goal was to extricate the U.S. from Vietnam rather than to achieve a military victory. For U.S. airmen, such subtleties of America's changing grand strategy mattered little. For them, the war in Southeast Asia simply ground on with the same deadly routine.

"A switchable faucet of firepower"

Most ground soldiers, from the generals in their war rooms to the grunts in their foxholes, thought of air power as flying artillery. Gen. Westmoreland's search and destroy strategy had relied heavily on air power to counteract the Communist tactic of engaging U.S. forces at close quarters in an attempt to wear the Americans down by inflicting heavy casualties. When they made contact with the enemy, U.S. ground commanders would often back off

and call in an air strike, then move back in to mop up.

But as U.S. troops began withdrawing in mid-1969 and the enemy shifted back to a strategy of hit-and-run guerrilla warfare, ground tactics changed considerably. Although a few major offensives were launched against Communist-controlled areas in early 1969, large-scale search and destroy sweeps of 1,000 men or more became less common as Vietnamese troops gradually replaced the withdrawing Americans. The emphasis was now on securing populated areas and military installations. Operations tended to be mounted at the company level and by small patrols of ten to fifty men who concentrated on gathering information to help maintain the security of rear areas and base camps.

For U.S. pilots this shift in tactics brought increased responsibilities. As more ground troops withdrew, air power was called upon to shoulder more of the burden. U.S. air-

craft now became a major source of protection for military installations throughout South Vietnam. In response to stepped-up guerrilla attacks and the enemy's increased use of lightweight 107mm and heavier 122mm and 140mm portable rockets, which could be fired from improvised sites up to 10,000 meters away, air force AC-47 "Spooky" gunships, equipped with their own flares and three 7.62mm Gatling guns that could fire 18,000 rounds per minute, maintained a constant patrol over major military bases.

Gunships and tactical aircraft were also held on alert to support remote U.S. Army aviation and fire support bases, isolated Special Forces camps, and small reconnaissance patrols when they came under attack. In addition, they flew an increasing number of combat missions in support of ARVN troops in the field as American units withdrew and the South Vietnamese took over more responsibility for ground operations.

When Communist troops attacked a Civilian Irregular Defense Group camp at Ben Het in the central highlands near the Laotian border on May 8, U.S. aircraft flew to the rescue. The heavily armed North Vietnamese force, supported by artillery and Soviet-built PT76 tanks, threatened to overrun the ARVN force, which had recently taken over responsibility for the camp's defense from the Americans as part of the Vietnamization program. U.S. fighter-bombers flew more than 30 sorties per day in support of the base until July 2, with B-52s providing an additional 804 sorties. The more than 20,000 tons of bombs they dropped day and night on Communist positions around the camp were decisive in breaking the back of the siege.

American air power was visible and audible everywhere in South Vietnam. In 1969, more than 700 U.S. Air Force tactical fighter-bombers and ten marine air squadrons were stationed at bases throughout the country and in neighboring Thailand while three navy aircraft carriers cruised offshore. Sophisticated radar-guided bomb delivery techniques and all-weather attack systems enabled U.S. aircraft to answer calls for air support in any kind of weather, day or night. In addition, the South Vietnamese air force was growing rapidly as the Vietnamization program proceeded.

Modernization efforts had begun in 1967 when the VNAF's 522d Fighter Squadron was equipped with the F-5 Freedom Fighter, a multipurpose supersonic jet. Although the small plane could not carry large payloads, its simple design made it easy to maintain and repair. The following year, the A-37 Dragonfly, a modified version of the T-37 trainer, was introduced into the VNAF's inventory to augment its aging fleet of A-1 Skyraiders. Powered by twin turbojets, with a 7.62MM minigun mounted in its nose and four bomb stations under each wing that could carry a total ordnance load of nearly 6,000 pounds, the A-37 was ideally suited for close air support. After an intensive pilot training program, three squadrons were equipped with A-37s in May 1969. By the end of the year, the VNAF had nearly doubled in size and strength.

With such an abundance of aircraft at their disposal and little in the way of Communist antiaircraft defenses to challenge them, there was never any doubt about allied air superiority in South Vietnam. "Air support in Vietnam is much like the faucet in your kitchen," said one forward air controller, "once you turn it on it just keeps flowing along." Indeed, Gen. Abrams equated it to a "uniquely switchable faucet of firepower."

No one was more appreciative of this vast arsenal of aerial firepower than embattled ground troops. For many of them, the screeching sound of a jet engine overhead often spelled the difference between life and death. While some infantrymen grumbled about the comparatively easy life pilots led, sleeping in beds with real sheets far from the battlefield, they held a grudging admiration for the unseen warriors who patrolled the skies overhead.

On the offensive

While they were given the highest priority, tactical air strikes in a "troops in contact" situation were the exception rather than the rule. According to a U.S. Department of Defense study for 1970, fewer than 10 percent of all combat sorties flown by fixed-wing aircraft in South Vietnam were direct close air support missions. This marked a significant decline in one of the traditional roles played by tactical fighter-bombers in wars past. It could be partly explained by the nature of the war in Vietnam where the majority of combat engagements tended to be small, brief firefights. The Pentagon study indicated that 53 percent of the total ground engagements reported up to 1970 were either too small or over too quickly to generate any requests for fire support.

Another factor was the development of helicopter gunships, which were now available in large numbers for close air support missions in Vietnam. Armed helicopters and artillery support were requested in 39 percent of the

On target. An A-37 Dragonfly attack aircraft from the Vietnamese Air Force's 520th Fighter Squadron dives to fire its rockets at an enemy bunker in the Mekong River Delta region of South Vietnam.

contacts while tactical air support was requested in only 8 percent. Army field commanders tended to rely more upon their own aviation units for air support rather than air force or navy fixed-wing aircraft. Many complained that fixed-wing aircraft often took up to an hour to arrive on the scene and argued that it was far quicker and less complicated to call upon their own organic aviation units rather than going through what they considered the rather lengthy chain of command for external air support. Army, and marine units as well, were much more comfortable calling upon their own helicopter gunships and marine aircraft flown by pilots who had worked closely with their units day in and day out. They also felt that their own aircraft were better suited for tactical close air support than the air force's and navy's multimission, high-performance jet fighter-bombers.

Although on the surface this seemed natural, it betrayed a certain degree of self-promotion on the part of the military service branches involved. If the army, for example, could show that its armed helicopters could do the job just as well as air force fighter-bombers, the army would be in a better position to gain more helicopters during the next procurement budget debate. Such turf battles were not uncommon during the Vietnam War. The kind of national emergency or sense of unity that had tended to mitigate interservice rivalries in past wars was lacking in Vietnam. This was partly because the war was a limited one in which the national security of the United States was not directly threatened and public support for the war was marginal at best.

While the air force found its traditional role of providing close air support to troops in the field being challenged in Vietnam, the use of air power as an offensive weapon increased dramatically. In 1969, with the decision to begin withdrawing American troops, General Abrams relied

Cobra

Speed, endurance, and firepower. These qualities characterized the AH-1G Cobra. Designed specifically to carry a variety of heavy weapons, this gunship and observation helicopter flew with almost two tons of ammunition to fire from its 7.62MM machine guns, 20MM cannon, and 40MM grenade launchers. Ground commanders likened the Cobra to a tank for its fire support capabilities. Easily recognized by its downturned nose and in-

sectlike profile, this swift and hardy craft became one of the most celebrated tools of the war.

In September 1965, Bell Helicopter completed the prototype for the Huey Cobra, and two years later, it replaced the standard UH-1C Huey in Vietnam as a faster, better-armed escort for the CH-47A Chinook and as a fire support helicopter. The Cobra's slim fuselage, stub wings, and improved rotor system enabled gunship crews to attack their targets at steeper dive angles and varying speeds, which made the AH-1s hard to hit with ground fire. Its speed, low-profile silhouette, and ability to perform the maneuvers of a conventional aircraft distinguish the Cobra.

Two drawbacks of the Cobra, the lack of side gunners and a virtually sound-

proof cockpit, lessened the security of the crew in hostile fire. However, the Cobra depended on its speed, profile, and weapon turret to compensate for this lack of protection.

The army had ordered 838 Cobras by the spring of 1968; by that time the craft was serving in the majority of armed aviation units in Southeast Asia. The marines ordered forty-nine and designated them AH-1J Sea Cobras.

The Cobra paired with the Loach light observation helicopter formed a formidable hunter-killer team. During the Tet offensive, Huey Cobras helped repel a Vietcong attack on the Bien Hoa Air Force Base near Saigon and provided

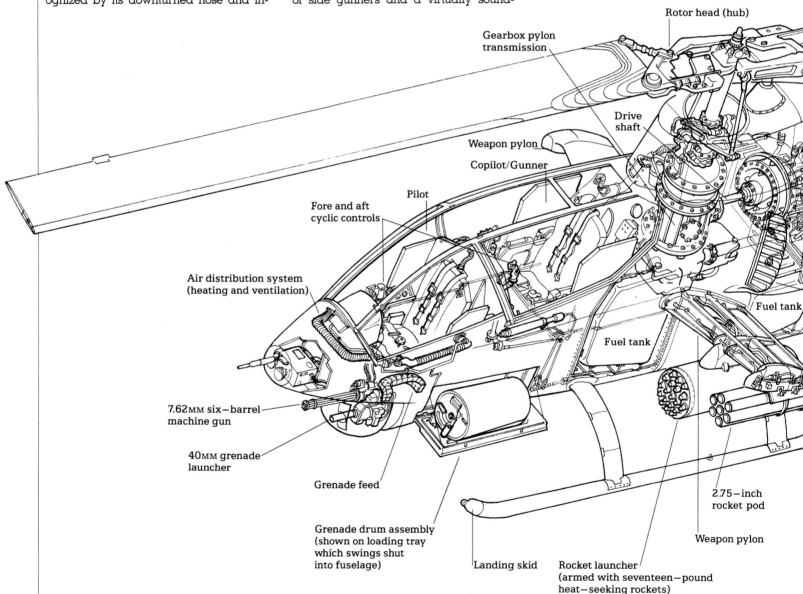

deadly close support fire to within fifty feet of friendly troops in Hue. Widely deployed by 1970, the AH-1G also provided support for daily small-unit actions in the countryside as well as for larger battles. During the invasions of Cambodia and Laos, the Cobras used their rocket and machine-gun fire to splinter enemy infantry formations, and even destroyed enemy PT76 light tanks while forced to operate under low-hanging rain clouds. This exposed them to fierce opposition from the NVA's heavy 12.7MM machine guns.

The Cobra also played a crucial role during the siege of An Loc. By this time, however, the North Vietnamese had learned to counter the Cobra, downing two at An Loc with the Soviet-designed SA-7 heat-seeking missile. This hand-held weapon significantly limited the use of the AH-1G and other slow-flying aircraft until exhaust shields, flares, and evasive tactics were developed to foil them.

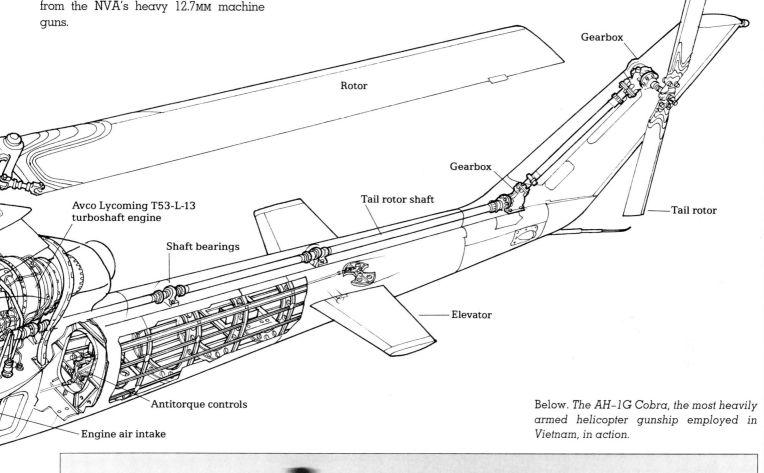

Rotor

Gearbox

Gearbox

Tail rotor shaft

Tail rotor

Avco Lycoming T53-L-13 turboshaft engine

Shaft bearings

Elevator

Antitorque controls

Engine air intake

Below. *The AH-1G Cobra, the most heavily armed helicopter gunship employed in Vietnam, in action.*

more and more on air power to carry the war to the Communists. Aerial "spoiling operations," intended to keep the enemy off balance and prevent them from massing forces, were stepped up to buy time for the Vietnamization program. A full 25 percent of tactical air support missions in Vietnam were flown in answer to requests from ground commanders or forward air controllers for immediate air strikes against "time sensitive" targets such as known enemy troop concentrations or active base camps outside of the immediate battlefield. Well over half were pre-planned strikes against suspected enemy locations, base areas, and supply caches in remote areas beyond the reach of conventional ground forces.

Observation and reconnaissance missions were the most important factors in a guerrilla warfare environment where there were no fixed battle lines and the enemy's greatest advantage was freedom of movement. Newer and more modern aircraft were introduced to supplement the unarmed, lightweight O-1 and O-2 Cessna observation planes used by forward air controllers and OV-1 Mohawk photo reconnaissance planes. In 1968, army and marine units were equipped with the AH-1 Cobra, a gunship and observation helicopter designed for high maneuverability at low altitudes. The air force introduced the OV-10 Bronco, a turbo-prop-powered aircraft that could carry bombs as well as marker smoke rockets. Its oversized cockpit canopy provided excellent visibility for the pilot and his back seater.

Many of these aircraft carried a variety of sensors designed to help them locate elusive guerrilla units that evaded conventional photo reconnaissance jets by moving under the cover of the jungle and at night. Starlight scopes, which magnified existing starlight and moonlight and could be held by hand, were widely employed by airborne FACs. Infrared detectors pinpointed heat sources such as campfires, while infrared photos could uncover heat variations in the terrain caused by the natural body warmth of a large group of men. Perhaps the most unusual device was something called the "people sniffer," which reacted to the scent of the human body.

These technological innovations were initially very effective, but eventually the Communists learned how to counteract many of them with elaborate camouflage and simple tricks. In the case of the people sniffer, the guerrillas simply urinated in tin cans and buckets which they placed at safe distances from their real positions, deceiving the Americans into raining tons of bombs upon empty jungle. By far, the most reliable source of reconnaissance intelligence for aerial interdiction missions was a FAC's own eyes and experience. "Although the enemy could expertly conceal himself in the jungle, we FACs knew a few

tricks too," according to Captain Henry S. Bartos, an air force pilot who logged 840 hours in an OV-10 in 1969. "We would look for recently used trails, a river with a muddied spot (indicating a recent crossing), a telltale wisp of smoke in the jungle, or even the type of clothing hanging on a line in a small village."

While air force, navy, and marine tactical fighter-bombers, guided by airborne FACs, flew a great number of these aerial interdiction missions, air force B-52s, with their far greater payloads, provided the lion's share of the bombs. Throughout the year, B-52s flew 1,800 sorties per month against targets in South Vietnam. During the last five weeks of the year alone, they unleashed more than 30 million pounds of bombs against Communist troop concentrations and base areas.

In 1969, air power reached its zenith in South Vietnam. The total number of combat and combat support sorties by U.S. fixed-wing aircraft and helicopters of all types during the year reached the 8.5 million mark, a million more than were flown in 1968. The statistics confirmed the assessment of General George S. Brown, who succeeded General William Momyer as commander of the 7th Air Force and MACV's deputy commander for air operations in August 1968. "While our overall objective is defensive, to deter continued enemy invasion, our tactics are very definitely offensive in nature," he claimed in a January 1969 interview. "[T]actically speaking, there is no question that we are on the offensive."

Fisheye view. Lieutenant Colonel R. E. Stratton, commander of the 23d Tactical Air Support Squadron, scans the ground for hostile forces from the cockpit of his OV-10 Bronco. South Vietnam, September 1972.

A navy OV-10 Bronco fires a Zuni rocket in the Mekong Delta, October 28, 1969. Primarily a reconnaissance craft, the OV-10 could double as a light attack plane.

The "Secret" Air War in Laos

"We march in the desolate gray of the forest. Around us, giant trees stripped of their foliage thrust out their stark branches. Their ghostly silhouettes march across a low, cloudy sky—heavy like a soaked quilt.... U.S. Air Force planes above never stop. Like masked gangsters, they hide above the clouds ... formations of Phantoms, the howl of death in their jet engines, and the continuous growl of the reconnaissance planes. The whistle and explosion of bombs thunder in every corner of the forest."

Thus read the diary of North Vietnamese war correspondent Tran Mai Nam, which was published in Hanoi in 1969. Although the preface indicated it was an account of the author's impressions during a mission to the two northernmost provinces in South Vietnam, the events recorded occurred not in South Vietnam but on the author's journey through the neighboring kingdom of Laos, where a bitter struggle was secretly being waged between Communist and U.S. forces.

Between 1964 and 1969, U.S. aircraft flew nearly half a million combat sorties over Laos, dropping nearly two million tons of bombs. During that time, nearly 380 planes were shot down. Approximately 200 U.S. military personnel, most of them airmen, died in combat, and another 200 were listed as missing or captured. The families of these servicemen were vaguely informed that they had been killed, shot down, or captured in "Southeast Asia." But as the numbers rose, so did the publicity surrounding efforts by mothers and wives to obtain further information.

While occasional articles would appear in Western newspapers, the American public knew little about U.S. air operations in Laos. American reporters were forbidden to visit U.S. Air Force units based in Thailand where most of the operations originated. American military advisers in Laos, many of whom worked under civilian cover, maintained a low profile and were under strict orders not to associate with the few journalists posted in the capital of Vientiane. When reporters questioned State Department officials at the U.S. Embassy, they were usually unable to get a straight answer. Not until late 1969 was the curtain lifted.

In mid-1969, Senator Stuart Symington (D-Mo.), a former Marine Corps pilot, announced that his Subcommittee of the Foreign Relations Committee on Security Arrangements and Commitments Abroad would hold hearings on U.S. involvement in Laos. "We have been at war in Laos for years," Symington said, "and it is time the American people knew more of the facts." The hearings, which began in October, confirmed the rumors that had been circulating for years. On March 6 the publicity forced President Nixon to acknowledge for the first time U.S. involvement in Laos. But since the hearings were held in closed session and the transcript released to the press was censored, the full extent of American activities remained obscure to the American public.

Neutrality in name only

A sparsely populated country of rugged mountain ranges, tropical jungle, and dense rain forests, Laos occupied a strategic location in the heart of Southeast Asia, sharing a common border with six other nations, including China and North Vietnam. Since the early fifties, Western proponents of the domino theory maintained that if the Communists gained control of Laos the security of Thailand, Cambodia, and South Vietnam would be seriously jeopardized. Although the Geneva accords of 1954 pledged to uphold Laotian neutrality, the newly independent country was wracked by internal divisions between Communist

Preceding page. Royal Laotian Army Rangers wait to board an American C-123 at Pak Se in February 1968 for transport to Saravane to reinforce government troops battling Communist Pathet Lao forces.

(that is, Pathet Lao), right-wing, and neutralist factions who jockeyed for power.

The fragile balance was shattered in 1960, when open war broke out between rightist factions in the Royal Laotian Army and neutralist forces who allied themselves with Communist Pathet Lao guerrillas in control of the northeastern portion of the country. North Vietnam, Russia, and China quickly closed ranks behind the Pathet Lao, while the U.S. threw its support behind pro-Western forces. The crisis was finally defused in 1962, when the U.S. and the Soviet Union reached an agreement in Geneva reaffirming their commitment to a neutral Laos.

But the second neutralization pact proved no more effective than the first. While the two superpowers were not prepared to risk an international crisis over the tiny kingdom, Laos figured prominently in Hanoi's grand strategy to unify Vietnam under its control. Hanoi's primary objective was to ensure the free movement of men and supplies along the Ho Chi Minh Trail in Laos to the main battlefield in South Vietnam. To achieve that goal, Hanoi sought to strengthen the position of the Pathet Lao as a buffer between the vital supply artery and anti-Communist Royal Laotian forces. The North Vietnamese supplied the Pathet Lao with arms and ammunition and reinforced their ranks with NVA advisers and specialized combat units in order to keep government forces in check along the strategically important Plain of Jars in the northeast.

Hanoi went to extreme lengths to conceal its military activities in Laos. The North Vietnamese were anxious to mask their extensive infiltration network in Laos not only because they were in flagrant violation of Laotian neutrality, but also to maintain the illusion that the war in South Vietnam was a popular uprising against the Saigon regime. General Vo Bam, who was assigned the task of opening the infiltration trails in 1959, recalled: "Absolute secrecy, absolute security were our watchwords."

Washington played a similarly clandestine game, secretly sending in American military advisers and providing arms and ammunition to the Royal Laotian Army. The CIA conducted extensive paramilitary operations throughout the country, recruiting its own clandestine army among ethnic Meo tribesmen in the mountainous eastern region under the leadership of General Vang Pao, who had fought with the French against the Vietminh. Washington also agreed to provide the Royal Laotian Air Force (RLAF) with thirty T-28 Nomad fighter-bombers. Early in 1964, USAF Special Air Warfare Commandos were sent to train Laotian pilots to fly the new planes. Known as Project Water Pump, the secret training operation was conducted across the Mekong River at Udorn Air Force Base in Thailand to avoid publicity.

While U.S. covert assistance to Laotian government forces managed to offset Hanoi's support of the Pathet Lao in the battle for the Plain of Jars, the North Vietnamese were free to enlarge and expand their infiltration network along the eastern border region and in the southern pan-handle. During the first five months of 1964, according to U.S. intelligence estimates, nearly 5,000 NVA troops traveled down the Ho Chi Minh Trail into South Vietnam. Unarmed American reconnaissance jets began daily surveillance flights over the trail in May and soon confirmed the Communist build-up.

Alarmed by the rising level of support for the Vietcong, President Johnson approved the idea of limited bombing operations against the trail. But the State Department objected to a proposal to use U.S. aircraft because if an American pilot was shot down and captured Hanoi would have hard evidence of U.S. neutrality violations. Instead, Washington approached the Laotians about employing Royal Laotian Air Force T-28s for the job, but Prime Minister Souvanna Phouma was reluctant. Although he was willing to accept covert U.S. aid for the war against the Pathet Lao, Souvanna Phouma considered traffic on the Ho Chi Minh Trail to be a U.S./South Vietnamese problem. The Laotian government feared that Hanoi would react ruthlessly to any attempt to cut its vital supply artery.

As an alternative, the United States hired a number of Thai pilots to fly U.S.-supplied T-28s. Operating under the control of the American ambassador, they were assigned and briefed on targets by CIA agents and U.S. Air Force personnel. But these Thai mercenaries proved extremely unreliable, often dropping their bombs indiscriminately from high altitudes to avoid the heavy ground fire from North Vietnamese AA guns guarding the trail. They rarely hit their assigned targets.

North Vietnam's growing antiaircraft defenses also harassed U.S. reconnaissance flights over Laos. The low-flying photo jets flew well within the range of the 37MM guns, 57MM guns, and smaller caliber heavy machine guns that protected the trail. Late in May, an RF-8A from the U.S.S. *Kittyhawk* was hit by ground fire on a routine mission. Lieutenant Charles F. Klusmann nursed the crippled plane safely back to the carrier, but on another mission two weeks later he was hit again and was forced to eject over enemy territory, just twenty miles from the North Vietnamese border. After an abortive rescue attempt, Klusmann was captured by the Pathet Lao and spent three months as a POW before he escaped with the help of a Communist deserter. A second navy jet met a similar fate on June 7, but this time the pilot was rescued.

The loss of two jets prompted Washington to dispatch a number of F-105 Thunderchiefs to Thailand to act as armed escorts for the photo jets. They were empowered to retaliate against AAA sites when fired upon and provide suppressive fire during rescue operations. But the idea of using U.S. planes in actual offensive operations was still considered too risky. Instead, the Laotians were finally persuaded to divert some of their T-28s to bombing operations against northern sections of the trail in exchange for more American military aid. U.S. Air Force advisers provided a list of key targets, mainly bridges and mountain passes, for the RLAF to destroy.

But the Laotian pilots and their tiny fleet of aging T-28s did not have the necessary experience or firepower. In one instance it took RLAF planes three tries before they were finally able to destroy a highway bridge outside the town of Nape along the North Vietnamese border. American air commanders argued that U.S. aircraft could do the job better. One officer boasted that "we can whomp them [the targets] all out in the first day." But when approval finally came, it was far more restricted than they had hoped for.

Operation Barrel Roll, as it was labeled, began on December 14, 1964. It was to consist of two bombing strikes per week, by no more than four aircraft in each instance, in keeping with President Johnson's desire for secrecy and minimum risk. Missions were conducted on a rotating basis by carrier-based navy aircraft and USAF F-105s stationed in Thailand. To avoid attracting unwanted publicity to the fact that U.S. planes were operating from Thai bases on combat missions, the F-105s had to fly to Da Nang and launch their strikes into Laos from South Vietnamese territory. American reporters in Thailand watched the bomb-laden F-105s taking off and returning a few days later, stripped clean. When they questioned officials on where the planes had been, they met with silence.

Initial Barrel Roll results were discouraging. Unacquainted with the jungle terrain and often assigned to targets that appeared in intelligence photos one day only to have moved on the next, U.S. pilots found Barrel Roll missions exasperating. Strict rules of engagement limited them to only certain targets within narrowly defined geographical boundaries. To avoid civilian casualties, they were instructed to fire only upon sites that unmistakably showed military activity. Trying to determine whether a hut or a moving truck contained military supplies was virtually impossible from the cockpit of a fast-moving jet.

Steel Tiger

Soon after his decision in February of 1965 to initiate a sustained bombing campaign against North Vietnam, President Johnson authorized a corresponding step-up in U.S. air strikes along the Ho Chi Minh Trail. While Barrel Roll missions continued harassing Pathet Lao and North Vietnamese supply lines and base areas in the northeastern section of the country, a separate air campaign, specifically targeted against Communist infiltration routes in the southern panhandle of Laos, began on April 3, 1965. The operation and the geographical territory it covered were both called Steel Tiger.

Two B-57s, accompanied by a C-130 flareship, flew the first Steel Tiger mission over the trail. Within a few months, air force and navy fighter-bombers were averaging twenty sorties per day. By mid-year the level had in-

creased to more than 1,000 sorties per month. By day, they blasted bridges, highways, and the narrow mountain passes that bisected the border with North Vietnam. By night, flying under the artificial glow of flares, they scoured the roads for signs of trucks or troops moving down the trail. In December, SAC B-52s began flying Steel Tiger missions as well. During the first half of 1966 they flew 400 sorties against suspected troop camps, supply depots, and truck parks.

Because of the political considerations involved, the aerial interdiction campaign in Laos was conducted through a complicated command structure and weighted down with numerous restrictions. Since there was no formal military command in Laos, like MACV in South Vietnam, overall operational control rested with the commander-in-chief, Pacific (CINCPAC), in Honolulu who had the ultimate responsibility for running all Asian air operations outside of South Vietnam. CINCPAC exercised his control through the 7th Air Force, headquartered in Saigon, which assigned aircraft on a daily basis against each ap-

proved target. Since the air wars in South and North Vietnam were given first priority, the 7th AF had a limited number of aircraft to work with.

While navy, marine, and army aircraft all participated in bombing operations in Laos, the majority of missions were flown by air force units based in South Vietnam and Thailand. The Thai government, however, objected to having American planes based on its soil while their commander was located in Saigon and insisted that commanders of U.S. forces based in Thailand also be located in Thailand. Reluctant to establish a duplicate command structure, the 7th Air Force solved the problem by assigning its deputy commander to the 13th Air Force based at Udorn AFB, which exercised administrative control of U.S. aircraft in Thailand. He became deputy commander, 7th/13th Air Force, reporting to the 7th on operational matters and to the 13th on administrative and logistical matters.

In addition to this awkward command arrangement, air operations were further complicated by the participation

Two American-supplied T-28s, one of which displays the Royal Laotian Air Force insignia, carry 200- and 500-pound bombs in July 1965. Although these planes were technically given to the RLAF, they were sometimes flown by USAF pilots and Thai mercenaries.

had men in the area that the air force did not know about.

MACV headquarters in Saigon, enthusiastically in favor of bombing the trail, also wanted a voice in the selection of targets. Each truck that was destroyed in Laos represented that many fewer troops or supplies that U.S. ground units would have to battle in South Vietnam. Army commanders also saw the bombing as a means of harassing Communist base camps across a border they were prohibited from crossing on the ground.

Late in 1965, General Westmoreland asked for operational control of bombing missions in the southern half of the panhandle directly adjacent to South Vietnam, claiming it as part of the "extended battlefield." CINCPAC approved the request and MACV became the primary agency for target selection in the area, which Westmoreland renamed Tiger Hound. The northern portion of the panhandle retained the name Steel Tiger and continued under air force control.

The ultimate authority for approving all air strikes in Laos still remained at the U.S. Embassy in Vientiane. All targeting recommendations had to pass through the U.S. air attaché's office in Vientiane where Colonel Robert L. Tyrell and his staff screened the requests to make sure they did not threaten populated areas or exceed the rules of engagement as set down by the U.S. ambassador, William H. Sullivan. Tyrell's staff, which was legally limited in size by the 1962 neutralization agreement to himself and only half a dozen enlisted men, soon was overwhelmed by the rising level of air operations. In 1966, Washington sent 117 additional military advisers, masquerading as civilians, to join the U.S. mission in Vientiane in what was known as Project 404. Nearly half were air force personnel, primarily intelligence and communications specialists, who worked in the secret operations center in Vientiane or in the air attaché's office in the embassy itself.

During his eighteen-month assignment as the chief targeting officer for Project 404, Captain Jerome J. Brown never once wore his air force uniform. Dressed in a conservative business suit and carrying an ID that identified him as an employee of the Agency for International Development (AID), Brown worked in a tiny cubicle cluttered with maps, reconnaissance photos, and film in the rear of the air attaché's office. Brown and his associates were ordered to keep a low profile and threatened with court martial if they were seen mingling with journalists. It was all part of the charade, the North Vietnamese denying the existence of the Ho Chi Minh Trail and the Americans denying bombing it. "North Vietnam lied to us and we lied to them," said Brown.

Ambassador Sullivan found himself in the extraordinary position of reconciling the bombing with official U.S. adherence to the 1962 Laos neutralization agreement. Although Souvanna Phouma approved of the bombing, he was reluctant to admit such publicly for fear of being labeled an American "puppet." Washington policy makers,

of various competing agencies who all had a voice in picking targets. The CIA, which had been running paramilitary operations in Laos for years, became heavily involved in the targeting selection process. The agency had recruited a number of ex-servicemen who acted as air war experts, providing the analysis to justify bombing operations that complemented the CIA's own activities in Laos. The agency's proclivity for secrecy created exasperating problems for air force planners. The agency would often request air strikes on short notice at certain times and places to support special teams it had infiltrated behind enemy lines on top secret missions and expect them to be carried out without question. Other times the agency would ask that a strike be cancelled because it

Air force Captain Jerome J. Brown, the chief targeting officer for Project 404, the U.S. air campaign in Laos.

anxious to avoid a direct confrontation in Laos when they considered the center of activity to be in South Vietnam, also preferred the covert arrangement.

In maintaining this Alice-in-Wonderland fiction, Sullivan shouldered the unenviable task of trying to satisfy the conflicting demands of the air force, CIA, and MACV and, at the same time, keeping a lid on the level of bombing. He had to satisfy not only the political guidelines imposed by Washington, but also a Laotian government concerned with the safety of its civilian population.

"I was restrictive not only on B–52 strikes but also on strikes of tactical aircraft," Sullivan commented during a Congressional hearing on U.S. bombing operations in Laos. "These were fast-moving aircraft and their navigational controls were not all that precise in those jungle areas, and we wanted to be absolutely certain that they were not indiscriminately striking into inhabited areas. This meant that we insisted on photography beforehand." Armed reconnaissance missions, in which pilots were allowed to hit targets of opportunity, were conducted within strictly defined geographical boundaries. In addition, all

air strikes not flown in areas that the Laotian government had designated as "free fire zones" had to be cleared by the ambassador or by Laotian observers who accompanied airborne FACs.

As a result, Sullivan won few friends among the military. "Everybody was sniping," said Col. Tyrell. "A lot of people felt that we should be running the Communists out of Laos and each one of them had his own ideas on how it should be done." General William Westmoreland, in particular, battled Sullivan over targeting requests. Exasperated by the ambassador's guidelines and restrictions, Westmoreland sarcastically referred to Sullivan as the "Field Marshal," while other critics labeled the trail "Sullivan's Freeway."

Faced with such a complicated set of rules of engagement, pilots who flew bombing missions in Laos found the experience extremely frustrating. One navy squadron commander complained that "you couldn't afford to miss the God–damned target, because if you did the Ambassador [became] involved." A number of his men were called on the carpet because they had knocked out a truck in an area where they were not supposed to be. "That used to really frost my guys," he said, "to go over there and throw their pink bodies at the ground and if they threw a bomb in the wrong place somebody put them on report."

Night mission over the trail

Because targets were usually moving vehicles, air strikes had to be mounted quickly and bombing accuracy was essential. Airborne FACs in air force O-1s and twin-seated A-1Es, as well as army OV-1 Mohawks, scoured the countryside for signs of enemy activity. Once they spotted a target, the FAC advised an orbiting C-130 crammed with radar and communications gear, which acted as an airborne command post. The C-130 would call in a strike force and direct it to the FAC in the area. At first, the so-called "fast movers," such as F-4s, F-100s, or F-105s, made the attacks, but pilots in these fast-moving, high-flying jets had difficulty seeing the minute details that were required for pinpoint bombing accuracy, especially at night when Communist activity was at its highest. Slower, conventional aircraft were considered better suited to the conditions that prevailed along the trail.

Since enemy antiaircraft fire was still relatively light in Laos (most AAA units were concentrated in the Plain of Jars, at the major supply hub at Tchepone, and near the mountain passes along the border), slow-moving planes could operate almost as safely as faster-moving jets, especially at night when the danger from enemy AAA gunners was a lesser threat. Piston-engined aircraft, with larger fuel capacities and lower fuel consumption, were able to remain airborne far longer and carried heavier ordnance loads which they could deliver with greater accuracy. Patrolling at night, in tandem with FACs in their O-1s or C-130 and C-123 flareships mounted with starlight scopes that could magnify existing starlight or moonlight, they could strike within minutes of the target's discovery.

A variety of older planes were used, including B-57 Canberra light bombers, A-1 Skyraiders, and T-28 Nomads. Even World War II-vintage B-26 Invaders were resurrected and modified for duty in Laos. On their way to the air force graveyard in Arizona, the last few Invaders remaining on active duty were rerouted to factories in California where they were fitted with eight external wing stations, eight .50-caliber machine guns, an enlarged internal bomb bay, and permanent wing tip fuel tanks. Redesignated the A-26, it could carry a maximum load of 11,000 pounds of ordnance and remain airborne for nearly three hours.

The added weight cut the plane's normal cruising speed in half, to 305 knots. But its slowness was, in fact, an asset in missions over the trail. A pilot could cruise at a low enough altitude to pick out reference points the FAC passed on to him, follow them to the target, and roll into his attack run from that same low altitude. On the night of April 5, 1968, Captain Michael Roth and his bombardier/navigator, Lieutenant Colonel Francis L. McMullen, who were assigned to the 609th Air Commando Squadron at Nakhon Phanom, showed just what the Invader could do.

After patrolling a stretch of the trail sixty miles east of Nakhon Phanom for a little over an hour, their FAC sighted two trucks rolling southward on a road below. Dropping a flare and marking the trucks' position with smoke rockets, the FAC pulled up and away as Roth made two bombing passes over the spot. Swooping in low again, the FAC found one of the trucks ablaze. But as he began searching for the second truck, the FAC's O-2 developed engine trouble, and he had to return to base.

Roth and McMullen decided to stay on patrol as long as they had fuel left. A half hour later they were still cruising above their assigned sector when a 37MM antiaircraft gun fired a couple of rounds in their direction. From the muzzle flash of the gun, they were able to pinpoint its position.

Checking their map references to find out the level of the terrain and to make sure there were no villages in the area, Roth and McMullen determined the best heading for a bombing pass. Although they had flares aboard, they decided against using them since that would make it easier for the enemy gun crew to track their approach. Rolling in over the site, Roth laid down a string of cluster bombs. One of the bomblets triggered a secondary explosion that lit up the jungle.

Realizing he had hit something bigger than an artillery gun, Roth contacted a C-123 orbiting a few miles away and asked its pilot to examine the area with its starlight scope. While he was waiting for the C-123, Roth noticed

Laotian Prime Minister Prince Souvanna Phouma and U.S. Ambassador William Sullivan. Sullivan had the difficult task of approving U.S. bombing targets in Laos while maintaining at least the appearance of American neutrality there.

he was running low on fuel and decided to unload the rest of his bombs on the same spot. After three more passes, a sheet of white fire rose. When the C-123 arrived on the scene, the starlight scope observer broke in excitedly over the radio. "My God," he exclaimed, "you found a truck park!" He counted eight vehicles and a cache of oil drums on fire as well as piles of ammunition that continued to erupt in secondary explosions.

Usually the best pilots could hope for on their nightly armed recon missions over the trail would be to catch a few trucks rumbling along open road. Many times they found nothing at all and had to content themselves with dumping their bombs to "crater" a strip of road. Truck parks and supply depots were rare finds. Roth and McMullen had hit a jackpot.

Hundreds of truck parks were scattered along the Ho Chi Minh Trail. Located a few hundred yards off the main roads and highways, hidden by elaborate camouflage nets, the parks proved elusive targets. Usually circular in shape, they consisted of a number of sandbagged revetments, roughly twenty feet long by fifteen feet wide and six feet deep, which sheltered trucks during the day.

When a low-flying reconnaissance jet occasionally uncovered an occupied truck park, by the time the recon photos reached the intelligence analysts who interpreted them and then a formal request for an air strike was approved by the U.S. ambassador, the Communists would have moved the trucks to another site. To make the situation more confounding, the enemy fabricated decoy truck parks, complete with papier-mâché trucks, to confuse photo interpreters.

Another tactic of the North Vietnamese was to leave empty oil drums stacked in the open alongside roads, interspersing a few full barrels among the empty ones to explode when hit. Pressured to provide targets, sometimes even when they did not have any, intelligence analysts would target the phony barrel depots although they knew the bombs would be wasted.

Before a bombing mission over the Ho Chi Minh Trail in Laos in March 1965, three American F-100 fighter-bomber pilots, their aircraft parked behind them, go over their flight plans.

An expanding network

Locating and destroying individual supply trucks as they traveled down the trail was an even more frustrating task. The biggest problem was monitoring the ever-expanding network of roads and trails that seemed to grow and change character overnight. Even at the height of the bombing, North Vietnamese road-building battalions laid one mile of road per day. Working at night, laborers would start on a stretch of jungle, chopping down trees, hauling in gravel to lay the road surface, then replacing the jungle cover back atop the road, making the new route virtually impossible to spot from the air.

The North Vietnamese later claimed they had built nearly 13,000 kilometers of new roads throughout Laos, creating an intricate system of bypasses and alternate routes that complicated the work of U.S. targeting analysts. According to one air force officer: "You'd have trucks coming down four different highway systems at one time. You'd have to find where the most trucks were coming and try to do some damage to them."

The air force countered with its so-called "choke point theory," which had been employed effectively against the Germans in World War II. Strikes were concentrated against key junctions, bridges, and narrow spots along sections of heavily traveled roads. Trucks caught in the resulting traffic jams would be sitting ducks for follow-up air strikes. "The idea was that if you put a hole in the road, theoretically a truck couldn't go past the hole," said an air force captain, "but they would drive around it." If the bombers cratered one road, the Communists simply opened up alternate routes.

A North Vietnamese soldier explained: "When Road 2A was the only passable road, the enemy concentrated their attacks on it. Although working day and night to repair it, the engineering corps combatants ... were unable to make it passable again. ... The commander came to the spot and ... decided to open Road 2C right away. While vehicles were running uninterrupted on Road 2C, he ordered the opening of Road 2D. ... The enemy learned of the existence of Road 2C only weeks after it was made passable. He attacked Road 2C. Our vehicles used Road 2D and the repaired Road 2A. The enemy was confused [and] stopped his attacks for a week, not knowing which roads to attack, or how to attack them."

Between 25,000 and 30,000 North Vietnamese served in Group 559 of the People's Army, whose transport, engineer, signal, artillery, and infantry units were responsible for keeping open the supply lines to South Vietnam. Another 40,000 to 50,000 laborers, many of them teen-age boys and girls, lived in camps along the Ho Chi Minh Trail and worked in repair gangs. These "young pioneers," said Ha Van Lau, who later became North Vietnam's first ambassador to the United Nations, "were ready at a moment's notice to repair the roads immediately after every bombing in such a way that despite strict surveillance by American planes this road network was never cut."

Routes were divided into twenty-mile segments, each with its own maintenance teams, trucks, drivers, and security forces. After traveling over the same route day after day, truck drivers came to know every inch of the terrain, including the locations of dense thickets, rock overhangs, and specially camouflaged lay-by sites where they could hide from reconnaissance planes. Spotters along the roads kept a lookout and relayed warning signals to nearby truck convoys when they heard the sound of an approaching aircraft. Warning signals varied from a sentry's rifle shot to a sophisticated system of flashing lights which indicated the plane's line of approach so that moving traffic could take appropriate evasive action.

Antiaircraft defenses, though intense in some areas, were fairly limited in total numbers until mid-1967, when the Communists began moving in more guns along the Ho Chi Minh Trail. By the end of 1968, an estimated 10,000 antiaircraft artillery pieces had been hauled across the border from North Vietnam. Aircraft vulnerability rates in Laos, previously only slightly higher than those for missions in South Vietnam, increased markedly, especially for slower propeller-driven planes. The enemy's introduction of 57MM and 85MM radar-directed guns also made it necessary to cover strike forces with EB-66 electronic countermeasures aircraft and F-105 Wild Weasels.

This drove the cost of the bombing campaign, which was already consuming millions of dollars a year, even higher. The average cost per fighter-bomber sortie in munitions alone was put at $3,190. B-52s, which carried a normal payload of 100 750-pound bombs apiece, were even more expensive and less cost-effective. Officials admitted that the estimated kill ratio for B-52 operations was one infiltrator for every 300 bombs at a cost of $140,000.

Despite the men, money, and aircraft that were poured into the interdiction campaign in Laos, the best the Americans could hope for was to harass the North Vietnamese and restrict the number of men and supplies that traveled down the trail. Even this limited goal seemed to be beyond their reach. Infiltration figures rose steadily, reaching an estimated level of 90,000 men per year in 1967. Ivan Delbyk, a member of a U.S. Special Forces unit that periodically ran clandestine surveillance missions into Laos, recalled: "At times the Ho Chi Minh trail ... was like the Long Island Expressway—during rush hour."

The inability of the Americans to cut the flow of traffic on the trail was painfully apparent to Project 404's chief targeting officer in Laos during 1967 and 1968, Captain Jerome Brown. One night his sergeant, who was looking through some film from a night recon mission, called over to Brown: "We got a boat down here." Brown stared at him in disbelief. "You're out of your mind," he answered, "how can you have a boat in a land-locked country?" But when he looked at the film, the captain saw it with his own eyes. "Sure enough, it was a yacht," he said. "It was beautiful, white and with all sorts of furnishings."

Brown later checked with National Security Agency personnel who conducted elaborate radio intercept operations throughout Southeast Asia to see if they had picked up any information that might explain the incongruous sight. They told him they had heard that the Chinese were sending Cambodia's Prince Norodom Sihanouk a yacht as a gift. "They delivered it by sending it down the goddamn trail," Brown said. "You've got to think of it now—a 60-foot yacht coming down the trail on the back of a trailer, through bombing missions and the whole works," he recalled. "It blew our minds."

Igloo White

The air force was constantly searching for ways to improve its interdiction effort along the trail. Attempts to turn the trails and roads into muddy quagmires by seeding rain clouds proved ineffective. Another ambitious scheme to develop a chemical mixture that would turn the damp soil into grease was also abandoned as impractical. Helicopters were rigged with flashing lights, sirens, and loudspeakers in an attempt to scare superstitious truck drivers.

Some of the more bizarre ideas never even got off the drawing board. Frank Snepp, a CIA analyst in Saigon, recalled "we discovered that the North Vietnamese loved Budweiser beer." The idea then developed "of dropping Budweiser beer along the infiltration areas in southern Laos because ... we thought it might slow them down." But the idea died when it was discovered that there was not enough beer available to drop on the entire road system. Another aborted scheme was to train pigeons to home in on trucks. A metal detector would trigger an explosive charge strapped to the bird once it landed on the vehicle. There was one big problem: the designers of the plan could not teach pigeons to distinguish a Communist truck from a non-Communist one.

The Americans also tried a variety of newly developed detection devices. Reconnaissance planes, fitted with infrared cameras, would fly over suspected truck parks just before dawn as enemy truck drivers began pulling off the roads to hide during the day. The theory was that the cameras would record the heat from the engines before they had time to cool off. But the infrared photos were difficult to interpret; analysts could not distinguish a campfire from a truck engine.

In 1966, Secretary of Defense Robert McNamara assembled a panel of civilian scientists known as the Jason Summer Study Group to assess the effectiveness of the

North Vietnamese trucks roll down a heavily bombed section of the Ho Chi Minh Trail. Even at the height of U.S. bombing, Communist road-building battalions constructed one new mile of road per day.

Barrel Roll Mission Over Laos

American pilots flying Operation Barrel Roll missions over northern Laos risked their lives every time they flew over the heavily defended Communist territory. Yet, though death might be only inches away in the form of enemy AA fire, pilots often felt curiously removed from the war, insulated from reality by an instrument panel full of high-tech gadgetry. The missions, most of them flown at night, were long, lonely excursions far beyond reasonable hope of return should something go wrong. The following is a description of a typical Barrel Roll mission, written by a former marine pilot who flew 118 missions over Laos and Vietnam.

The strangeness of the air war. Not more than two hours ago we had been watching *The Graduate* at the outdoor theater set up near our quarters in Da Nang. In an hour we'd be hundreds of miles away dodging tracers and airbursts over enemy territory. And an hour after that (with luck) we'd be back, hitting the officers' club for our usual 5:00 A.M. scotch.

It wasn't just a backward timetable that made our lives seem inside out. It was fighting a war—the same war the grunts fought face to face on the ground—from a distance, through an elaborate filter of technology. We went out at night, alone, each pair of men sealed almost hermetically in sleek black capsules. We didn't see our targets; the enemy didn't see us. Machines gave both sides the information that "indicated" our presence to each other and "suggested" the proper course of action. Almost every mission was like that: Life-and-death drama coolly played to blips and hums and streaming colors in the night.

On this particular night my call sign was Manual 74. The ready room clock showed 1:00 A.M., just forty-five minutes before our scheduled takeoff time. The atmosphere was busy, but quiet and somewhat tense. Gallons of coffee were being consumed, as usual, and cigarette smoke hung in the hot, humid air. It was rainy outside: the usual monsoon drizzle.

We were to operate along Route 6 in northern Laos, one of the northernmost segments of the Ho Chi Minh Trail, about 125 miles west of Hanoi and 175 miles south of China, 400 long miles away from anyone who'd consider us friendly. We'd be well out of helicopter range and well within range of a lot of NVA AA artillery.

I ignored the activity to continue the preflight brief with my bombardier/navigator. We briefed for about an hour, covering every detail as though it were our first flight together instead of our thirtieth. Route of flight, approach to the target, weather over the target, enemy gun positions—every contingency had to be considered. If we were hit but could still fly, should we turn east and head for the water? That meant having to eject over North Vietnam if the jet didn't make it. We would be held captive—if we survived—for months, maybe years. Or should we try to turn west toward Thailand? The risk there was ending up in northern Laos, which was Pathet Lao territory. They were notorious for not taking prisoners.

On our approach to the target, should we go in high to avoid the 23MM and 37MM antiaircraft barrage fire or stay low to avoid radar detection? No one was sure which was the better method, but everyone had an opinion, and differing opinions caused many a pilot and navigator not to want to fly together.

Are there radar-guided 57MM guns in the area? How about MiG reports? Are they flying down from their "safe" bases in China? Have any SA-2 surface-to-air missile launches been reported near the target? The questions went on and on.

As takeoff time approached we climbed into the forty-five layered pounds of flight gear: G-suit, torso harness, and survival vest to start. With helmets, oxygen masks, and flight bags in hand, the Manual 74 crew walked over to the squadron schedules board and chalked out at 1315, due back at 0330.

We picked up pistols and survival radios at the para loft on our way to the flight line. Two returning flight crews passed us as they walked back into the hangar. Their flight suits were wringing wet, partly from the light rain, mostly from nervous sweat. "Good luck, guys, but plan on being hosed a bit," they said. The NVA must have received their monthly allotment of ammunition from the Russians, and they were spending it all that night.

We walked to the aircraft, each of us privately rehearsing the mission. A lousy night. Rain, some thunderstorms, overcast at 200 feet, visibility half a mile at best. Not only would it be difficult over the target; takeoff and landing wouldn't be much fun either.

Our A-6A Intruder had already been taken through its preflight check list by the ground crew. It was dry, shielded by the cement revetment which protected the aircraft from the rocket attacks that seemed to come about every third night, usually between midnight and 3:00 A.M. Using flashlights we checked over the plane and then concentrated on the ordnance fusing. Eighteen 500-pound bombs and ten Rockeye canisters hung from the wings. Each Rockeye canister contained 247 explosive darts—very effective against trucks, and trucks were our target tonight.

The plane captain helped us strap in, and soon the cockpit came to life with electrical power provided by the ground power unit. The A-6, with its inertial navigation, terrain-avoidance radar, and ballistics computer, was one of the most advanced aircraft used in Vietnam.

I pushed the "press to test" button, illuminating forty different emergency lights. The test was to ensure that all the bulbs were working, but the glow of all those red and orange lights reminded us how many things could go wrong with this state-of-the-art flying machine.

We finished the check list quickly; it was long, but we had been through it hundreds of times and knew it cold: oxygen on, master arm off, fuel master on, GTC on, crank switch depress, throttle around the horn. ... Two powerful J-52 engines whined and rumbled beneath us.

There we were, sitting on top of 18,000 pounds of roaring thrust, surrounded by tanks containing over 2,400 gallons of fuel, which in turn were surrounded by miles of tubing containing everything from pure oxygen to highly flammable hydraulic fluid. Not to mention the 14,700 pounds of bombs hanging under the wings. No wonder few jets survived even a single hit: Virtually every part of the aircraft was vital—and explosive.

Takeoff was uneventful, or as uneventful as getting 60,000 pounds off the ground can be. For the first twenty seconds or so that aircraft didn't really want to fly; it was loaded to capacity. But with the gear and flaps up and the airspeed passing through 300 knots, she started handling like an airplane.

The flight north was quiet—and lonely. No radio chatter, no formations of jets for company, no nothing. The A-6 was a loner, always solo, generally flying at night. This was a dark, moonless night. We ran into thunderstorms, and it seemed that whenever our eyes began to adjust to the darkness another bright flash of lightning destroyed whatever night vision we had managed to acquire.

Vertigo became a problem, as it did almost every night. The jet's acceleration would force the inner ear fluid aft, giving us the sensation of lying flat on our backs as though we were climbing. The turbulence further confused our sense of balance, and soon I was feeling as though the aircraft was flying 30 degrees nose up, 20 degrees left wing down—but the instruments indicated straight and level flight.

After almost an hour, we approached the high-threat area within range of enemy radar, and I descended to a lower altitude hoping to avoid radar detection. I hadn't yet shaken the vertigo, but smooth precision flying was necessary now, for the Intruder had to stay low, and the terrain over northern Laos was rugged, with ridges ranging from 3,000 to 6,000 feet.

While heading north along Route 6, about seventy miles north of Ban Ban, the navigator picked up four "movers" on the ground via his AMTI radar. The unsuspecting trucks were heading south from China. My instrument panel read: "distance to target: 18 miles; time to target: 2 minutes."

We moved in, but the guns along the trail began to provide cover for the trucks. Gunners on the ground often couldn't see, or ever hear, an approaching jet, but one thing was certain: They knew the jet had to fly over the road to hit the trucks, so up went the barrage fire. A pilot had no choice but to fly through it.

The last thirty seconds of the attack grew even more tense. My navigator and I exchanged quiet, terse instructions, punctuated by a growing number of expletives. "Got a track-lock on the movers." "We're taking heavy 23/37MM from the right; I've got to get lower." "Not much lower, ridge line ahead; 37MM at ten o'clock." We hadn't fired a shot.

I yanked the aircraft left and right to evade the AA, and the resulting G forces made our vertigo worse. The cascading red, white, and green tracers made us feel that we were in an amusement park fun house. Strobe lights from the flashing airbursts completed the effect.

Flying lower and faster now, the trucks just one mile ahead. The barrage fire was heavier. The cockpit glowed as the red tracer balls passed noiselessly overhead and to the rear. Finally, the computer went into its attack mode. Lights began flashing on the instrument panel: "Attack, In Range." The hum in my headset indicated that the aircraft's radar had a lock on the trucks and that the trucks were continuing to move. The ballistics computer calculated the lead; it would release the bombs automatically when we were in precisely the right position.

Airspeed: 550 knots; altitude: 1,500 feet. The trucks were less than two miles ahead.

The navigator, his head buried in the radar scope, tried to ignore the red tracers shooting past the aircraft; I could hardly see anything else through the dense black clouds. I tried to line up the plane with four trucks that we were fast approaching.

"System looks good, about twenty seconds till bomb release."

"I'm gonna break left after release—how high is the ridge line to our left?"

"About 3,500. Get above 4,000, but don't get higher; we're picking up enemy radar on the APR-25."

"Christ, what's that?" As I spoke, four unguided 122MM rockets appeared dead ahead, exploding above us at about 3,000 feet. The NVA were throwing up about as much as they could at us, even unguided surface-to-surface rockets set to explode seconds after being launched.

We could see the road below in the flash of the airbursts overhead. "What must those truck drivers be thinking?" I thought. "They've got to know the guns are shooting at something that's coming after them." The hum continued in the headset; the trucks were still moving.

The bombs began releasing. So did the Rockeye canisters. "Those damn canisters," I shouted. As they fell away from the aircraft, explosive charges blew open the pods to release the darts, six small explosions lighting up the bottom of the Intruder for every gunner in the valley to see. The damned engineer who designed these things should try dropping them at night.

Sure enough, the tracers that had been trailing the jet now began to lead us. I pulled up and to the left, a 6G turn to 4,000 feet. "I'm gonna race for altitude. We've got to get above this 37MM stuff. You work the ECM gear so the radar-guided guns don't lock us up."

Just then our bombs hit far below us, slightly aft and to the left, one in front of another on the road. Two secondary explosions, puffy orange balls. Must have hit at least two trucks. I remember having it register in my mind that two or more of the drivers had probably just died.

A 37MM gun on top of a 3,000-foot mountain picked us up as we were breaking away. We both saw it coming, in spite of the weather. We were so close to the gun that we even saw the muzzle flashes as the eight rounds left the barrels. The right wing obscured my view of the approaching red balls as I again broke hard to the left. I was sure we were going to take a hit, and all I could think was "What's it going to sound like when they hit?"

But all eight rounds missed. The red balls passed about fifty feet to the right and turned into airbursts above and behind us.

The trip home, like the trip out, was quiet, uneventful. Almost two hours in the air, most of it routine and somewhat boring. But those twenty minutes or so in the middle—that was pure terror.

Our mission was about over; we were almost home, and I could feel us both beginning to relax. Maybe tomorrow night we'd be lucky and draw a flight "down South."

As we came in sight of the base, the navigator broke the calm silence with a single question, the kind of question you could ask only coming out of a mission, not going in: "How are we gonna do this for another six months without sooner or later catching one of those red balls?"

bombing strategy in Southeast Asia. Their pessimistic report suggested an alternative to what they considered a costly and ineffective bombing campaign—an anti-infiltration barrier of electronic sensors along with conventional barbed-wire fences and minefields to be strung across the DMZ and the Laotian panhandle to the Thai border. McNamara assembled a secret team of military and civilian scientists at the Pentagon called the Defense Communications Planning Group to research and develop the concept and other aspects of military technology.

What air force generals derisively referred to as "McNamara's Fence" was never built. Instead, the planners settled upon the idea of seeding electronic sensors along the trail to detect and monitor enemy movements. The sensor system, named Igloo White, was put into operation in November 1967 by Task Force Alpha, a special team of air force personnel and civilian analysts.

Specially designed acoustic and seismic sensors were airdropped along key transportation routes in Laos and across the DMZ. Some of these battery-operated sensors were shaped in the form of spikes that buried themselves in the ground on impact, leaving only flexible antennas disguised as weeds above ground. Others were equipped with tiny parachutes that snagged in trees. The sensors were activated by ground vibrations or nearby sounds of troops or truck movements. Once activated, they transmitted signals to electronic monitoring equipment aboard an EC-121R aircraft orbiting overhead. The EC-121R relayed the signals to a huge computer complex at Nakhon Phanom just across the Thai border, where Task Force Alpha analysts interpreted the information. When the surveillance center got a fix on large troop concentrations or truck convoys, strikes could be launched immediately by air force, navy, and marine fighter jets held on constant alert as part of Operation Commando Bolt.

Besides immediate targeting intelligence, the sensors provided analysts with a broader picture of enemy activities along the trail. At Nakhon Phanom, signals were sorted out by computer and the data analyzed along with reconnaissance photos and other intelligence reports. The combined results were plotted on detailed maps which were studied to detect patterns of movement along the trail. Air commanders could then coordinate their strategy accordingly. Segments of the trail were seeded with mines or delayed-action bombs, while American pilots focused bombing efforts on natural "choke points," such as the Mu Gia Pass between North Vietnam and Laos, where Communist truck convoys could be destroyed en masse.

Two of the most effective weapons against trucks were the BLU-31, a 700-pound land mine that buried itself into the ground upon impact, and the Mark-36 Destructor, a 500-pound delayed-action bomb which detonated if moved, or if reached by vibrations of nearby movement. Flat, three-inch-square gravel mines, about the size and shape of a tea bag, were liberally scattered in areas known to be heavily traveled by ground troops. Once a mine was stepped on, a twenty-gram charge of black powder would detonate with enough force to blow off a man's foot. Although these weapons were employed in increasing numbers as they became available, the mainstays of Igloo White's destructive power were conventional general purpose bombs, cluster bombs, and Mark-35 incendiary bombs.

Commando Hunt

In November 1968, bombing missions in southern Laos more than tripled. Tactical sorties by air force, navy, and marine aircraft jumped from 4,700 in October to 12,800 in November. SAC B-52 sorties jumped from 273 to nearly 600 during the same period. In part, the increase could be attributed to the normal ebb and flow of weather conditions. October brought the end of the rainy season in Laos which meant both better flying weather for U.S. pilots and drier roads for Communist trucks. But the advent of the dry season in 1968 also coincided with the bombing halt over North Vietnam, which left Hanoi with a large pool of manpower, weapons, and supplies for use in Laos and South Vietnam. Intelligence sources registered a sharp jump in infiltration figures and discovered the enemy was building a POL pipeline directly into the panhandle.

The end of the Rolling Thunder campaign also meant that more U.S. aircraft were now available for missions in Laos. As one official noted: "We had all these planes sitting around and couldn't just let them stay there with nothing to do." Since military commanders had often argued that bombing operations along the Ho Chi Minh Trail directly affected the level of Communist operations in South Vietnam and, therefore, the number of U.S. casualties, they had a natural argument for employing these

Pathet Lao soldiers position an 85MM D-44 field gun on the Ho Chi Minh Trail, adding to the trail's increasingly intense AA defenses.

A reconnaissance photo reveals the positions of three enemy trucks along the Ho Chi Minh Trail in Laos in 1970.

planes in air operations in Laos. The idea also appealed to the Nixon administration as a way to buy time for its Vietnamization program. Air force, navy, and marine aircraft formerly directed against North Vietnamese targets now joined the ranks of American warplanes that layered the skies above Laos.

At 2,000 feet were the lightweight O-1 and O-2 Cessna observation planes. Propeller-driven A-1s, A-26s, and T-28s droned above them at 5,000 feet. Jet-powered F-4s, F-100s, F-105s, and B-57s roamed at 10,000 feet, along with EC-47 and EC-119 electronic detection aircraft. KC-135 refueling tankers cruised at the 20,000-foot level, while SAC B-52s thundered by another 10,000 feet above. EC-130 command and control aircraft circled at 35,000 feet, while black, needle-nosed SR-71 reconnaissance jets streaked past at 70,000 feet.

With virtually unlimited resources at their disposal, the U.S. high command launched a series of successive bombing campaigns beginning with Operation Commando Hunt I, which lasted from November 1968 through the end of the dry season in May 1969. Initially, the operation was limited to a 1,700-square-mile area adjacent to the South Vietnamese border. Its major objectives were to destroy supplies, tie down enemy manpower, and test the effectiveness of the sensor system. Commando Hunt II maintained the pressure through the following rainy season (May-October 1968) when Communists traditionally concentrated on expanding and repairing roads and augmenting AAA defenses in preparation for the next dry season. American aircraft were now flying 400 sorties per day in Laos, nearly 100 more than were flown in North Vietnam at the height of the Rolling Thunder campaign. By January 1970, during the middle of Commando Hunt III, the 7th/13th Air Force alone was averaging 14,000 sorties per month.

Statistically, Commando Hunt was a spectacular success. The air force claimed 7,332 trucks destroyed or damaged in 1968 compared to 3,291 in 1967. The totals for 1969 rose to 9,012 and peaked in 1970 at 12,368. The statistics aroused some skepticism, however. A Congressional investigating committee, for example, noted that the total number of truck kills claimed in 1970 alone far exceeded the number of trucks believed to be in all of North Vietnam. In addition, bomb damage assessment (BDA) reports by pilots were considered highly unreliable.

It was extremely difficult for pilots, especially those flying fast-moving jets, to tell whether they had hit anything worth hitting, particularly at night, and, if so, with what effect. Many times the enemy's practice of setting decoy fires tricked pilots into reporting a truck as destroyed. Although most airmen took great pains to confirm a truck kill, some deliberately padded their claims for advancement purposes, while others told intelligence debriefing officers what they wanted to hear. "There's a tremendous satisfaction in doing the job, counting up the ordnance dropped,

filling out the kill charts," one pilot told a reporter from the *New York Times.* "Of course, you never even see if you've hit anything most of the time."

An air force officer attached to the embassy in Vientiane later recalled the self-ingratiating atmosphere of weekly meetings between air force and CIA officials at Udorn, Thailand, every Tuesday. "The first thing we had was a summary of the weekly targets struck. ... Every mission always reported secondary explosions, because the pilot got brownie points for secondary explosions. ... It made everybody happy ... everybody would sit back and say, 'Oh, boy, it was a great week. We really hurt them!' By the end everybody had [his] say and everybody felt good. We really knew we had the North Vietnamese in a horrible position. ... Everybody was doing a fantastic job, everybody was patting everybody else on the back; the meeting was adjourned and we all went home."

This tendency toward self-promotion and self-deception among the air managers was confirmed by Col. Tyrell. He got the impression that Laos became a "dumping ground" for the air force after Rolling Thunder was halted. "They were looking at it in terms of what could be generated to keep things going rather than what was needed," the air attaché said. "It was my feeling in a few cases that people were using this situation for their own personal gain." A number of generals, frustrated by the bombing halt over North Vietnam, considered Laos their last chance to show what they and air power could do. "Goddamn," Tyrell overheard one exclaim in the embassy dining room one day, "this is the only war we've got now."

The "other war"

Commando Hunt, in fact, was not the only game in town. Parallel to the sophisticated electronic air war in the southern panhandle, the U.S. waged a very different campaign in northern Laos. There, the early Barrel Roll missions, begun in 1964 to support Royal Laotian troops in their battle against the Pathet Lao, had evolved into a separate air campaign with a life of its own.

Barrel Roll operations ranged from Route 7, which stretched westward from North Vietnam into the Plain of Jars, north to the Chinese border. Its objective was similar to that of Commando Hunt operations, namely interdicting the northernmost avenues of the Ho Chi Minh Trail and Communist supply lines supporting the Pathet Lao. Because these northern supply lines were close to the North Vietnamese and Chinese borders, the missions were usually flown by long-range jet fighter-bombers, such as navy and marine A-6 Intruders with more sophisticated radar and navigational equipment (see sidebar, p. 36). But in 1969, U.S. air activity in the Barrel Roll zone took on another objective. American planes began to fly close air support missions for loyalist ground forces in what Ambassador Sullivan termed the "other war" in Laos.

North Vietnamese soldiers, captured by Laotian government troops after a two-day battle at Lao Ngam, Laos, in February 1968, are displayed to reporters in Pak Se before being flown to South Vietnam.

For nearly eight years, the war between the Pathet Lao and the Royal Laotian Army had been a stalemate, featuring little more than seasonal exchanges of real estate in the Plain of Jars. The Communists advanced during the November–May dry season, while government forces normally retook lost ground during the June–October wet season. One of the reasons the Pathet Lao were never able to fully gain control of the plain was the chain of mountain strongholds in and around the region held by General Vang Pao's Meo irregulars. Many were equipped with rough airstrips that were known as Lima sites (a designation given to all airfields in Laos, which were assigned numbers to mark their locations for U.S. pilots). Although Vang Pao's clandestine army had been integrated into the Royal Laotian Army, it continued to receive airlifts of arms and supplies by CIA owned and operated Air America aircraft (see sidebar, p. 47).

These loyalist ground forces were supported by RLAF T–28s divided into five wings of ten planes each. American and Thai advisers trained the Laotian pilots and also supervised maintenance and ordnance handling. While most of their missions were flown in response to requests

from Laotian ground commanders, effective control of the RLAF lay in the hands of the U.S. ambassador and U.S. Air Force advisers. Although American bombing operations concentrated against Communist supply lines and base areas behind the battle lines, U.S. aircraft had also been called in on occasion to assist RLAF T–28s in providing close air support for ground troops.

That direct American participation increased dramatically in the spring of 1969, after the stalemate on the ground was suddenly shattered by a combined Pathet Lao–North Vietnamese drive through the Plain of Jars backed by artillery and tanks. On March 1, the Communists captured Lima Site 36 at Na Khang and began closing in on Vang Pao's headquarters at Long Tien. Vang Pao requested more American aircraft to support a counteroffensive aimed at seizing Xieng Khouang, the Pathet Lao's provisional capital on the Plain of Jars. The 7th Air Force obliged, flying more than 700 sorties in support of the advancing troops, who captured the town late in April.

Vang Pao's success was short-lived. The Communists counterattacked during the rainy season in June, capturing Vang Pao's stronghold at Muong Soui (Lima Site 108).

Encouraged by his American advisers, the Meo leader tried to retake the town. But poor flying conditions doomed the attempt. Not until the weather cleared in mid-August did Meo and Royal Laotian forces begin reversing the Communist tide.

Supported by an average 200 Barrel Roll sorties per day, government forces managed to regain control in the southern portion of the Plain of Jars. Vang Pao's guerrillas expanded their control around their Lima sites, cut enemy supply lines along Route 7, and recaptured Muong Soui in September. This was achieved through tactics designed to counter the Meo's poor performance in conventional warfare and exploit their excellent capabilities as counter-guerrillas. According to General Robert L. Petit, deputy commander of the 7th/13th Air Force, "Vang Pao and his troops would move out, identify the enemy, pull back and then the airpower would come in."

U.S. Air Force fighter-bombers based in Thailand were often used against concentrations of troops or to soften up enemy positions prior to a ground attack. But pilots flying these F-4s, and especially pilots flying F-105 Thunderchiefs, which were designed for high-altitude bombing missions, lacked the equipment or training necessary for close air support work. One F-105 pilot whose squadron was diverted to flying Operation Barrel Roll missions after the bombing halt over the North admitted that "we as crews were rather reluctant to engage in a troops-in-contact situation. The primary reason was they wanted us to drop high drag weapons [from low altitudes] and we just couldn't drop them accurately enough . . . most of us had no training in it."

The majority of close air support missions were flown by conventional fighter-bombers of the 633rd Special Operations Wing based close to the Laotian border at Nakhon Phanom. The wing's A-1 Skyraiders and T-28 Nomads, with large ordnance loads, slower speeds, and greater maneuverability at low altitudes, were much better suited for these low-level missions. When incoming pilots asked the old-timers what the preferred angle for bomb delivery was, they were told "roll in so steep that it scares you to death." The steeper the angle, the fewer problems with distance and accuracy.

Finding the target was another matter. U.S. radar sites in South Vietnam and Thailand, which aided pilot navigation in the nearby Steel Tiger and Tiger Hound zones, could not reach into northeastern Laos. To remedy the deficiency, a few unmanned TACAN (tactical air navigation) sites, which provided pilots with fixed geographical reference points via a continuous radio transmission, were erected atop high mountains in northern Laos. Usually located in disputed territory, they made inviting targets for the enemy.

One of the more bizarre events of the war occurred at Lima Site 85, atop a 5,200-foot mountain near Phou Pha Thi, twenty-five miles west of the Communist stronghold of Sam Neua and only seventeen miles from the North Vietnamese border. When the TACAN site there was replaced, late in 1967, with an all-weather navigational system operated by nineteen USAF technicians, the enemy became suspicious of an increased level of activity. On January 12, 1968, four Soviet-built AN-2 Colt biplanes appeared over the site, and North Vietnamese machine gunners on board began firing out the plane's windows.

This first North Vietnamese Air Force foray into Laos proved less than satisfactory, however. The pilot of an Air America H-34 helicopter, who happened to be delivering a load of supplies at the time, lifted off immediately to avoid the mortar shells being lobbed from the planes by hand. Once in the air, the Air America pilot and his mechanic/loadmaster realized their chopper was faster than the biplanes, and they decided to take after the Colts.

Pulling out an AK47 automatic rifle he had acquired as a war trophy, the helicopter's mechanic sprayed one of the planes with a burst of fire. The pilot was killed and the biplane crashed to the ground. The chopper pilot then chased a second Colt, which crash-landed. A third was shot down by ground fire from the radar site. Three months later, the North Vietnamese attacked the installation from the ground. A small force of sappers scaled the supposedly invulnerable side of the mountain, surprised the 100 Meo tribesmen guarding the site, and destroyed the radar equipment. Twelve of the USAF technicians got out by helicopter, but the remaining seven were not seen again and were listed as missing in action.

Since there were few reliable ground radar sites to provide navigational assistance in the Barrel Roll area, pilots virtually "flew by the seat of their pants," relying on geographical landmarks by day and little more than instinct at night. "It was really hairy in Barrel Roll," said Major James Costin, an A-1 pilot with the 602d Special Operations Squadron at Nakhon Phanom. "Everything was dead reckoning up there. Most of the people knew the Barrel like the back of their hand toward mid-tour at least." If they did not, they more than likely ended up as statistics on the casualty lists.

The combination of rough terrain and poor weather made flying conditions in Laos a hazardous proposition for even the most experienced pilots. Deep valleys interspersed with jagged limestone formations, known as karst, and surrounded by menacing mountain peaks became invisible obstacle courses when shrouded in clouds and fog. A number of pilots were lost to unexplained accidents, becoming disoriented when flying in bad weather and crashing into the side of a mountain. "In the rainy season the sun could become a memory to those on the ground and something a pilot might occasionally see between clouds," according to one pilot. "Sometimes the weather scared me as much as enemy gunners."

There was also danger of running into other flights operating in the area, particularly at night. Air traffic was theoretically controlled by airborne command posts, which assigned various aircraft differing altitudes to keep them separated. Since, to avoid detection by the enemy, none of the pilots flew with their plane's lights on, they had to trust each other to keep to their assigned altitudes. "But people were departing their altitude and flying wherever they wanted to fly out there," noted Maj. Costin. "I have had sets of fighters come right through my strike."

As in southern Laos, many of the strikes were pre-planned affairs assigned by higher headquarters against "picture" or "paper" targets, usually suspected enemy troop locations or supply lines that had been uncovered by intelligence reports or aerial reconnaissance. The time delays involved in analyzing and disseminating the information often gave the enemy time to disappear before the strike hit.

Far more effective were strikes controlled by the so-called Raven FACs, American pilots who flew O-1s, U-17s, and T-28s. Operating directly from bases in Laos close to the battlefield and with a Laotian observer on board who could immediately validate targets, a Raven FAC's intelligence tended to be far more timely and reliable. "When you worked with a Raven," said Maj. Costin, "you probably weren't going to bomb something that you shouldn't be bombing. With the rules of engagement, as they changed and as inflexible as they were, that was something that was always a concern. . . . We lived in fear of bombing the wrong people up there all the time."

Most American close air support missions resulted from calls for help from Laotian ground units themselves. This meant that pilots had to rely heavily on forward air guides (FAGs) on the ground, mainly Laotians or Meo tribesmen attached to ground units or positioned behind enemy lines. Operating on designated FM frequencies, forward air guides kept in constant touch with aircraft in their areas, providing intelligence on Communist troop movements and passing on requests for close air support strikes. Aircraft pilots came to know the FAGs by their individual call signs, usually words from the names of various bars and bordellos in Vientiane.

While the pilots developed amiable relations with the Laotian spotters, working with them was not easy. Communications tended to be less than precise when conducted in the broken English most FAGs were able to master. The problem was compounded when a FAG or ground troops had no marker smoke rounds for their mortars. The location of the target then had to be passed on by the less reliable method of map coordinates or a physical description, a problem in view of the language barrier. This often forced pilots into the hit-or-miss situation of firing marker rockets until they finally stumbled on the target the FAG was trying to describe.

Voice recognition was also important. Since the enemy monitored communications between the FAGs and pilots, they were able to pick up the jargon and would some-times try to trick American pilots. "On two occasions," recalled one pilot, "they tried to put me in on what I think were loyalist teams in the field, friendly positions. So you had to be very careful."

Yet another problem was the undue emphasis Laotian ground commanders placed upon air power. "They had the feeling that they could do anything if they had air support," said Col. Tyrell. There was a marked tendency to use this new weapon as a sort of life insurance policy. If ground units spotted something on a nearby ridge or suspected someone was over the next hill from them, they would call in an air strike. Operating under these less than ideal conditions, it was no wonder that Barrel Roll missions achieved erratic results.

"Good guys and bad guys"

Captain Richard S. Drury, an A-1 pilot with the 1st Special Operations Squadron at Nakhon Phanom, recounted a night Barrel Roll mission he flew three days before Christmas in 1969. He and his wingman were given a set of coordinates for contacting a FAG whose call sign was Kingpin. Flying by instruments, which in the unsophisticated A-1 merely meant estimating the time and distance required to reach a given spot, Drury tried to establish radio contact in a crude form of pidgin English.

"Hello Kingpin. This is Hobo. You hear me?" After a few more tries, a distant voice finally broke through the static. "Hobo. Kingpin. You come help Kingpin?" "Yes, Kingpin," replied Drury, "Hobo come help you. You have bad guys?" "Roger, roger, Hobo. Have many, many bad guy. They all around. They shoot big gun at me."

Although Drury could not see any muzzle flashes through the murky night sky, he knew that small-arms fire was usually invisible to a pilot. He had often landed after what appeared to be an uneventful mission only to find his plane peppered with holes. The "big gun" Kingpin referred to could be a mortar. Drury now began a tedious game of "hide and seek" to pinpoint the FAG's position. As often occurred, the map coordinates Kingpin had given him were wildly inaccurate. The two pilots slowly circled the area waiting for Kingpin to hear the sound of their engines. Finally, they narrowed the position down to a deep valley surrounded by towering mountain peaks.

"Kingpin; Hobo see big valley. Where are you?" "Roger, Hobo," replied the FAG. "Bad guy in valley. You put bomb in middle of valley." Captain Drury asked Kingpin again to locate his position. Although he knew that any attempt to get a more accurate description of the target would be useless, he at least wanted to be sure he was not dropping live ordnance on top of Kingpin. "Hobo, Kingpin on top of mountain," came the reply, "OK, Hobo drop bomb in valley."

By the dim red glow of the instrument panel inside the cockpit, Drury activated the release mechanism for one of

Pathet Lao workers in Sam Neua Province blast caves out of the mountains to shelter supplies from American bombing. The blasted rock, in turn, was used for road repairs.

the bomb stations underneath the A-1's left wing, which held a 500-pound napalm bomb. Turning off all but one of his external lights to present less of a target to the enemy gunners below, Drury began his descent past the mountaintops into the valley.

Rolling into a forty-five-degree dive, Drury peered into his gun sight looking vainly for signs of life in the inky darkness. Although the possibility of antiaircraft fire nagged at the back of his mind, as his altimeter spun down he worried more about hitting the ground. Punching the release button on his control stick, Drury felt the loss of 500 pounds before the three "G" pull up flattened him into his seat. The napalm "splashed like one giant flashbulb" in his rearview mirror and Drury concentrated on his instruments until his night vision returned.

"Hobo! You have number one bomb!" came the cry from Kingpin. "Ver-ry good. You do same again." Drury and his wingman obliged. They made a few more passes until the valley sparkled with the flames from little fires and 20MM tracer fire. As with most night missions, Drury flew home wondering whether he had done any damage to the enemy at all.

Although FAGs often provided pilots with immediate bomb damage assessment reports, Drury claimed they were usually so exaggerated that they became a running joke among the squadron. To show their appreciation to the pilot and to encourage him to return,

Caves housed Pathet Lao schools, command posts, and other operations, such as this printing press.

FAGs picked a nice high figure, thinking that the higher the kill rate the better both they and the pilot would look in reports to higher headquarters. "You kill one hundred bad guy," became the standard BDA report. This appeared to impress the brass, who measured success in terms of body counts, until they noticed that every mission seemed to turn up a body count of 100. Apparently the FAGs got the word that their numbers were not being taken seriously and began changing their BDA reports.

Following the standard routine after a Barrel Roll mission one night, Colonel George Miller called the FAG he had been working with and asked for the BDA. "You killed ninety-eight bad guy," came the serious reply. "Oh come on Pogo," Miller said to the FAG. "Whatdya mean, ninety-eight?" After a moment of silence, Pogo responded, "Okay, you kill one hundred and two."

During 1969, U.S. Air Force planes flew an average of 300 sorties per month in northeastern Laos, most of them against Communist positions in and around the Plain of

Jars. But direct American aerial intervention in the ground war failed to have any lasting effect. In December, the Communists took to the offensive once again. By January 1970, they had wiped out the government's gains and recaptured control of the Plain of Jars. The situation began deteriorating so rapidly that in February Washington took the unprecedented step of approving the use of B-52s for Barrel Roll operations. In the first raid on the eighteenth, thirty-six B-52s dropped 1,078 tons of bombs on enemy positions. This extensive infusion of U.S. air power managed to prevent a total Communist victory in Laos, but the enemy kept his advantage on the ground.

The results were limited at least in part because of the complex command and control structure and the fact that Barrel Roll strikes were even more restricted in scope than those in southern Laos. Since the ground war gravitated around relatively heavily populated areas, a Foreign Service officer at the embassy carefully evaluated all targeting requests, even the types of ordnance employed, against a strict set of guidelines. No strikes were to be targeted within 500 meters of "active villages" not validated by the embassy for a strike, and a village could be defined as a single hut. The use of napalm was permitted only in zones designated as Special Operating Areas which the embassy had confirmed were free of any civilians or "friendly" personnel.

For all the stringency of these rules of engagement, reports of civilian casualties as a result of U.S. air strikes frequently appeared in the press. A *Washington Star* article, for example, stated that air strikes near Xien Khouang in May of 1969 killed 200 civilians. When questioned about the story during a Senate hearing later that year, Col. Tyrell claimed he had talked to Laotian refugees after the battle and heard no such accounts. "I am not saying that civilians have not been killed as a result of the air strikes occasionally," he told the senators, "but I do not think that there have been a significant number."

"The bombs fell like rain"

Others disagreed, including Fred Branfman, an American serving with the International Voluntary Services relief organization, who interviewed hundreds of refugees. "Every individual interviewed—without exception—has said that his town or village was destroyed by American bombing," Branfman claimed. "Tens of thousands of peasants have been killed and wounded, hundreds of thousands have been driven underground." One teen-age refugee told Branfman: "Our village was filled with bomb craters. . . . Each day, news came about such and such a village being bombed, more and more deaths and wounded. . . . [We] learned another form of civilization: the holes. We dug day and night, the planes bombed day and night." According to another villager, "they came like birds and the bombs fell like rain."

In any event, an area the size of the state of New York, once a fairly prosperous region of some 3,500 small villages inhabited by subsistence farmers, became a barren wasteland as its residents fled from the constant bombing. Nearly 50 percent of the area's population moved into government refugee camps in the Vientiane plain. The number of refugees on the rolls of the U.S. Agency for International Development, which averaged 130,000 between 1964 and 1968, jumped to 230,000 in February 1969.

The increased reports of civilian refugees and casualties were partially explained by the quickened pace of the ground war in 1969 and the corresponding increase in bombing, but State Department and air force officials attributed another cause to the wide-ranging activities of the CIA. Besides the usual use of clandestine espionage and sabotage teams, the CIA exercised a great deal of influence with Vang Pao's forces, whom they had recruited, trained, and supplied since the early sixties. When they began suffering setbacks in 1969, the agency pressed for more air strikes and a relaxation of bombing restrictions, citing Vang Pao's threats to pull his forces out of the battle if he did not get more air support. Although Ambassador Sullivan agreed to loosen some of the restrictions, he continued to monitor CIA targeting requests very closely.

But the situation changed in June 1969, when Sullivan was succeeded by G. McMurtrie Godfrey. A devoted advocate of the bombing and a close friend of the newly appointed CIA station chief in Vientiane, Godfrey relaxed the bombing restrictions even further. Air force officers noted a sharp rise in the number of Communist-controlled towns and villages targeted for air strikes. George Chapelier, a Belgian adviser with the UN, reported widespread bombing of small villages in areas controlled by the Pathet Lao late in 1969. "Jet planes came daily and destroyed all stationary structures. Nothing was left standing. The villagers lived in trenches and holes or in caves. They only farmed at night." There was no question in Chapelier's mind that the "bombings were aimed at the systematic destruction of the material basis of the civilian society."

After interviewing a number of U.S. and Laotian officials in the fall of 1969, veteran war correspondent Robert Shaplen noted in an article in *Foreign Affairs* magazine in April 1970 that the apparent objective of the bombing was to "destroy the social and economic fabric in Pathet Lao areas." A number of other un-

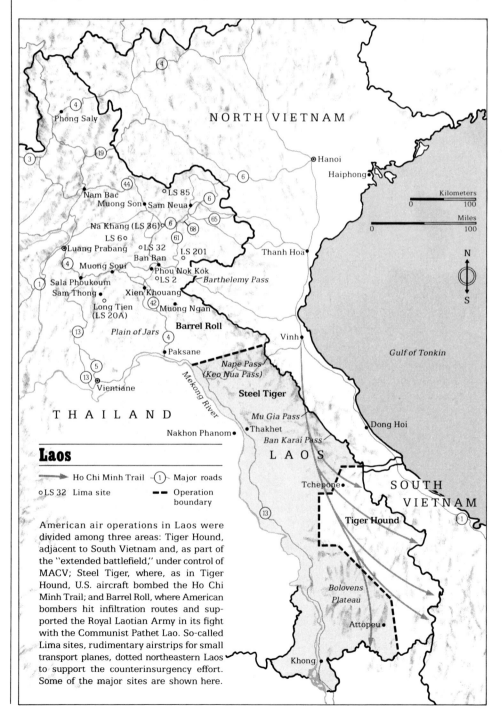

Laos

→ Ho Chi Minh Trail   ①— Major roads
○LS 32 Lima site   ▬ ▬ Operation boundary

American air operations in Laos were divided among three areas: Tiger Hound, adjacent to South Vietnam and, as part of the "extended battlefield," under control of MACV; Steel Tiger, where, as in Tiger Hound, U.S. aircraft bombed the Ho Chi Minh Trail; and Barrel Roll, where American bombers hit infiltration routes and supported the Royal Laotian Army in its fight with the Communist Pathet Lao. So-called Lima sites, rudimentary airstrips for small transport planes, dotted northeastern Laos to support the counterinsurgency effort. Some of the major sites are shown here.

Air America

Throughout U.S. air bases in Southeast Asia, a number of civilian aircraft mingled alongside the sleek fighters and bomb-laden jets. They belonged to air transport companies such as Continental Air Service and Bird and Son Air, which worked under government contracts to meet America's burgeoning transportation requirements in Indochina. The foremost among these was Air America, whose vast fleet of aircraft made it one of the largest and most profitable airlines in the world. One of the major reasons behind Air America's success was that it was secretly owned by the CIA.

The airline offered a perfect cover for the CIA's extensive paramilitary operations throughout Indochina. On the surface, Air America appeared to be a legitimate transport service. Many served with the company for years without realizing it was owned by the agency. While the bulk of the airline's contracts were aboveboard, nearly a quarter involved secret "black" flights in unmarked aircraft flown by pilots who were well aware of who their employers really were.

They airlifted intelligence agents and sabotage teams into North Vietnam. In South Vietnam, they transported VC prisoners, CIA payrolls, and operatives of the CIA's antiterrorist Phoenix Program. In Laos, Air America acted as the CIA's own clandestine air force, carrying out a number of the agency's pet projects. Air America planes were also the agency's sole link with the irregular armies they had recruited among the Meo and other ethnic tribes to fight the Pathet Lao.

Crude landing strips were hacked out of the jungle for the regular supply runs that shuttled in weapons, ammunition, and other supplies. To navigate these runways, Air America acquired a number of short takeoff and landing (STOL) helo-courier aircraft and PC-6 Pilatus Porters. But the majority of Air America aircraft employed in these secret missions were conventional planes and helicopters they either "bought" or received on "loan" from the U.S. military, which were "sanitized" to conceal their identity.

Through a series of complex accounting subterfuges, the CIA acquired surplus military aircraft without using budgeted funds which could easily be traced. The agency kept the auditors even further at bay by "laundering" the planes through a series of ownership arrangements in dummy corporations. Another method was to simply borrow the aircraft from the U.S. military.

The military planes were carefully sanitized before they were handed over to Air America. They were painted a different color from the official colorings and had a screw-on USAF insignia and scotch-tape markings that could be removed within a few minutes. While some were repainted with Air America insignia, others were left completely unmarked. Since each aircraft's tail, engines, and instruments carried serial numbers, they were often taken apart and reassembled in different combinations to make them harder to trace.

Air America pilots were an odd assortment of old China hands, aviation purists who loved the thrill of flying old-fashioned, propeller-driven aircraft, and a sprinkling of mercenaries. The majority were ex-military pilots who had seen combat duty in Vietnam. The fact that an Air America pilot could make up to $1,000 a week was an extremely enticing bonus. But they earned their money the hard way, risking their lives daily to fly "anything, anywhere, anytime—professionally," as their company motto boasted. "We went into places the military wouldn't dream of going," said chopper pilot Mel Cooper. Their unarmed and unprotected aircraft were constant prey for Communist small-arms fire as well as conventional 23MM and 37MM antiaircraft guns as they flew into Pathet Lao and North Vietnamese controlled territory time and time again.

If they were shot down over enemy territory, remarked one pilot, "our status would have been SOL—Shit Out of Luck." Dressed in civilian clothes, flying in unmarked planes, and often carrying incriminating cargoes, they were more likely to be executed as spies than be taken prisoner. "When an Air America bird went down it was official company policy, but also a pilot to pilot policy, that you busted your ass and risked being shot down yourself to pick up the pilot," said Mel Cooper.

Among the most dangerous missions were night drops of special espionage and sabotage teams of three to twelve men dressed in Pathet Lao or North Vietnamese uniforms, occasionally accompanied by a CIA case officer. Air America pilots in unmarked light planes and helicopters would fly them in, keep them supplied, and pick them up again after their work was completed. The teams were constantly on the move and, as a rule, maintained a strict radio silence. Supply pilots flew over a predesignated area at the appointed time, searching for a prearranged signal on the ground, usually a ring of flashlights and a strobe. "It was the most exacting flying I've ever done," said one pilot. "You were strung out there on the border way the hell away from everything with absolutely no navigational aids, working yourself down among a bunch of fog-shrouded hills looking for four or five damn flashlights."

Pickups were even trickier. Pilots never knew when a Pathet Lao patrol might be lurking in the jungle along the edge of an LZ, their guns trained on the descending chopper. "They would stay out for a week or a month or whatever and very often they were late or hadn't given the right signals or they hadn't been heard of for a couple of weeks when all of a sudden they would show up in the pick-up zone," said Tom Grady. "And they're wearing enemy uniforms so you don't know for sure who they are."

"Hardly a day went by that some aircraft didn't come back with a hole in it," recalled Bob Dawson. "I was subjected to greater hazard during my time with Air America than at any time I was a combat pilot in any of the three wars I was in. And I was a fighter pilot."

named air force sources interviewed by journalists confirmed Shaplen's view, noting that the CIA continually pressed for air strikes against towns and villages controlled by the Pathet Lao. The agency believed the strategy would deprive the Pathet Lao of food grown by local villagers and weaken their control over the local population. The result, however, was to cause the Pathet Lao to turn to Hanoi for more assistance and to drive thousands of dislocated farmers and villagers into the arms of the Communists. As one Laotian reported, the attitude was "better to die fighting than die hiding from the bombs."

An exorbitant price

This example of the differing rationales and objectives for the use of American air power in northeastern Laos was symptomatic of the entire bombing campaign in Laos. The U.S. was fighting two separate wars in Laos, one against the Pathet Lao and another against the Ho Chi Minh Trail. Within each, various U.S. agencies advocated their own strategies, which were often based on differing operational assumptions and objectives. While the North Vietnamese never lost sight of the fact that their activities in Laos were subservient to their main strategic objective of reunifying Vietnam under their control, the Americans' efforts tended to be overly compartmentalized.

The results of U.S. bombing operations were as vague and contradictory as their rationale. Bomb damage assessment reports from pilots, photo reconnaissance aircraft, and other sources were often unreliable and open to differing interpretations. Lacking any concrete way of assessing the actual effectiveness of bombing strikes, success tended to be measured in terms of the numbers of sorties flown and bombs dropped by statistically minded analysts. While this presented American strategists with an imperfect view, some general assumptions could be drawn about the impact of American bombing operations in Laos.

American air power had unquestionably helped maintain the fragile balance in the ground war in the northeast, but at a heavy cost in civilian casualties. However, it had failed to cut the flow of men and materiel down the Ho Chi Minh Trail to the battlefield in South Vietnam. It had made things increasingly difficult for the North Vietnamese, forcing them to commit a significant pool of manpower, weapons, and supplies in Laos to keep the infiltration routes open. This reduced somewhat the level of enemy pressure in the South and bought valuable time for the Vietnamization program. But at a cost of some 400 men killed, captured, or missing, and an estimated $2 billion a year in operational expenses, the U.S. was paying an exorbitant price for such limited results.

Pathet Lao forces on the offensive during their successful effort to recapture the Plain of Jars in December 1969.

Laos:
The "Other War"

Laos became neutral by declaration of the Geneva Conference of 1962, which also called for the removal of North Vietnamese and U.S. forces from the country. By the mid–1960s, however, the conflict in Vietnam had spilled into Laos, where the two sides fought an increasingly intense shadow war. To help support their main supply line to South Vietnam, the Ho Chi Minh Trail in Laos, the North Vietnamese supported local Communist insurgents known as the Pathet Lao, who controlled Laos's two northeastern provinces. The Pathet Lao, backed by the NVA, battled the Royal Laotian Army for control of the strategic Plain of Jars.

The U.S. secretly provided government forces with arms, but stopped short of sending troops. Instead, beginning in 1964, the Americans relied on limited bombing of the Communists in support of government forces. After the bombing halt over North Vietnam in 1968, more U.S. planes became available for missions in Laos, and the North Vietnamese stepped up their support as well. By 1969, over 100,000 tons of American bombs had rained down on the Plain of Jars, an area inhabited by more than 50,000 people.

Insets. *Having reached refuge in camps in the Vientiane Plain in 1970–71, survivors of bombings in the Plain of Jars related their experiences in images such as these. Each drawing had a caption. One read: "We had to go dig holes in the side of the mountain and in the big forest so that we never saw the sunlight."*

Left. *Smoke rises from a Communist mortar position in Laos following a strike by a U.S. Air Force A–1E Skyraider on August 11, 1970.*

The CIA recruited its own clandestine army to counter the Pathet Lao. The agency found ready recruits among the ethnic minorities inhabiting the mountainous terrain in northeastern Laos, the foremost being Meo tribesmen who over the years had developed a reputation as natural fighters, stubbornly defending their mountain villages against all comers. CIA agents offered the villagers guns, rice, and money in exchange for recruits for its irregular army and organized the construction of crude landing strips (known as Lima sites) to link by air the remote fortified villages. Under the leadership of General Vang Pao, the clandestine army infiltrated behind Pathet Lao lines and blew up bridges, ambushed patrols, and disrupted Communist supply lines.

Left. *USAF CH-53 helicopters at Vang Vieng, the northernmost airstrip under government control.*

Inset. *A young Hmong (Meo) recruit, still dressed in black tribal garb, poses with his new M2 carbine in late 1965 at Sam Thong.*

Above. *One of the many landing strips hacked out of the jungle for use by Air America aircraft to supply Meo irregulars.*

The CIA's main link with Vang Pao's army was Air America, a commercial transport airline owned covertly by the agency. Air America pilots flew their unarmed planes and helicopters deep into enemy territory to keep remote outposts supplied with arms and ammunition. Meo soldiers and their families also became dependent on Air America paradrops of sacks of rice and other foodstuffs. According to Air America pilot Porter Hough, "it got to be an old joke up there that when the school teachers asked the children where rice came from, they pointed up to the sky."

Left. *By 1970, CIA-chartered planes were dropping 8 million pounds of supplies a month to villages and refugee camps in northern Laos.*

Inset. *A crewman, known as a "kicker," pushes a load out a rear cargo door. A kicker was usually equipped with a parachute in the event that his momentum carried him out the door with the rice.*

Below. *At a refugee camp near Sam Thong, Meo civilians collect sacks of airdropped rice.*

55

In 1968, as the war intensified on the ground and in the air around the Plain of Jars, a large-scale program of civilian relocation was initiated and financed by the Department of Defense, USAID, and the CIA.

Right. *As government troops and the Pathet Lao engage in battles near their village in eastern Laos, these Meo civilians are evacuated by Air America CH-34 helicopter to locations south and west.*

Above. *Meo refugees, dressed in their best clothes, wait to board an Air America chopper in September 1968.*

The Supporting Cast

On June 9, 1969, President Nixon announced that 25,000 American GIs would be withdrawn from South Vietnam by the end of August. Another 35,000 were scheduled to be pulled out by the end of the year as part of the president's strategy of gradually withdrawing U.S. combat troops while training and equipping the South Vietnamese to fight their own war. But the withdrawal did not pertain to U.S. air units. American air power continued to flood the skies over Southeast Asia, shielding the South Vietnamese from external attack during the transition by escalating bombing operations in Laos and offsetting the U.S. troop cutbacks within South Vietnam.

By the end of the year there were 1,164 air force aircraft deployed in South Vietnam. Additional army, navy, and marine detachments brought the total to 2,000 aircraft based at ten major air bases and some sixty smaller airfields scattered throughout the country. Another 200 planes operated off navy carriers in the Gulf of

Tonkin. The air force also maintained three tactical fighter, two special operations, and two reconnaissance air wings at seven airfields in Thailand. In addition to a wing of B–52s at U-Tapao, the Strategic Air Command (SAC) also operated two more out of Guam and Okinawa. By April 1969, the number of air force personnel stationed in Southeast Asia reached a record high of 61,400 men.

Only a small percentage of this vast air armada in Vietnam was directly involved in combat operations. All the rest were supporting actors and props. Thousands of support personnel were required to maintain and defend these sprawling air bases. Millions of dollars and thousands of man-hours were spent to build and service the runways, hangars, ammunition and fuel dumps, control towers, mess halls, living quarters, and offices. Bases were ringed with cyclone fences, barbed wire, minefields, guard towers, and bunkers against enemy saboteurs and sporadic Vietcong raids. Ten squadrons, 5,000 USAF security police, equipped with sentry dogs, patrolled the bases day and night. By the end of 1969, 1,000 concrete revetments and 373 shelters protected aircraft from mortar and rocket attacks.

The number of personnel required to sustain the normal routine at these large airfields was staggering. There were staff officers who planned the air operations, clerks and typists who handled the paperwork, communications specialists, photo processors, intelligence analysts, computer technicians, equipment specialists who maintained the aircrews' flight gear, not to mention the local Thai and Vietnamese laborers who ran laundry and housekeeping services and staffed the mess halls. The highly technical nature of aircraft and their weapons systems also required large numbers of specialized ground crews to maintain the planes and load the bombs they carried to their targets.

Munitions and maintenance

Each bomb that a U.S. pilot released over an enemy target in Southeast Asia traveled the last few thousand feet of a 10,000-mile journey that involved thousands of man-hours of work. The job began at the Ogden Air Materiel Area at Hill AFB in Utah where Air Force Logistics Command personnel acquired and stockpiled ordnance for the war effort. From there, the bombs traveled through a supply pipeline that stretched from the Concord Naval Weapons Station in California, through Clark AFB in the Philippines, to bases in Southeast Asia.

Commercial transport ships, working under Defense Department contracts, ferried the explosives across the Pacific to Clark AFB in the Philippines, where a 120-day

back-up stock was maintained. Munitions ships shuttled the bombs from the Philippines to Saigon, Cam Ranh Bay, and ports in Thailand, where they were transported to major airfields and forward bases. The bombs were shipped in their component parts, so munitions experts and ordnance men at the bases then had to assemble them. At the large SAC base at U-Tapao, Thailand, the work was done by the men of the 635th Munitions Maintenance Squadron and a number of Thai workers. Working in teams, they moved down long rows of bombs, screwing in fuses and bolting on tail fins in assembly line fashion. Team supervisors reported the exact sequence of assembly over walkie-talkies to controllers who monitored every step of the process.

Loading bombs onto the B-52s based at U-Tapao was the job of the 4258th Munitions Maintenance Squadron. Thirty B-52s took off from the airfield every day, carrying an average load of one hundred eight 500-pound or sixty-six 750-pound bombs apiece—more than 21,000 bombs a week. At first, each bomb was individually loaded onto the aircraft, a delicate and time-consuming process. Eventually detachable bomb racks were developed which could be preloaded in the munitions area. Three bomb racks, each holding twenty-eight 500-pound or fourteen 750-pound bombs, were hoisted into the B-52's internal bomb bay by a five-man team using a hydraulically operated loader. Ordnance handlers attached the racks inside the bomb bay and rechecked each bomb to make sure it was secure before the hydraulic lift was lowered. Another team attached four smaller racks of three bombs apiece to two external bomb stations located under each wing.

Before the bombs were loaded, each plane had been carefully checked over by aircraft maintenance men who worked around the clock to keep the aircraft in perfect working order. Foremost among them were the crew chiefs, noncommissioned officers who supervised everything from changing tiny light bulbs on instrument panels to major engine overhauls.

Unlike pilots, who were usually assigned to fly different aircraft, a crew chief worked on one plane alone. He came to know every inch of the plane as well as its particular idiosyncrasies. A crew chief grudgingly allowed pilots to "borrow" his charge, but he "owned" it.

The B-52s, which crew chiefs affectionately called "pigs" (because they were big, ugly, and greasy), were among the oldest aircraft in the air force fleet and needed constant attention. Maintenance vehicles operating on the flight line at U-Tapao chalked up 20,000 miles per year just traveling the half-mile ramp along the runway.

For the crews, mostly short-term enlisted men in their late teens and early twenties, it was a monotonous job of long hours and poor working conditions. But, according to crew chief Sergeant Charles J. Smoak, "when you get right down to it every man on the line will do the job despite the bitchin' and moaning. Everybody gripes, but

A link along the munition supply chain. Part of the U.S.S. Evergreen State's cargo of 23,000 bombs is unloaded in slings in the harbor at Guam for storage at Andersen Air Force Base in 1965. The bombs are destined for use over Vietnam.

Air Drop at An Loc

Among the many risky air missions in Vietnam were low-level supply drops in combat areas by C–130s and other cargo planes. These became vital to ground troops during the Communists' siege of the town of An Loc during the Easter offensive of 1972.

At right, the crew of a C–130 waits tensely for a mechanical problem to be solved so they may fly their thrice-delayed drop on An Loc. Before dawn the flight got under way and soon (far right) a bright yellow parachute drops like a fallen soufflé with supplies for the embattled ARVN troops.

when it's necessary they will do the job properly." They knew they were ultimately responsible for an expensive piece of machinery and, more important, the lives of its crew. Staff Sergeant Al Mills, another crew chief at U-Tapao, told a visiting reporter, "We take care of them just as if they were the airplane taking us home."

Airlift

On an average day, 1,500 U.S. servicemen completed their tours of duty in Vietnam and headed stateside while another 1,500 arrived to replace them. Nearly 6,000 more were either traveling to or returning from R&R leaves outside the country. They flew on specially contracted commercial air carriers or transport planes of the air force's Military Airlift Command. MAC's long-range transports maintained a continuous strategic airlift of personnel and materiel from the U.S. to Southeast Asia while its smaller tactical transports flew thousands of sorties ferrying supplies and troops within the combat theater.

Initially, MAC's strategic airlift relied on C–124 Globemasters and C–133 Cargomasters, which were both nearing obsolescence. C–130 Hercules and C–135 Stratolifters were also employed, but the C–130 lacked sufficient speed and range while the C–135 had a relatively small load capacity. A number of Air Force Reserve and Air National Guard units were activated as early as August 1965 to

keep pace with expanding strategic airlift needs. But most of their planes were twelve- to fifteen-year-old C–97s, C–119s, C–121s, and C–124s, which were troublesome to maintain and carried no more than ten tons at a time.

Delivery of new C–141 Starlifters in mid-1965 helped relieve some of the burden. The Starlifter could carry 67,600 pounds of cargo 4,000 miles, or 31,000 pounds nonstop from the U.S. to airfields in the Far East more than 6,000 miles away. The biggest boost came in 1969 when the controversial C–5 Galaxy finally entered the service. Plagued by huge cost-overruns that drove the price tag for each of the giant transports to the $44 million mark, the C–5 was the largest and costliest aircraft in the world. It could transport 164,000 pounds over 3,000 miles or 80,000 pounds over 6,500 miles. Just seventeen Galaxies could have accomplished the work of the 300 or more transports employed each day of the 1948–49 Berlin airlift.

Additional cargo and passenger terminals had to be created in the U.S., at transshipment points throughout the Pacific, and in South Vietnam to handle the growing volume of traffic. MAC also employed hundreds of tactical aircraft to distribute supplies and transport personnel between bases within South Vietnam. Since land travel was a risky affair, most cargo and passengers went by air. The transports also allowed ground commanders to shift large numbers of men around the country rapidly. In addition to the thousands of troops shuttled from place to place, ap-

proximately 500 reporters, photographers, and radio and television commentators traveled back and forth across the country by air every day.

By the end of 1968, there were fifteen squadrons of C-130s and four squadrons of C-123s attached to the air force's 834th Air Division, which was responsible for tactical airlifts within South Vietnam. Additional C-124s, C-141s, and smaller C-5s brought the 834th's total strength to some 250 aircraft and 7,500 men. The 834th could also draw on aircraft from transport units operating from nearby bases in the western Pacific.

The 834th also acquired six squadrons of C-7A Caribous, purchased by the army in the early sixties to support its air-mobile units. Designed to operate from short, rough airstrips, the C-7 was ideally suited for resupply missions in support of forward bases and remote Special Forces camps. The air force objected to the army's acquisition of the C-7 transports and maintained that all tactical airlift should be consolidated under its control. After a bitter internal debate, the army consented to transfer the Caribous to the air force in 1967, in exchange for the right to continue to develop and operate its large helicopters, which were used for intratheater airlift and supply, and fixed-wing reconnaissance aircraft such as the OV-1 Mohawk.

Air transport units of all the service branches, plus a Royal Australian Air Force contingent of one squadron of Caribous and two squadrons of C-130s, were integrated into the Common Service Airlift System and its Airlift Control Center (ALCC) at Tan Son Nhut. The ALCC coordinated and scheduled the daily missions through a countrywide network of local airlift control units and mobile combat control teams that coordinated airlift requirements with ground units in the field. Most missions consisted of little more than the monotonous routine of hauling passengers and cargo from base to base. Twenty-four hours a day, transport crews shuttled troops, ammunition, food, fuel, spare parts, and mail from major ports and supply depots to smaller bases throughout the country. Sometimes they were called upon to deliver foodstuffs, including live pigs and chickens, to isolated villages. Although it was not glamorous duty, on occasion it could be extremely dangerous, especially the resupplying of remote bases under enemy attack.

Transport crews often risked their lives landing on exposed airstrips inside besieged outposts, unloading cargo and taking on wounded while under fire. Low-flying transports braved heavy ground fire to air-drop vital supplies by parachute to embattled troops in the field. Aerial resupply missions proved extremely valuable during the battle for Khe Sanh, providing the besieged garrison's only external source of supply. When the odds became too great, the transports were also called in to help evacuate bases under attack.

One of the largest such aerial evacuations occurred on

May 12, 1968, at Kham Duc, a Special Forces camp located forty-four miles southwest of Da Nang along the Laotian border. After holding off a superior enemy force for three days, the defenders were at the end of their rope and prepared to evacuate. Throughout the day, air force C-130s and C-123s assisted army and marine helicopters in airlifting out 1,500 troops. While fighter-bombers kept the enemy at bay, eight transports landed at the base's airstrip. One C-130 was shot down with 100 civilian passengers aboard, and another was damaged so badly that it was abandoned on the runway. By 4 P.M. the last of the camp's survivors had been evacuated. Controllers aboard the C-130 acting as an airborne command post for the operation declared the camp abandoned and directed fighter-bombers to destroy the base.

Just then a voice broke in over the radio net. Three air force combat controllers who had been landed earlier in the day to coordinate the airlift were still on the ground. Their radio jeep had been destroyed by enemy fire. A C-123 was sent in to see if its crew could locate the men, but as its wheels touched down on the runway it drew heavy fire from Communist troops who were closing in around the airstrip. Lieutenant Colonel Alfred J. Jeannotte, Jr., quickly rammed the throttles of his C-123 forward and roared off the strip through the hail of gunfire. Halfway down the runway, crewmen aboard the C-123 spotted the stranded airmen crouched in a ditch. But Jeannotte was too far down the runway to stop. Low on fuel, he was forced to return to base.

The airborne controllers then called Lieutenant Colonel Joe M. Jackson, whose C-123 was still orbiting the area. Would he make a try? Below, exploding ammunition dumps and smoke from fighter-bomber strikes created a chaotic scene. The airstrip was littered with debris and burning aircraft, and surrounded by hostile forces ready to foil another rescue attempt. The three men on the ground had resigned themselves to their fate. "We figured no one would come back and we had two choices," said Technical Sergeant Mort Freedman. "Either be taken prisoner or fight it out."

Jackson and his crew had made up their minds. "There wasn't any question about it," said the C-123 pilot, who had been a fighter pilot in Korea. Realizing that enemy gunners expected him to follow the normal low-level approach of the previous C-123, Jackson decided on an unorthodox maneuver. From 9,000 feet, he banked the heavy transport into a nearly vertical dive. Descending at 4,000 feet per minute (well over the normal rate of 500), Jackson pushed the plane's control surfaces to the limit.

Pulling out of the dive at 500 feet, Jackson skimmed the treetops and settled into an abbreviated landing run. Although his bizarre approach had temporarily shaken off the enemy gunners, Jackson now had to thread his way through the obstacle course in front of him, including the wreckage of a downed helicopter halfway down the runway. He knew he had to stop quickly to avoid the burning chopper, but he could not reverse the props on his two engines to slow the plane's momentum; that would automatically shut down the two auxiliary jet engines he needed for a quick getaway. Standing on the brakes as hard as he could, Jackson brought the C-123 to a shuddering halt only a few yards from the disabled helicopter.

The three stranded airmen ran toward the C-123 as enemy gunners opened up on the idling plane. Staff Sergeant Manson L. Grubbs and Technical Sergeant Edward M. Trejo quickly lowered the rear cargo door and pulled the men aboard. Just then a 122MM rocket roared straight down the runway at the C-123. It skipped off the tarmac and came to a stop twenty-five feet in front of the transport but failed to explode.

Taxiing carefully around the dud rocket and coaxing the plane around shell craters and debris, Jackson applied maximum takeoff power. Ten seconds later mortar shells slammed into the spot where Jackson's C-123 transport had been standing. "That was a real thriller," Jackson later recounted. "I figured they just got zeroed in on us, and that the time of the flight of the mortar shells was about 10 seconds longer than the time we sat there taking the men aboard."

The old C-123 still had to run a deadly gauntlet. As it slowly gained speed and altitude, the plane drew a storm of fire from gun positions on either side and at the end of the runway. "We were scared to death," said Jackson. But miraculously the plane escaped without a single bullet hole. "I'll never understand that," he said. For his valiant rescue, Lt. Col. Jackson received the Medal of Honor.

Flying gas stations

In addition to cargo and transport planes, a variety of specialized combat support aircraft traversed the skies above Southeast Asia. There were reconnaissance jets, electronic countermeasures (ECM) aircraft, airborne command posts, search and rescue planes and helicopters, and the giant KC-135 aerial refueling tankers with blue spangled bands wrapped around their fuselages. These specially configured Boeing 707s were fitted with internal tanks holding 31,200 gallons of fuel which could be transferred at a rate of 1,000 gallons per minute to other aircraft. Known as "flying gas stations," the KC-135 Stratotankers of the Strategic Air Command were assigned in 1964 the responsibility for airborne refueling operations for all air force aircraft in Southeast Asia.

On June 9, 1964, four KC-135s, weighted down with a full load of 100 tons of JP-5 jet fuel, took off from Clark AFB in the Philippines. The multi-engined jets headed west to Da Nang where they were to rendezvous with eight F-100 Supersabres en route to strike Communist antiaircraft sites in Laos in retaliation for the downing of a navy RF-8 recon jet and an F-8 Crusader escort. This was the first time that SAC tankers directly supported tactical aircraft in combat and the first of nearly one million such refueling operations KC-135s would perform during the war.

When the air war in Vietnam began in earnest in 1965, SAC organized the 4252d Strategic Air Wing at Kadena AFB, Okinawa. Its tanker force of fifteen KC-135s, nicknamed Young Tiger, would provide refueling for all combat aircraft operating in Vietnam and Laos. Two forward operating forces were soon established in Thailand, at the air force base in Takhli and Don Muang airport, to refuel fighters operating from Thai air bases as the air campaign against North Vietnam heated up. SAC tankers also provided in-flight refueling during the 10,000-mile trip across the Pacific for the increasing number of tactical aircraft deployed to Southeast Asia from bases in the U.S.

In mid-1966, the burgeoning refueling operations in Thailand were consolidated into the 4258th Strategic Air Wing. All KC-135s were moved to the newly constructed air base at U-Tapao where the wing was headquartered. By the end of the year, the 4258th took over all tactical aircraft refueling operations in Southeast Asia from the 4252d at Kadena, which took over sole responsibility for supporting Arc Light B-52 operations. By 1968, more than ninety KC-135s were engaged in refueling operations in Southeast Asia, including thirty-five at Kadena, forty at U-Tapao, and fifteen tankers of the 4200th Air Refueling Squadron at Ching Chuan Kang Air Base in Taiwan. Additional tankers were kept on emergency alert at Andersen AFB in Guam.

There were six major aerial refueling tracks in Thailand, two in the Gulf of Tonkin, one south of Da Nang, and two more in southern South Vietnam. Known as "anchors," each was identified by a color (i.e., White Anchor, Blue Anchor, etc.). The KC-135s stationed in these color-coded anchors flew in a continuous racetrack pattern. Pilots timed their circuit to begin the elongated lap of the anchor just as a receiving aircraft entered the same pattern so that the actual transfer of fuel could be completed while flying a straightaway portion of the circuit.

Each tanker was manned by three officers and an enlisted man. In addition to their normal duties, the pilot and copilot controlled the distribution, balancing, and unloading of fuel. They also monitored environmental controls, such as fuel tank temperatures and pressure, and the hydraulic pumping systems. The navigator operated a bank of radar and electronic equipment that allowed him to plot the precise course necessary to rendezvous with receiving aircraft. A technician stationed in the aft end of the plane controlled the forty-seven-foot retractable metal pipe, or "boom," through which the fuel was transferred.

Upon entering the refueling pattern, a pilot throttled back his engines and braked his plane to match the tanker's slower air speed. The boom operator talked the pilot into position twenty feet behind and fifteen feet below the tanker, then maneuvered the boom into a receptacle

located atop the plane's fuselage. In the case of older aircraft, such as the F-100, and many navy and marine planes that were fitted with probes rather than receptacles, the KC-135s employed a funnellike device known as a drogue which was attached to the end of the boom or to a flexible hose. The boom operator lowered the drogue and kept it stable while the pilot flew the receiving aircraft's probe into place. Whichever system was used, precise timing and coordination were essential. When flying in such close proximity the slightest error by either pilot could result in a midair collision.

Both pilots had to concentrate on maintaining a stable air speed and heading, taking into account wind and weather conditions. Strict radio silence was observed to avoid any distractions. "Turbulence makes refueling difficult," said Technical Sergeant Bob J. Merkle, a ten-year veteran boom operator. "When we run into it, our pilot has to make a lot of turns and the fighter pilots have to keep up with him. That takes a lot of skill." Sometimes pilots were forced to rely on their instruments and radar to grope through thick clouds and heavy rainstorms and hook up with the tankers.

While most refueling operations were precisely planned and plotted well in advance, sometimes the tankers were called to respond to emergency situations. Battle-damaged aircraft and planes critically low on fuel that could not reach one of the prepositioned refueling anchors had to be intercepted by tankers. To effect a recovery, KC-135s sometimes flew deep into enemy airspace, often disregarding SAC directives to avoid exposing the slow-moving planes to North Vietnamese AA guns and missiles. If a plane's tanks were damaged or a fuel line blown away by antiaircraft fire, the tankers would literally tow the aircraft to the nearest airfield, pumping fuel into the stricken bird as fast as it leaked out. The procedure introduced a new term into the aviators' vocabulary—an "aircraft save."

One of the more remarkable saves occurred on July 5, 1966. A flight of four F-105s was extremely low on fuel after a lengthy engagement with enemy MiGs deep in North Vietnam. An emergency call brought a KC-135 from the 301st Air Refueling Squadron on an intercept course at maximum speed. The KC-135 was well across the North Vietnamese border when it drew within range. The flight leader radioed that all four jets had only 200 to 500 pounds of fuel left. Two of the F-105 pilots had already resigned themselves to abandoning their planes and were, in fact, preparing to eject just as the tanker arrived.

Captain Howard G. Stalnecker quickly began turning the KC-135 onto the same course and called in the number four aircraft, which had only 100 pounds (roughly fifteen gallons) of fuel left. The situation was so critical that the F-105 pilot made the hookup while still turning in a thirty-degree bank. He was on the boom only a few seconds when another of the F-105's gauges hit empty. With

just enough fuel on board to keep going, the number four aircraft pulled away to let the other F-105 "take a drink." Stalnecker rotated the tanker through all four fighters the same way, first giving each enough to keep flying then rotating through again to provide enough fuel for the jets to make it safely back to base. Stalnecker and his crew were credited with saving all four F-105s and, very likely, the lives of their pilots.

By 1968, KC-135 crews had been credited with over 100 such saves of tactical aircraft. By the end of 1969, SAC tankers had flown more than 110,000 sorties in Southeast Asia, performing 481,908 refueling operations in which 5.3 billion pounds of fuel were transferred. At the end of the war in 1972, the totals reached 194,687 sorties and 813,878 refuelings, with nearly 9 billion pounds of fuel transferred.

Although they did not receive the kind of recognition earned by the fighter pilots, refueling crews knew that the fighter jocks depended on them to make it back home to fly another day. Hundreds of letters of appreciation from fighter squadrons, tacked up on bulletin boards at refueling bases, were reminders of the appreciation they earned.

Aerial traffic cops

On an average day in South Vietnam, more than 14,000 aircraft took off or landed. Coordinating the movements of so many aircraft was a giant task in itself, even without the combat conditions that prevailed in Vietnam. Fighter jets constantly moved in and out of corridors being used by hundreds of military transports and civilian aircraft. Shifting artillery barrages and naval gunfire, which usually occurred with little warning, had to be constantly avoided. Usable airspace was further limited because vast corridors were blocked off for B-52 operations exclusively.

Air traffic controllers had their hands full trying to sort out this massive aerial traffic jam. They monitored more than 53,000 air traffic "movements"—takeoffs, landings, and major flight pattern changes—in South Vietnam every day. Controllers at the three major airfields at Tan Son Nhut, Bien Hoa, and Da Nang alone handled nearly 70,000 air traffic movements every month. As a comparison, controllers at Chicago's O'Hare International, considered the busiest airport in the world at the time, handled 55,000 per month.

Orchestrating this cacophony of air activity was the job of the air force's 1964th Communication Group, which employed three types of air controllers. Flight tower and radar operators at each airfield launched and recovered aircraft. Air traffic controllers at six air traffic regulation centers controlled all aircraft over distant and intermediate range flights en route to and from their destinations,

While flying a bombing mission to North Vietnam in 1966, an F-105D Thunderchief receives fuel from a KC-135 tanker.

Air traffic controllers at work in the control and reporting center at the big air base in Udorn, Thailand. Known as Brigham Control, the center was jointly manned by American and Thai personnel. *Right.* With luminous hieroglyphics, Thai technicians record positions of hostile and friendly aircraft on a transparent plotting board. *Below.* In the center's radar room, lighted blips on the scopes show aircraft in motion.

providing "flight following" assistance such as weather information, navigational instructions, and collision avoidance warnings. Air weapons controllers directed the action in combat strike zones, as well as directing air rescue missions, assisting in recovery operations for battle-damaged aircraft and aerial refueling hookups.

The two major air traffic control centers in South Vietnam were Paris Control at Tan Son Nhut and Panama Control at Da Nang. Other smaller centers were located at Ban Me Thuot (Pyramid), Hon Tre (Portcall), Pleiku (Peacock), and Dong Ha (Waterboy). U.S. controllers worked alongside South Vietnamese counterparts who controlled all VNAF operations. All were plugged into an extensive air defense radar net operated by the 5th Tactical Control Group.

A similar setup existed in Thailand, where the 1974th Communications Group operated four control centers, the primary one being Brigham Control at Udorn. They controlled air activity in Thailand and Laos, as well as missions over North Vietnam. Airborne EC-121s of the 552d Airborne Early Warning and Control Wing, crammed with six and one-half tons of radar and communications equipment manned by up to twenty technicians, also acted as airborne air controllers in addition to their primary responsibility of monitoring enemy MiG activity. Code named College Eye, the EC-121s maintained continuous patrols over Laos and the Gulf of Tonkin.

Except for those who manned the flight control towers, most controllers never saw the aircraft they were controlling except as dots on radarscopes. Monitoring the blinking strobe lights and bouncing radar blips on their ground-controlled approach (GCA) or radar approach control (RAPCON) units, they communicated with pilots through radio headsets. To stare into the yellow eye of a radarscope for hours on end and make split-second, life-or-death decisions required physical and mental stamina.

"Work came in spurts at Paris," said Major Charles V. Durham, who worked as a weapons controller at Tan Son Nhut for six months. "There were days when we would assist fewer than 100 airplanes in a twelve hour shift. At other times, it seemed we talked to that many simultaneously. On those busy days, we would contact and flight follow or control about 250 aircraft. I have seen controllers sit at one scope for hours at a time, providing information to as many as 25 pilots at once. When you finally get up, you feel like you never want to sit down again, and you walk around for a couple of hours seeing little radar blips in front of your eyes."

Controllers were responsible for "talking" pilots into safe landings at night when optical illusions such as autokinesis, the illusory phenomenon of movement that a static light exhibits when stared at for a long time in the dark, could disorient them. Pilots sometimes maneuvered their aircraft into dangerous altitudes because they mistook ground lights for stars and vice versa. During the monsoon season in particular, when rain and clouds forced a pilot to rely solely on his instruments and radar, controllers carefully monitored the aircraft to warn if a pilot was becoming disoriented.

Assisting planes returning from combat missions was the diciest, most draining task for a controller. A pilot dangerously low on fuel might be clamoring for a refueling tanker, another in a seriously damaged aircraft would be calling for air support and rescue helicopters. A controller had to deal with both at the same time, arranging a refueling tanker for one while alerting search and rescue teams for the other. If a plane went down, he also was expected to pinpoint the spot and provide navigational assistance for the rescue force. In 1968 alone, air controllers were credited with saving the lives of 660 crewmen and passengers, as well as 221 aircraft valued at $260 million.

Captain Peter M. Dunn, who commanded the first detachment of air controllers assigned to Brigham Control in Thailand, recalled the relentless pressure the men worked under. Most of his men were young lieutenants who worked eighty- to ninety-hour weeks, handling "40 or 50 aircraft of different makes and missions, going in different directions, with different demands. And they did it for 12-13 hours a day, talking until they were hoarse, eating sandwiches at their scopes, sometimes 30 to 40 days at a stretch without a day off."

Offshore airfields

The air war from offshore required thousands of sailors to man the floating airfields of Task Force 77 cruising off the Vietnamese coast. Unlike servicemen ashore, they could not head for a drink at the club or sample the distractions offered by a nearby town after their fifteen- or sixteen-hour workdays. Except for rare liberty calls in the Philippines or Hong Kong, the monotonous routine ground on month after month. They lived in a world of gray steel and stale air in cramped bunk rooms far removed from the battlefield. Every day they watched the ship's planes take off and return with only the vaguest idea of where they had been or what they had done.

Out of a total of 4,000 officers and enlisted men assigned to a carrier, only a handful were airmen. The majority performed a multitude of routine tasks. Enlisted men in the engineering department ran the ship's engines and handled repairs and general maintenance. Communications operators handled 1,000 messages a day. All worked with one objective: everything and everyone aboard the huge, gray warships, from the captain down to the lowest rating, were there to maintain and project the carrier's aerial striking power.

Staff officers at wing and squadron level plotted and planned each mission. The wing's weapons coordinator and aviation fuels officer carefully calculated ratios of bomb and fuel weights for each plane to maximize weapons' loads yet ensure there would be enough fuel for the return trip. Maintenance crews worked on the planes at night in the hangar deck to prepare for a morning launch. Further below decks, armorers assembled bombs and rockets and transferred them topside where they would be loaded on the waiting planes.

During a launch, hundreds of crewmen wearing jerseys, whose colors denoted their various duties, swarmed over the flight deck. Yellow-shirted flight directors shouted orders to men in blue who manhandled the planes into their prearranged launch sequence. Sailors in purple jerseys filled fuel tanks while red-shirted munitions men loaded bombs onto aircraft by hand.

The men in brown jerseys were the "plane captains," warrant officers who performed the same function as air force crew chiefs. Before takeoff, the plane captains strapped the pilots into their cockpits and took them through their prelaunch systems checks. One by one the idling planes were led to the catapults by the yellow-shirted flight directors. Crewmen in green and usually grease-stained coveralls attached the heavy restraining cables and hooked up the steam-powered shuttle that would send each plane shooting off the carrier's deck at the signal of the catapult director.

From a glassed-in control tower that jutted out over the flight deck from the ship's superstructure, the aircraft carrier's air officer choreographed the entire operation. He also directed recovery operations, sorting out the landing order for incoming aircraft, many of which were low on fuel or damaged by enemy fire. One accident could foul up the entire flight deck, making it impossible for other planes to land.

Landing signal officers on deck literally "talked" each pilot down onto the rolling and pitching carrier deck, providing speed and directional adjustments. Crewmen stretched across the flight deck heavy arresting cables which were snagged by the planes' tail hooks, bringing them to a jarring halt. Fire and damage control teams stood by, ready to assist in any emergency.

Night landings were especially tense both for pilots and flight deck crews. Guided by radar controllers and a landing signal officer, an incoming pilot lined up his plane with rows of dim red lights that outlined the carrier's flight deck. On the side of the runway was an orange searchlight that shined into a large mirror bordered with green lights, which bobbed up and down with the pitching and rolling motion of the carrier. By keeping the ball of light, referred to as the "meatball," lined up inside the box of green lights pilots kept their planes on the correct angle of approach. The slightest mistake could send a pilot crashing into the flight deck or shooting past the arresting cables into the sea. Navy flight surgeons discovered that a pilot's pulse rate and respiration rose during night landings even higher than when he was flying over enemy territory under fire.

While airborne, the carrier's aircraft were under the control of the ship's Combat Information Center, whose radar operators and controllers monitored all air activity in the area. One hundred miles north of Yankee Station, in what was labeled the Positive Identification Radar Zone (PIRAZ), radar operators aboard navy destroyers took over the guidance function. They tracked all navy aircraft operating over North Vietnam during the Rolling Thunder campaign, providing them with navigational assistance, hookups with refueling tankers, and warnings of approaching enemy aircraft. After the bombing halt, the controllers at PIRAZ Station continued to maintain an early warning radar net against possible attacks by enemy aircraft or PT boats against the carriers.

Besides its combat aircraft, each carrier also operated a number of support planes. A-3 Skywarriors, built in the 1950s as the navy's first all-jet bomber, now doubled as transports, aerial refueling tankers, and electronic coun-

termeasures aircraft. The RA-5 Vigilante, developed as a high-speed nuclear bomber in the late fifties, was refitted in 1965 to become the navy's main reconnaissance and photo surveillance aircraft. EA-2 Hawkeyes, with distinctive radar domes, acted as airborne radar controllers. Aircraft carrier task forces also required a vast array of supporting ships.

Supply vessels and refueling tankers shuttled to and from shore bases with the stores necessary to maintain the giant, gray warships, their crews, and their aircraft. During a seven-month tour of duty at Yankee Station, the U.S.S. *Coral Sea* consumed 17 million gallons of fuel and an additional 9.5 million gallons of aviation fuel. The carrier also took on nearly 1,300 tons of stores, from food to spare parts, and more than 2,000 tons of bombs, rockets, and ammunition. Everything had to be manhandled onto cranes and winches, which transferred the cargo onto the carriers while they were under way.

A screen of destroyers and submarines protected each carrier. Although there was little threat from the tiny North Vietnamese navy, Soviet intelligence-gathering ships disguised as commercial trawlers monitored every move the carriers made. On a number of occasions, the trawlers attempted to disrupt launch and recovery operations by steering on a collision course with the carrier, which had to remain on a steady course and speed. Destroyers and attending tugs ran interference for the carriers, engaging in a battle of nerves with Soviet trawlers, which sometimes closed within a few feet before sheering off.

Shore-based P-2 Neptune, P-3 Orion, and P-5 Marlin naval surveillance aircraft patrolled the Gulf of Tonkin in search of enemy PT boats and monitored the thousands of small junks that sailed up and down the Vietnamese coast, on the lookout for ships carrying arms and supplies to the Vietcong. Navy pilots also flew long-range EC-121 Warning Stars on electronic surveillance patrols.

Aviation Boatswain's Mate Third Class Schonig scrambles out of the path of a navy A-4 Skyhawk about to launch from the flight deck of the U.S.S. Bon Homme Richard *in the Gulf of Tonkin in August 1968.*

A new breed

In addition to all of these various fixed-wing aircraft, there were thousands of helicopters stationed in Southeast Asia. First employed on a limited scale during the Korean War, helicopters had come of age in Vietnam, where American strategists considered mobility to be the key to winning a counterinsurgency war. This was particularly true for the U.S. Army, whose infantry and air-mobile divisions depended heavily on helicopters to transport combat troops and supplies.

Of the 4,000 different types and models of American helicopters, the most common was the UH-1 Huey series. The first Hueys deployed in South Vietnam, in early 1962, were the helicopter ambulances of the 57th Medical Detachment. By 1968 there were some 116 UH-1 medevac choppers; they could land directly on the battlefield, take on up to six wounded soldiers on stretchers, and in a matter of minutes evacuate them to the safety of mobile surgical units and base hospitals. Some were equipped with special hoists to evacuate wounded men from areas where there was no clearing to land.

Between 1965 and 1969 the helicopter ambulances medevacked 372,947 casualties from battlefield sites in Vietnam to medical facilities, with a speed that greatly reduced the number of combat fatalities. Fewer than 1 percent of those casualties who reached hospitals died as a result of their wounds. In Korea, where helicopters were first employed to medevac casualties, the rate was 2.5 percent. In World War II, without helicopters to help, the rate had been 4.5 percent.

The UH-1's primary role in Vietnam, however, was that of a troop transport. A variety of different models served as armed troop transports and covering gunships for U.S. Army and ARVN units. When they were not flying combat support missions, Huey pilots often found themselves assigned to ferry VIPs and supplies in what they labeled "ash and trash" missions, along with other UH-1s that were permanently assigned to a noncombat transport role. But the majority of helicopter transport missions were flown by specialized medium- and heavy-duty choppers.

The army's primary heavy transport helicopter was the twin-engined CH-47 Chinook, which could carry its crew of three and thirty-three passengers or twenty-four litters and two medical attendants for a range of 230 miles. Occasionally, Chinooks carried bombs, napalm, and tear gas canisters, which were rolled out the rear cargo ramp and fused by a static line once they were clear of the ship. A few, nicknamed Go-Go Birds, were even fitted out as gunships, with a grenade launcher, 20MM cannon, and rocket pods.

The Chinook's greatest contribution was in logistical support. The cargo compartment on the C model could hold nearly 20,000 pounds of cargo and equipment. External loads of up to 28,000 pounds could be hung from a cargo hook underneath the CH-47's fuselage. Chinooks loaded in this fashion often hauled artillery batteries up to the tops of inaccessible mountains to create easily defended firebases. During the war CH-47s retrieved more than 11,400 disabled aircraft, worth roughly $3 billion, that had crashed or been shot down.

Another valuable cargo craft was the CH-54, an oddly shaped helicopter that was called a Skycrane. Its crew consisted of a pilot, copilot, and a crewman who operated the cargo hook and winch controls. The Skycrane, which had a 20,760-pound load capacity, was commonly used to carry heavy engineering equipment such as bulldozers, prefab bridges, howitzers, or two-and-one-half-ton trucks. It also could carry detachable cargo pods that could be used as mobile field hospitals, command posts, or maintenance shops.

The Marine Corps flew its own fleet of transport choppers, including the versatile CH-46 Sea Knight, which was the marine equivalent of the army's Huey. The CH-46 could carry seventeen combat-equipped troops in addition to its three crewmen or fifteen litters for medical evacuation. When employed as a cargo ship it could haul up to 6,000 pounds inside or as much as 10,000 pounds on its cargo hook. By July 1969, marine Sea Knights had transported more than 1.3 million troops, lifted nearly 100,000 tons of cargo, and ferried more than 120,000 casualties to base hospitals. For heavy transport there was the CH-53 Sea Stallion. Its thirty-foot-long cargo cabin could accommodate a one-and-one-half-ton truck, a 105MM howitzer, or a Hawk missile battery.

The navy and the air force also operated their own helicopter units. SH-3 Sea King and UH-2 Seasprite helicopters based aboard destroyers, cruisers, and carriers acted as search and rescue aircraft. CH-3 Sea King and CH-53 Sea Stallion cargo choppers were modified by the air force's Air Rescue Service for rescue operations. Redesignated the HH-3E and the HH-53B, they came to be known by their respective nicknames—the Jolly Green Giant and the Super Jolly Green Giant. These two helicopters formed the backbone of the 3d Aerospace Rescue and Recovery Group, which held the primary responsibility for rescue operations in Southeast Asia (see photo essay, p. 74).

When added together, this vast supporting cast of personnel, equipment, and aircraft was a vital component of the United States' air effort in Southeast Asia. Although they did not receive the same recognition combat pilots did, support personnel on the ground, at sea, and in the air were equally vital to the American air war in Southeast Asia.

A UH-1 medevac helicopter swoops down on an AH-1 Cobra crash site to pick up the destroyed craft's crew. The soldiers at right, 173d Airborne troopers who picked up the Cobra's "Mayday!" and summoned the Huey, depart the scene, leaving the injured crew in the hands of the medical team.

Search and Rescue

The USAF 3d Aerospace Rescue and Recovery Group was responsible for coordinating all search and rescue (SAR) efforts throughout Southeast Asia from the Joint Center at 7th Air Force headquarters at Tan Son Nhut. The 3d ARRG consisted of four squadrons based at Tan Son Nhut, Da Nang, Tuy Hoa, and Udorn, Thailand, with smaller detachments at fourteen additional sites in South Vietnam and Thailand. The backbone of the ARRG's fleet consisted initially of HH-3 Jolly Green Giant rescue helicopters equipped with auxiliary fuel tanks to give them a maximum range of 625 nautical miles. In 1967, larger HH-53 Super Jolly Green Giants were introduced. Armed with three 7.62MM miniguns, the HH-53 was the largest, fastest, and most powerful helicopter in the air force's inventory. Refueled by specially designed HC-130 aerial refueling tankers, the helicopters would effect recoveries deep in enemy territory.

Right. *Two HH-53 Super Jolly Green Giant rescue helicopters of the 37th Aerospace Rescue and Recovery Squadron based at Da Nang are accompanied by an HC-130P refueling tanker on a long-range rescue mission in June 1970. Inset. A door gunner aboard an HH-53 fires one of its three 7.62MM miniguns during a rescue mission off the coast of North Vietnam.*

SAR operations over enemy territory required precise planning and execution. Once a pilot was reported down, rescue controllers had to act quickly, assembling and coordinating the SAR task force. A pair of A-1 Skyraiders, known as Sandies, were sent in first to contact the downed airman by radio, pinpoint his exact location, and scout the area. While the Sandies circled over the downed airman's position, a rescue helicopter sped in at treetop level guided by another pair of Sandies providing covering fire. Sometimes the pilot had already been killed or captured and the enemy was using the airman's emergency survival homing device to lure SAR helicopters into a trap.

Left. A helicopter crewman watches as a parajumper rides into the jungle via a winch during a rescue in 1968. Above. USAF pilot Lieutenant Glenn Fleming and a parajumper are hoisted from the jungles of Laos by an HH-43A Huskie on April 28, 1971. Right. Tension runs high in the operations center of the 40th ARRS at Udorn as a back-up team listens in to radio transmissions during a large SAR mission.

Their motto was "That Others May Live," and SAR crews constantly risked their own lives in pursuit of that goal. According to Colonel Royal A. Brown, an HH-53 pilot, "whenever a guy went down the whole war would come to a stop [for us]." Some SAR missions lasted two or three hours, others two or three days. "You never quit until you got him out regardless of ... how many people got shot down," Brown said. "As long as that guy was there, he knew we were going to keep trying to get him out." Between August 1964 and August 1973, American SAR crews saved the lives of 3,883 men, nearly half of whom were American airmen.

Left. *USAF Captain John A. Corder, shot down on his ninety-sixth combat mission, flashes a grateful smile to his rescuers. Below. Before ejecting, pilots hit during missions over North Vietnam often tried to nurse their crippled planes over the Gulf of Tonkin, where their chances of rescue were greater. After bailing out of his damaged F-8 Crusader in the gulf, Lieutenant Cody A. Balisteri clambers directly aboard a navy rescue helicopter after its cable hoist failed to pull him out of the water.*

Buying Time

Lieutenant Rick Curtin, a UH-1 pilot with the 118th Assault Helicopter Company, was on duty in the operations office at Bien Hoa on April 30, 1970, when he received a telephone call from headquarters. He was to fly to Long Binh to pick up a parcel. Although it was only a five-minute hop each way, Curtin welcomed any relief from the boredom and paperwork of his dual assignment as the unit's assistant operations officer.

At Long Binh, Curtin was handed a cardboard tube of maps. "I couldn't understand why we were getting new maps," he recalled. They already had plenty of their assigned area of operations around Saigon in III Corps. Besides, they hardly used their maps anyway. Curtin had been in country for only two months, but like the other chopper pilots in his company he had quickly memorized distinctive geographical landmarks so that he knew their area of operations by heart.

While flying back to Bien Hoa, Curtin's curiosity got the better of him. He opened the end of the

tube and glanced inside. The writing on the map was in a foreign language. "I couldn't recognize the alphabet," he said. Not until he spread the map out on his desk did it finally click. The script was Khmer, the native language of Cambodia. "Hot shit," Curtin thought to himself, "we're finally going in there to kick ass."

Nixon's gamble in Cambodia

The next day in Washington, President Nixon made the stunning announcement that U.S. and South Vietnamese forces had crossed the border into Cambodia. Only ten days before he had announced the impending withdrawal of another 150,000 American troops from Vietnam. The invasion, which was certain to provoke a storm of protest at home, was in fact a huge gamble on the part of the president, a gamble made possible by a sudden turn of events in Cambodia.

For years, Prince Norodom Sihanouk had managed to keep his nation insulated from the conflict in Southeast Asia. But in 1968, as the Americans escalated their aerial interdiction campaign against the Ho Chi Minh Trail in Laos, Cambodia became an increasingly attractive alternate supply route for Hanoi. Soviet and other Eastern bloc ships stepped up their use of the port at Sihanoukville where supplies were unloaded and transported by truck to Communist support bases along the South Vietnamese border. The tonnage of supplies flowing along the Sihanoukville route soon was reported by U.S. intelligence to be enough to support enemy activities in two-thirds of South Vietnam.

By mid-1969, an estimated 40,000 North Vietnamese and Vietcong troops in Cambodia were reportedly providing arms and ammunition to local Communist insurgents, the Khmer Rouge. The growing North Vietnamese presence in Cambodia alarmed Sihanouk and triggered anti-Vietnamese protests in the capital of Phnom Penh. In July, under increasing domestic pressure, Sihanouk announced he was ready to restore diplomatic relations with Washington. He also turned a blind eye to the secret U.S. Menu B-52 bombings of Communist bases which had begun earlier in the year. Sihanouk apparently hoped to gain some diplomatic leverage by his tilt to the West. In the following months, he lobbied Moscow and Peking for support in persuading Hanoi to withdraw its forces.

His efforts were too little and too late. On March 18, 1970, Sihanouk was ousted as head of state by Lieutenant General Lon Nol, the pro-Western army chief of staff. Lon Nol closed the port of Sihanoukville and ordered the North Vietnamese out of the country. Sporadic fighting soon broke out between the Communists and the poorly trained

American transport helicopters at the ready on their pad at Khe Sanh as the invasion of Laos, Operation Lam Son 719, gets under way in February 1971.

and inadequately equipped Cambodian army of some 35,000 men. Lon Nol turned to Washington and Saigon for arms and support. This was not enough. North Vietnamese troops quickly rolled back the Cambodian army, and by April 20 the Communists effectively controlled most of the northern and eastern portions of the country. The Cambodian army appeared ready to collapse.

The commander of American forces in South Vietnam, General Creighton Abrams, was alarmed. On April 18, he requested authority to use U.S. tactical aircraft for a thirty-day period, in addition to the ongoing B-52 Menu strikes, against Communist forces across the border in Cambodia. Two days later the Joint Chiefs of Staff, with White House approval, granted his request. The strikes were code named Operation Patio, and all communications regarding them were to be sent through special, secure channels. Aircraft were assigned cover targets in Laos in the same way that Menu B-52 operations employed phony targets in South Vietnam.

On April 24, the first Patio missions hit a narrow, eight-mile strip of northeastern Cambodia along the South Vietnamese border, where intelligence sources reported heavy enemy activity. Within a few days, however, the boundaries were expanded to a uniform depth of eighteen miles inside the country. Some were flown in support of stepped-up, clandestine cross-border raids by Special Forces teams. Patio was only a prelude for more drastic action: the full-scale invasion of Cambodia by American and South Vietnamese forces.

American military leaders were convinced that a Communist victory in Cambodia would have a deleterious impact on the war in South Vietnam, especially in light of continuing U.S. troop withdrawals. The creation of a secure Communist base of operations along their western border would present an even more dangerous threat to the South Vietnamese.

President Nixon viewed Hanoi's aggressive moves in Cambodia as a direct challenge. In spite of his decision to begin unilaterally withdrawing U.S. troops, the North Vietnamese had spurned renewed American negotiating efforts. Hanoi apparently was convinced that rising antiwar sentiment at home would preclude any American escalation of the war.

According to NSC staff member Roger Morris, the president became "obsessed with the idea that the other side was trying to push him around." Nixon was convinced that Hanoi would never acquiesce to a negotiated settlement of the war if the U.S. could not convince the Communists that they could not win on the battlefield. In an April 22 memorandum to Kissinger, the president wrote: "We can't let them do this. . . . We need a bold move in Cambodia." Nixon rationalized that since any move into Cambodia would cause an uproar at home, he might as well go all the way. "When you bite the bullet," he told Nelson Rockefeller, "bite it hard—go for the big play."

The Joint Chiefs of Staff furnished a plan that called for a simultaneous attack by ARVN forces into an area along the border known as the "Parrot's Beak" while American troops hit a section of the border further north known as the "Fish Hook." By attacking the enemy's exposed supply lines and bases along the border, the generals hoped to disrupt the Communist offensive against Lon Nol and buy precious time for the Vietnamization program. Once again the JCS also dangled the promise of uncovering COSVN headquarters. On April 26, after silencing or ignoring any opposing viewpoints, Nixon approved the plan, which called for a combined force of 48,000 ARVN and 40,000 U.S. troops. At a Pentagon briefing on April 30, the day after the invasion began, the president exhorted the generals to "blow the hell" out of the Communists. This was easier said than done.

Although the burgeoning Vietnamization program had achieved some measure of progress, the South Vietnamese still lacked sufficient support assets, such as artillery, helicopters, and tactical aircraft, to mount their part of the operation without American help. The South Vietnamese Air Force possessed only four squadrons of UH-1 Hueys and had no heavy-lift helicopters. Although the VNAF had expanded its combat aircraft inventory to five squadrons, they consisted mainly of A-37s, F-5s, and older, slower-moving A-1 Skyraiders, which were not well suited for long-range missions. In addition, the F-5 had a limited ordnance load capacity. American aircraft would have to provide airlift, resupply, medevac, and close air support for ARVN troops, as well as for U.S. troops in the Fish Hook operation.

Tay Ninh, located just twelve miles from the Cambodian border, was the jumping-off point for the ARVN operation against the Parrot's Beak. On the morning of April 29, the day of the invasion, the runway came alive with activity. O-2 Bird Dogs, doubling as airborne FACs and artillery spotters, constantly took off and landed. Hundreds of transport and medevac choppers were revving their en-

While American armored cavalrymen look on, an F-100 Super Sabre jet pulls up after dropping bombs and napalm on Communist positions near the town of Snuol in Cambodia, May 1970.

gines on the flight line. Among them was Lt. Rick Curtin's UH-1D, which took off in the first wave. "You looked to your left and you looked to your right and there was movement everywhere," Curtin later recalled, as the fleet of choppers headed west toward Cambodia.

During the next few weeks Curtin logged seven to ten hours of flying time a day, ferrying troops back and forth across the border. He knew of some pilots who flew as many as sixteen hours per day. Initially, the helicopters met with little resistance. But as the invasion progressed, it became apparent that ARVN units were running up against stiff opposition. One day Curtin's company commander was asked to provide a Huey with a cargo hook for a special detail. For the next four hours Curtin found himself "ferrying cargo nets full of bodies and parts of bodies" of ARVN soldiers from Cambodia to a mass grave near Saigon.

American tactical aircraft flew more than 6,000 sorties in support of both ARVN and U.S. ground forces, an average of 210 per day. Every night three U.S. gunships patrolled overhead, expending a total of 1.5 million rounds of ammunition and 8,600 flares. In addition, air force C-130s flew twenty-one Commando Vault missions in which they rolled 15,000-pound bombs out their rear cargo doors to blast enemy positions or create instant helicopter landing zones in dense jungle.

Air force B-52s continued the work they had begun in Operation Menu, flying 186 missions against targets along the border in support of the invasion force. The most effective raid occurred on May 11 against a suspected enemy base area northwest of the town of Mimot. Troops who swept the target zone after the raid found 101 bodies and the ruins of a large underground shelter.

In the short run, the invasion appeared to achieve most of its tactical and strategic goals. Although the much-talked-about enemy COSVN headquarters had again eluded the allies' grasp, according to MACV officials the enemy had been dealt a severe setback. They reeled off impressive statistics citing the thousands of tons of weapons, ammunition, and supplies that had been captured or destroyed, and estimated the number of Communists killed at 4,776 men. As the generals had predicted, the invasion resulted subsequently in a sharp drop in U.S. casualty rates in South Vietnam.

The invasion of Cambodia, however, produced a number of long-term side effects that would haunt the Nixon administration for the next three years. It had provoked the most serious backlash of public opposition yet to the war. An anxious Senate passed the Cooper-Church amendment, prohibiting U.S. combat troops from entering Cambodia and Laos after June 30. Caught between his public commitment to the withdrawal program and growing Congressional checks, Nixon saw his options in Southeast Asia rapidly dwindle, locking the U.S. even more firmly into the Vietnamization program.

At the same time, the boundaries of war had been irreversibly widened. Just as the escalated bombing campaign against the Pathet Lao had drawn the Americans deeper into the conflict in Laos, the invasion of Cambodia committed them to supporting Lon Nol in his fight against the Communists. The overt extension of the war into the two neighboring countries benefited Hanoi in the long run, allowing it to extend its control over larger portions of territory while the United States was forced to divert more of its dwindling resources to support pro-Western forces in both countries.

Operation Freedom Deal

Although President Nixon pulled American forces out of Cambodia by the June 30 deadline, U.S. and South Vietnamese forces continued to operate in the country. In August, the VNAF detached twelve Skyraiders, several observation planes, and two AC-119 gunships to Pochentong airfield at Phnom Penh. There the VNAF set up an Air Support Operations Center at Khmer air force headquarters to coordinate VNAF missions in support of Cambodian forces. Washington and Saigon also supplied the tiny Khmer air force, which consisted of a handful of MiG-15s and MiG-17s, with additional T-28 fighters, C-47 transports, and six UH-1 Hueys.

Cambodian pilots flew more missions than an air force its size could have been expected to, but they were constantly hampered by maintenance problems and a lack of spare parts. VNAF mechanics and CIA-contracted Air America personnel were sent to service the planes, and the U.S. Air Force helped further by swapping new C-47s for ones that needed extensive repairs. Then, in one strike on January 21, 1971, Communist saboteurs virtually wiped out the entire force during a raid on Pochentong airfield, and the Cambodian army became totally reliant on VNAF and U.S. air support.

Although the Cooper-Church amendment passed by the Congress barred American ground forces from Cambodia, the 7th Air Force continued to conduct tactical air strikes against Communist supply lines in eastern Cambodia. The interdiction strikes, code named Operation Freedom Deal, were restricted to a thirty-mile-deep area between the South Vietnamese border and the Mekong River, but within two months they were, without public announcement, expanded to include targets west of the Mekong. Between July 1970 and February 1971, approximately 44 percent, or 3,634 of the more than 8,000 sorties flown in Cambodia, struck at targets outside the authorized Freedom Deal area of operations.

Many of these strikes were in direct support of Cambodian troops engaged with North Vietnamese and Khmer Rouge forces, although officials denied the fact. Journalists reported seeing American planes dropping napalm and bombs within 300 meters of friendly ground troops. The missions were directed by USAF airborne command and control aircraft and controlled by American FACs who worked with Cambodian forward air guides on the ground. Since few spoke English, French-speaking volunteers accompanied the FACs as translators.

The U.S. Army circumvented restrictions on engaging in combat on the ground in Cambodia by employing its helicopters in "hunter-killer" missions. Mark Hilton, a warrant officer pilot in Charlie Company, 1st Squadron, 9th Regiment, of the 1st Air Cavalry Division stationed at Tay Ninh, recalled flying such missions in Cambodia until his tour was up in July 1971. They ranged as far west as the Mekong River, but mainly operated within twenty miles of the Cambodian border.

Hunter-killer missions consisted of an AH-1 Huey Cobra gunship and a QH-6A Light Observation Helicopter (known as a Loach) working in pairs nicknamed "pink teams." Together they scoured the countryside for signs of enemy activity. While the Cobra circled overhead at 2,000 feet, Hilton flew his Loach in low "to find the bad guys." First he checked the area by making a high-speed pass at treetop level, then a slower, curving "S" pattern. If he didn't draw any fire, he brought the Loach in under the trees for a closer look.

While cruising at a slow speed just three to four feet off the ground, Hilton inspected the trails and paths like an old-fashioned cavalry scout. "You almost became one with your environment," Hilton said. "You could sense people out there in the bush. Even if you didn't see evidence of people, you knew they were there." As a precaution, Hilton always kept the nose of his Loach pointed to the side as he flew down the trails to throw off concealed enemy gunners who had a tendency to "lead" a helicopter, aiming a few feet in front of the chopper's nose expecting the pilot to fly straight into the hail of fire. While he studied the trail, his two crewmen kept a lookout.

In the seat behind Hilton, his crew chief manned an M60 machine gun with a sawed-off barrel while an enlisted observer in the left seat held a small automatic weapon and a smoke grenade. If they drew fire, Hilton executed a rapid escape maneuver while the observer marked the spot with the smoke grenade for the circling Cobra gunship, which immediately dove in to blast the site with its rockets, miniguns, and cannon. If they uncovered a large body of troops or an extensive cache of supplies, they called in air force fighter-bombers.

Due to the political sensitivity of these missions, rules of engagement prohibited hunter-killer teams from firing unless fired upon first. "You would have to call in to headquarters to get authority to hit a force that didn't fire on you," said Hilton. But sometimes there was not enough time and Hilton had to make a split-second decision. In situations where there was any doubt, he usually opened fire immediately. "If you hesitate," he said, "you're dead."

Despite the liberal use of U.S. air power, the Commu-nists occupied half the country by late 1970 and had cut the land routes leading to and from the capital of Phnom Penh. All supplies for the capital had to be shipped from Saigon up the Mekong River in convoys escorted by South Vietnamese patrol boats. USAF fighter-bombers and army helicopter gunships were assigned to fly cover for the convoys as they came under attack from enemy gunners hidden along the river banks. Navy jets also were called in when the air force could not keep up with requests for air support and interdiction missions elsewhere in the country.

Before long, the U.S. found itself committing more and more of its air power to the struggle in Cambodia. In 1971, missions in Cambodia made up nearly 15 percent of the total number of U.S. combat sorties in Southeast Asia, up from 8 percent in 1970. From his government-in-exile in Peking, Prince Sihanouk remarked that the Lon Nol regime continued to exist "only through the intervention of the U.S. Air Force."

"Vietnamizing" the air war

While U.S. air units were busy propping up Lon Nol's forces in Cambodia, the VNAF was beginning to stand on its own in South Vietnam. Since mid-1969, U.S. advisers had been accelerating the Vietnamization effort, as Washington provided additional aircraft to enlarge and modernize the VNAF's air fleet. By mid-1970, the VNAF had expanded from 428 aircraft and 29,000 officers and enlisted men to nearly 700 aircraft and 35,000 men in a little over a year.

The enlarged VNAF had a solid corps of battle-hardened South Vietnamese pilots. A number of the VNAF's senior pilots had served with the French in the fifties, while others received training in the United States in the early sixties. Unlike their American counterparts, who rotated in and out on one-year tours of duty, the South Vietnamese were in the war for the duration. Those pilots who survived were extremely good. Many had logged incredible amounts of combat flying time over the years. "I've got 300 combat flying hours," said Colonel Peter Van Brussel, chief of the Air Force Advisory Team at Nha Trang. "That's a respectable amount for a U.S. pilot but hardly a start for Vietnamese airmen. Many of the men I work with have more than 3,000."

There were too few of these veteran combat pilots to go around, however, and most of them had logged their time in A-1 Skyraiders, the VNAF's primary combat aircraft until 1968. The introduction of more sophisticated A-37 and F-5 jets, as well as AC-47 and AC-119 gunships, required specialized training. That meant either withdrawing older pilots from combat duty to train in these new aircraft or starting from scratch with new recruits. A lack of qualified pilots to man the increased number of combat aircraft was not the only problem. Pilots were also needed for the

VNAF

To beef up the South Vietnamese air force in preparation for America's withdrawal, U.S. advisers accelerated their efforts to train Vietnamese in the maintenance as well as the flying of combat aircraft. By mid–1970, the VNAF had grown into a force of 35,000 men and nearly 700 aircraft.

Above. *Vietnamese mechanics unpack and assemble newly delivered F-5 "Freedom Fighters" at Bien Hoa airport in November 1972.* Right. *A Vietnamese pilot gets the feel of his F-5's cockpit at Bien Hoa.*

transport, reconnaissance, and observation aircraft the VNAF acquired from the Americans to support the expanding needs of ARVN units. Technical and logistical support requirements for this expanded air fleet were enormous. While the VNAF had recruited large numbers of support personnel, nearly half of them were unskilled.

The U.S. Air Force sent two mobile training teams to the Vietnamese Air Training Center at Nha Trang in early 1971, to help set up and teach an enlarged curriculum of courses. In March, 243 Vietnamese technicians went to bases in the U.S. to learn seventeen basic maintenance skills and help translate complicated aircraft manuals from English into Vietnamese. Within fifteen months, 6,000 Vietnamese graduated from these courses, and many of them became instructors at Nha Trang.

At the same time, the U.S. Air Force established on-the-job training and integrated crew programs at bases shared by U.S. and VNAF units. They provided practical experience to recent graduates and also familiarized older pilots and mechanics with new aircraft and upgraded their skills. In the integrated crew program, members of USAF units who were scheduled to be withdrawn from Vietnam were assigned to fly with the Vietnamese who would eventually take over the aircraft. U.S. advisers also provided on-the-job training in thirty different specialized skills, including air traffic control, communications, electronics, reconnaissance photo processing and analysis, weather, air base security, and fire and damage control. By June 1971, more than 7,300 VNAF personnel had completed courses in these two programs.

U.S. Army advisers conducted similar training programs for Vietnamese helicopter pilots. Although officially part of the VNAF, South Vietnam's four UH-1 squadrons were under the effective control of local ARVN corps commanders, who employed them interchangeably as transports, gunships, medevacs, and resupply ships. This inhibited pilots from developing specialized skills and left little time for training in night operations or formation flying, which were essential for large-scale heliborne assaults. At the urging of U.S. advisers, the VNAF gradually began assigning aircraft and crews for specialized roles and instituting night and close formation training exercises.

The biggest task facing the VNAF and its American advisers was to develop a coherent command structure to manage this greatly expanded force. In essence, at the time the Vietnamization program began, the VNAF was merely a collection of pilots and planes parceled out to various army corps commanders who were often reluctant to release them for missions outside their own corps areas. The VNAF possessed no real command and control structure capable of running the air force on a countrywide basis because of a shortage of experienced staff officers and the air force's lack of influence within South Vietnam's military hierarchy. Lacking any representation on the Joint General Staff, the VNAF remained a junior partner to the army, with little voice or experience in planning joint operations.

As the Vietnamization program progressed, the increased size and strength of the VNAF necessitated structural changes that helped to alleviate these problems. In mid-1970, the VNAF was reorganized into five air divisions under the overall command of General Tran Van Minh. Each division consisted of two mixed wings of fighter-bombers, helicopters, and gunships. In addition, there were five maintenance and supply and seven airbase support wings. By developing its own command and support structure, the VNAF achieved a degree of independence from army control and greater flexibility in managing the air war countrywide.

Throughout 1971, as American air units departed, VNAF aircraft flew more combat sorties in South Vietnam than all U.S. air arms combined, nearly a 70 percent increase over their operations in 1970. While the encouraging statistics appeared to indicate the VNAF were now capable of holding their own in the low-level conflict against the Communists in South Vietnam, events in Laos would cast a shadow of doubt on the effectiveness of the Vietnamization program.

Lam Son 719

Following the loss of their Cambodian supply routes, the North Vietnamese heightened their activities in Laos. During the first six weeks of 1971, an estimated 31,000 troops and 1,800 trucks filtered down the Ho Chi Minh Trail, a substantial increase over the previous year's levels. While some of these resources were channeled to the battle in Cambodia, the majority were earmarked for South Vietnam. General Abrams and the South Vietnamese chief of staff, General Cao Van Vien, feared that a major Communist invasion was in the making and planned a preemptive strike of their own, Operation Lam Son 719—the invasion of Laos.

Lam Son 719's initial objective was Tchepone, an important supply hub on Route 9, twenty-five miles inside the Laotian border. Intelligence sources believed Tchepone housed a major communications center, complete with sophisticated Russian equipment, for guiding traffic along the Ho Chi Minh Trail. Although the Cooper-Church amendment prohibited the use of U.S. ground troops, President Nixon authorized unlimited air support for the ARVN invasion force. The 7th Air Force temporarily diverted aircraft from missions against the trail to provide close air support while 600 helicopters were assigned to transport ARVN troops across the border and for resupply and medevac missions.

Lam Son 719 swung into action on February 8, when ARVN armored units drove across the border along Route 9 into Laos. Helicopters of the 101st Combat Aviation Group airlifted other ARVN units into flanking positions

Raid
on Son Tay

by Kevin Generous

By the spring of 1970, American military disengagement from Southeast Asia was in full swing. But for those 1,463 Americans listed as either prisoners of war or missing in action, there was no scheduled rotation home. As the war wound down, the Pentagon's concern over American POWs held in North Vietnam increased, while Hanoi made obvious its intention to use the POWs as "bargaining chips" at the Paris peace talks—in effect, hostages for continued American withdrawal from Southeast Asia.

Public awareness in the United States over the plight of the POW/MIAs was at an all-time high. Thousands of citizens wore a one-quarter-inch aluminum bracelet inscribed with the name and date of an American POW/MIA and pledged not to remove the bracelet until his liberation. Other Americans launched intense letter-writing campaigns in an attempt to pressure Hanoi for more information and better treatment for the imprisoned Americans.

This sort of activity did not seem enough to American military leaders. The Pentagon had long considered attempting a POW rescue operation that, according to JCS Chairman Admiral Thomas Moorer, could provide a "focal point, something dramatic" that would give the nation a more positive per-

spective on the war. "If we could get 50 or 60 of those boys back in the U.S. and let them tell in their own words what happened to them," Moorer stated, "it would throw a lot of light on the character of North Vietnam."

But a POW raid into North Vietnam would be more than just a Pentagon public relations gimmick; after the release of three Americans by Hanoi in 1969, U.S. military leaders heard firsthand the horror stories of systematic North Vietnamese psychological and physical torture of POWs, confirming what had always been suspected. The tales sufficiently impressed the Joint Chiefs of Staff to order the special assistant for counterinsurgency and special activities (SACSA), Brigadier General Donald Blackburn, to study the possibility of a dramatic POW rescue operation. Such a raid, it was thought, would raise POW morale and force Hanoi to improve treatment for remaining POWs. It would also demonstrate that the U.S. would not stand idly by while its fighting men were abused by a signator of the Geneva Convention.

Blackburn, former commander of MACV-SOG, the special operations group that ran covert cross-border operations, realized the difficulty of a successful raid on a POW camp behind enemy lines. In fact, the U.S. had secretly conducted numerous but mostly unsuccessful POW rescue attempts in South Vietnam. The only American POW freed from a Vietcong camp later died of wounds inflicted by his captors during the rescue. Air force search-and-rescue teams and SOG agents had conducted many quick-in-and-out rescues of downed pilots in North Vietnam, but none to pluck POWs out of prison camps. Even with the full backing of the Pentagon brass and U.S. military resources in Southeast Asia, a rescue raid on a POW camp in the North would be risky, demanding daring speed, perfect execution, and most important, good intelligence. A Joint Contingency Task Group was formed in May 1970. From a number of possible POW camps the group picked Son Tay, some twenty-three miles west of Hanoi. There were said to be fifty-five American captives

there. Photographic intelligence from low-altitude unmanned Buffalo Hunter drones and high-altitude SR-71 strategic reconnaissance aircraft showed signs of life at Son Tay. Although three NVA military installations and 12,000 NVA troops fell within ten kilometers, Son Tay was relatively isolated, and planners felt that a surprise nighttime raid could be executed before the North Vietnamese could react.

The rescue operation, code named Ivory Coast (a name picked at random by a Pentagon computer), was put in the command of air force Brigadier General Leroy J. Manor, chief of the USAF Special Operations Force at Eglin AFB, Florida. Eglin was the home of the Aerospace Rescue and Recovery Service (ARRS), the elite pararescue organization responsible for rescuing more than 3,800 American pilots and air crews during the Vietnam War. Manor himself had flown 275 combat missions as commander of the 37th Tactical Fighter Wing, based in Phu Cat.

At General Blackburn's insistence, Special Forces Colonel Arthur "Bull" Simons was picked as Manor's deputy and ground commander of the raid. Simons was a legendary figure among the Green Berets, a noted expert on unconventional warfare who had served as a World War II Ranger, as commander of the 1960-62 "White Star" missions that organized the Meo guerrilla tribesmen in Laos, and, in Vietnam, as chief of SOG's OPLAN 35 covert cross-border operations. When word went out at Fort Bragg's JFK Special Warfare Center that Simons wanted men for a special mission, more than 500 men volunteered. Simons handpicked a fifty-nine-man assault force, divided them into three groups, and chose two SOG veterans to command the first two groups. Simons himself would lead the third.

Both air crews and Simons's raiders trained at Eglin Auxiliary Airfield No. 3, an isolated, vacant cantonment at which Jimmy Doolittle's B-25 Tokyo Raiders had trained in 1942. During the rigorous six-week training, air crews and raiders were kept in the dark about their actual mission. One air force pilot was certain he was training for a helicopter assault on Cuba. The raiders practiced on a full-scale mockup of the Son Tay camp, made of lumber and target cloth that could be rolled up to mask the operation from twice-daily passages overhead of Soviet COSMOS satellites. Simons's men trained in surprise raiding tactics and with bolt cutters, chain saws, and axes for breaking into locked cellblocks.

Pilots and assault teams also studied "Barbara," an exact, $60,000 CIA-built scaled model of Son Tay compound, rigged with special viewing devices to duplicate precise light effects from varying angles of approach. Simons wanted his assault force intimate with every detail of Son Tay. Helicopter pilots trained extensively for night contour flying and navigation, while trailing a specially modified C-130 Combat Talon equipped with a new forward-looking infrared radar system. Another C-130 Combat Talon practiced guiding a flight of supporting A-1 Sandy attack planes, while a HC-130 rescue ship rehearsed as tanker for refueling and for navigation support.

Flying in radio silence from five bases in Thailand, the C-130s and a helicopter assault force of five HH-53 Super Jolly Green Giants and an HH-3 Jolly Green Giant would have to link, refuel in midair, and penetrate carefully picked "blind spots" in North Vietnamese and Chinese radar coverage. An essential ingredient for a successful rescue was, of course, timely and accurate intelligence. Although the Son Tay raiders had the full support of the CIA, DIA, NSA, and the National Reconnaissance Office, the cumulative record on POWs held in North Vietnam was thin and based largely on aerial photographs from low-level 147SC remotely piloted aircraft and SR-71s taken from 80,000 feet. As the raid planning continued in June 1970, the photos duly noted such details as guard towers, volleyball nets, and, in midsummer, the flooding of the river adjacent to the camp to within two feet of its walls.

As training got under way in August 1970, planners were told of "decreased activity" in the Son Tay camp. Highly abnormal weather conditions over North Vietnam, plus North Vietnamese persistence in shooting down the reconnais-sance drones, interfered with efforts to get good photographs, but some clearly showed weeds growing inside the compound. Planning for the raid continued anyway. As the raid's planned deadline approached, some other disconcerting in-intelligence came in. A covert source smuggled a cigarette pack out of Hanoi that contained a list of active North Vietnamese prison camps. Son Tay was not on the list.

Son Tay was indeed empty of American POWs. In mid-July unusually heavy monsoon rains had flooded the camp and forced the evacuation of the POWs held there. Later, Blackburn would remember that someone had suggested to him that Son Tay might be empty, but the planners preferred to believe that the POWs were merely being kept inside the compound.

General Manor and Colonel Simons, now based in Thailand, were never told to expect an empty camp. On November 20, Bull Simons told his men: "We are going to rescue 70 American prisoners of war, maybe more, from a camp called Son Tay. This is something American prisoners have a right to expect from their fellow soldiers. The target is 23 miles from Hanoi."

The raiders were silent for an instant, then stood up and applauded loudly. At 6:00 P.M. on November 20 the rescue team departed from Udorn Air Force Base for a flight through Laos and then into North Vietnam. One hour before their arrival at Son Tay, 100 navy planes headed for Haiphong Harbor in the largest night air operation ever flown over North Vietnam. The planes, however, were dropping not bombs, but flares, designed to divert Hanoi's air defenses from Son Tay. The diversion worked, and Simons's small helicopter fleet was able to slip through Hanoi's radar undetected.

With one exception, the raid proceeded according to plan. One small helicopter landed inside the compound, knocking out the guard towers and guard barracks. The other two choppers were supposed to land outside the camp, blow a hole through the wall, and then reinforce the initial assault group. One of them did, but Simons's own helicopter veered off course and dropped down at what U.S. planners had thought was a secondary school 500 yards away from the camp. There the raiders found a large group of foreign military advisers (Chinese or Asians from the U.S.S.R., they could not tell which) and shot several of them before moving on.

By the time Simons reached Son Tay itself the bad news was apparent. No POWs. Sporadic fire from North Vietnamese defenders injured one raider, and the raiders in turn killed or wounded several North Vietnamese guards. Another American broke an ankle during the initial landing. They were the only two casualties among the raiders, other than the men's spirits. "You build your heart up for something like this," one man said later. "Every nerve in your body wants it. Then there's no one there."

The results of the raid reached the White House less than one hour after the men had left Son Tay. President Nixon and Secretary of Defense Melvin Laird decided to make the mission public and portray it in the best light possible, before word of it could leak out.

Recriminations over the Son Tay failure came quickly. Within hours after the raid was announced publicly, Son Tay was called an "intelligence failure," a "first-magnitude blunder" that radically decreased the chances of better treatment of POWs through negotiation.

While it saved no American POWs, the raid on Son Tay may at least have ameliorated their plight. Not long after the raid, the North Vietnamese herded all the POWs into prisons in central Hanoi to make them less accessible to future raids. As one of them, Colonel Robinson Risner, later wrote: "The raid may have failed in its primary objectives, but it boosted our morale sky-high! It also put all the POWs captured in North Vietnam together for the first time. This would have a major impact on us."

Kevin Generous has published a book and several articles on special operations and unconventional warfare in Vietnam.

astride Route 9 ahead of the armored column. Within three days, 16,000 ARVN troops had poured across the border. Heliborne ARVN units moved westward toward Tchepone in a series of leap-frogging maneuvers, setting up a string of fire support bases to pave the way for the armored column. At first they encountered only rear echelon and antiaircraft units guarding the trail. But within three weeks, the North Vietnamese sent in elements of three regiments supported by artillery, tanks, and AAA to blunt the ARVN advance. The Vietnamization program was now put to the acid test, as the South Vietnamese faced heavily armed, conventional NVA forces for the first time in the war.

The Communists took advantage of ARVN's dependence on helicopters to move and resupply troops in the thick jungle terrain. Unfamiliar with the terrain and plagued by poor weather conditions, chopper pilots tended to travel predictable paths along which the enemy stacked his defenses. Whereas in Cambodia ground fire had tended to come from small-caliber 7.62MM and 12.7MM machine guns, in Laos the choppers ran into heavier 23MM, 37MM, and 57MM antiaircraft guns.

Since there were few natural clearings suitable for use as landing zones for large-scale helicopter assaults, the enemy was able to mass its AA guns at these obvious sites. The guns were cleverly concealed in the surrounding jungle and carefully positioned to provide overlapping fields of fire against incoming helicopters. Troop-carrying "slicks," highly vulnerable during landing and takeoff, were the hardest hit. Their Huey Cobra gunship escorts had a difficult time silencing the North Vietnamese gunners. Nearly twenty-five allied helicopters were destroyed and at least that many damaged in the first fifteen days of the offensive. As the fighting intensified, the losses skyrocketed. According to one American chopper pilot, "We were the hunted in Laos."

David Groen, a Huey pilot, recalled Lam Son as being far worse than the Cambodian invasion. "Crippled slicks suspended from the bellies of Sky Cranes or Chinooks were a common sight," he said. "The missions were so bad that crews taped 'chicken plates' [steel body armor] down on the chin bubble and on the floor to stop the bullets. Door gunners wore chest and back armor plates and sat on pieces of armor."

Frequently, U.S. pilots would unload ARVN troops at a seemingly "cold" landing zone only to have the woods around the LZ explode with enemy fire once the choppers were gone. The ARVN commander would radio them to come back and pick up the troops. Such a mission was a nightmare for a chopper pilot. Not only did he have to return to a hot LZ but also to contend with ARVN troops who were often too disorganized to provide any supporting fire. The helicopters' precisely timed close-formation approaches, essential to successful evacuation missions under fire, broke down as panicking soldiers gave them little room to land and mobbed the choppers as soon as they touched down.

Without the support of U.S. fighter-bombers and B-52s, the invasion force would certainly have met with disaster. Continuous air strikes prevented the North Vietnamese from massing their forces for a knockout blow. When they did try to mass, U.S. aircraft took a heavy toll. Air force, navy, and marine tactical bombers flew more than 8,000 sorties during the invasion, dumping 48,000 tons of bombs in support of ARVN units. Another 1,352 sorties were flown by B-52s in advance of ARVN assaults and against rear staging areas. Together they killed an estimated 4,800

North Vietnamese troops, nearly a third of the total Communist casualties inflicted during the entire invasion.

But the bombers could not stop the continual ambushes or prevent isolated fire bases from being overrun. The collapse of air-to-ground communications and a lack of coordination between ground commanders hampered effective air support. Although most U.S. FACs who directed the air strikes were accompanied by ARVN interpreters, language difficulties aggravated the communications problems. Navy A-4 pilots from the U.S.S. *Hancock* complained there was so much confusion that they often ran out of gas and had to head back to the carrier before the FACs assigned them a target.

Still, despite heavy losses, ARVN commanders pressed toward Tchepone. On March 7, after U.S. B-52s and fighter-bombers laid down a covering barrage, 120 transport helicopters airlifted two ARVN battalions into Tchepone itself. It was the largest and longest heliborne assault of the war. But ARVN's stay was brief. North Vietnamese reinforcements poured in, bringing their committed force to an estimated 35,000 experienced troops. They hacked away at the string of vulnerable ARVN fire support bases, and by the second week in March the invasion force beat a hasty retreat. Under an umbrella of fixed-wing air support, U.S. helicopters began evacuating ARVN troops.

Relentless enemy pressure threatened to turn the evacuation into a rout. Panic broke out and discipline collapsed among many ARVN units. South Vietnamese soldiers crammed aboard helicopters while others clung desperately to the skids. Many isolated units surrendered or were captured. By March 24, Saigon reported all its troops had been evacuated. But in the hasty retreat, many stragglers and wounded had been left behind and large numbers of tanks, trucks, and other heavy equipment were abandoned.

President Thieu blamed the Americans for the breakdown of the invasion. "The Americans would not accept the high price both in helicopters and pilot losses," he claimed. "After the first week the Americans had so many casualties that they reduced the number of helicopters being used." U.S. officials denied the charge, claiming their pilots had flown more than 96,000 sorties during Lam Son. But Thieu's accusation held a kernel of truth. U.S. losses were high in aircraft and men. Air crew losses were officially placed at 55 dead, 178 wounded, and 34 missing and, according to U.S. Army sources, approximately 100 choppers were lost and another 618 damaged. U.S. Air Force officials claimed the number of choppers lost was closer to the 200 mark.

The statistics fueled yet another round in the perennial controversy between the air force and the army over the vulnerability of helicopters in combat. One air force official questioned whether the relatively slow-moving, lightly armored and armed helicopters could survive in a "truly heavy AA environment" without fixed-wing air support. Army officers countered that their Huey Cobras had performed well. Lieutenant Colonel Robert Molinelli, commander of the 2d Squadron, 17th Air Cavalry, claimed that his Cobras "flew right down the barrels" of NVA 37mm guns to knock them out.

According to official army statistics only 4,900 helicopters were lost during the entire war. Others, including some veteran pilots, maintained that

As dawn breaks on a February day in 1971, a file of American helicopters carries South Vietnamese assault troops to their positions near Fire Support Base A Luoi in Laos.

upwards of 16,000 were shot down or lost due to accidents. They claimed that the army distorted its statistics by retrieving the tails from wrecked choppers, which carried the aircraft's serial number, and shipping them back to the U.S. where they were attached to new fuselages. The story may not have been true, but the fact that the men who flew helicopters in Vietnam believed it says a great deal. While critics and proponents argued back and forth, one thing was certain. Without American helicopters Lam Son 719 and the hundreds of other such airborne assaults mounted during the war would not have been possible.

Allied commanders claimed that the invasion was a success, citing a 9 to 1 "kill ratio" in favor of ARVN forces. President Nixon later admitted that a 5 to 1 ratio was probably more accurate. The invasion apparently did succeed in its original purpose as a preemptive strike, thwarting any major Communist offensive for the rest of the year, but the price in casualties and equipment losses was high for such modest and temporary results. ARVN's performance was shaky at best and cast serious doubts on the effectiveness of the Vietnamization program.

The invasion also failed to achieve its objective of disrupting traffic along the Ho Chi Minh Trail. Although 176,000 tons of ammunition were captured or blown up by air strikes, according to official claims, the numbers were highly suspect since intelligence sources calculated the average monthly flow of supplies along the trail at only 14,000 tons. Allied military officials also claimed between 3,000 and 4,000 trucks destroyed, mainly by B–52s, and large portions of the trail around Tchepone were made impassable. But the extent and resiliency of the enemy's logistics network had again been underestimated. The North Vietnamese rerouted supplies west around Tchepone along smaller roads and trails while some 4,000 to 8,000 reinforcements arrived and quickly repaired damaged sections of the trail. Within two weeks of the withdrawal, reconnaissance pilots saw trucks moving down the trail at the preinvasion pace.

Following Lam Son's failure to cut Communist infiltration routes in Laos, American aircraft resumed their aerial interdiction efforts against the trail. With the exception of brief incursions on the ground in Cambodia and Laos,

An American medevac helicopter kicks up dust as it arrives at Fire Support Base A Luoi in Laos to pick up ARVN soldiers wounded in the Lam Son 719 fighting. March 1971.

U.S. air power remained America's primary line of defense in Southeast Asia, providing a shield against any Communist threats from outside South Vietnam's borders while Saigon's forces continued their build-up and consolidation within the country. American aircraft were also virtually all that stood between pro-Western governments in Laos and Cambodia and the Communists.

Air power appeared to be the perfect instrument for Nixon's strategy. It cost fewer American lives than a ground war and was fought from the skies above Laos and Cambodia away from press or public scrutiny. At the same time the president could bring American fighting men home without altogether abandoning his commitment to defend the Saigon regime. But this politically beneficial strategy could not work forever.

The Nixon doctrine committed the U.S. to pulling out of Southeast Asia and letting the South Vietnamese fight their own battle. That meant the withdrawal of U.S. air units as well as ground troops. By late 1971, after two years of gradual cutbacks, fewer than 500 U.S. aircraft would be left in Southeast Asia as opposed to nearly 2,000 in the peak year of 1969. In an effort to keep pace with its growing responsibilities with fewer aircraft, the 7th Air Force came to rely more and more on technology. This was particularly true in Laos where the battle against the Ho Chi Minh Trail evolved into a fully automated war.

The electronic battlefield

Task Force Alpha's sensor system and air force gunships became the principal mainstays of the anti-infiltration campaign. After its entry into the war in the midsixties, the gunship evolved far beyond its mission of nighttime base defense. The early AC-47 "Spooky" gunships were followed by the larger and more heavily armed AC-119G Shadows. The AC-119K "Stinger" carried a pair of 20MM cannon in addition to the four 7.62MM miniguns mounted along its port side. Following the Tet offensive in 1968, a number of Stingers fitted with rudimentary radar and infrared sensors flew against enemy infiltration routes in Laos. But the slow-moving gunships were too vulnerable when the North Vietnamese moved in heavy 37MM and 57MM AA guns.

The gunship program reached its most sophisticated stage in Laos in mid-1969, when the first three AC-130 Spectres were deployed to the 16th Special Operations Squadron at Ubon Air Base in Thailand. The AC-130 packed two miniguns, two 20MM Gatling guns, and two 40MM cannon which could be fired manually or integrated into the ship's computerized firing system. Occasionally, the gunships were used to support government troops in northern Laos and Cambodia. But they were most effective over the Ho Chi Minh Trail, where they became known as "truck killers."

Gunships operated continuously over Laos from dusk to dawn, two aircraft patrolling an assigned sector in alternating shifts. Their ability to remain on station for five to six hours at a time provided overlapping coverage throughout the night when traffic on the trail was heaviest. The AC-130's real edge lay in its sophisticated system of sensors operated by five technicians who sat in a booth at the rear of the plane. One was a low-light-level television (LLLT), which projected an image of the terrain by magnifying existing moonlight. Its wide- and narrow-angle lenses could cover an area the size of a football field or close in on a small, specific target which could then be illuminated with flares or a searchlight.

An infrared detector (IR) had a limited capacity to detect heat sources beneath jungle foliage where the television could not see. It was particularly useful for spotting the heat radiated from truck engines, though a trained eye was needed to interpret the readings. A number of times gunships opened up on what they thought was a convoy of trucks only to see the images scatter on their scopes, zigzagging erratically through the jungle. Only then did they realize that they were shooting at a herd of water buffalo or elephants.

Another ingenious device was the "Black Crow" ignition detector, which could pick up static from a gasoline internal combustion engine within a ten-mile range. Although the signal often faded in and out like a radio signal, it was enough to direct a pilot to the general area where he could bring his other sensors into play. Once a truck was located by one of these sensors, the gunship's computerized fire control system took over. All the guns were synchronized with the movement of the sensors, which "locked on" to the target. All the pilot had to do was roll in above the spot, start flying a left-handed circle around it, and let the gunners begin firing. If the target was a convoy of trucks, the gunners hit the lead vehicles first, then the rear truck to prevent any escape, then they picked off those bottled up in between.

Using these tactics, an AC-130 gunship could make short work of a Communist truck convoy. Lieutenant Colonel Loyd King, the operations officer for the 16th Special Operations Squadron, recalled a particular mission in the fall of 1971 when he was assigned to check a segment of Route 7 east of Ban Ban near the Plain of Jars. "I was making a beeline for this road segment, but we found so many trucks before we got there that we couldn't pass them up," King said. "They were running around the countryside like bees making honey. They were all over the place." King and his crew reported bagging twenty-five enemy trucks that night.

The gunships were not always that successful, for the North Vietnamese were an elusive prey. They abandoned the practice of traveling in large convoys in favor of smaller groups of three to four trucks and gradually learned ways to confound the gunship's sensors. A North Vietnamese newspaper article in August 1971 provided an alarmingly accurate description of American gunships' sensor capabilities and weaknesses. It warned truck drivers to keep their vehicles camouflaged with freshly cut brush to confuse sensor operators. The article instructed that "fresh tree leaves strongly reflect infrared radiation for their color is very bright" and would clutter the image on an infrared screen. Camouflaged vehicles "will blend with the surrounding trees and be very difficult to see" on the gunship's television screens.

North Vietnamese drivers tried to mask the heat of their engines as well. According to Lieutenant Colonel William B. Hartman, an AC-130 fire control officer and navigator, "they were using things over their hoods to shield the heat, apparently something like wet canvas or burlap." Drivers also learned to wrap their ignition wires in aluminum foil to shield against the Black Crow sensors.

Once they heard the distinctive sound of an AC-130's engines, spotters situated along the trail passed on warning signals to truck drivers and AA gunners. A pilot knew he had been spotted when he saw a single AA round go off a few miles ahead as he approached a suspect area. Gunships also faced a formidable network of antiaircraft defenses, particularly in the Steel Tiger area where it was "wall-to-wall AAA," according to Lt. Col. King. "Every road segment over there was covered to some extent." Enemy gunners knew that the gunships had to fly in a steady and predictable circular orbit to bring their guns to bear once they located a target and would often bracket the aircraft with AA fire.

In these high-threat areas, a flight of F-4 Phantom escorts flew "flak suppression" support, bombing and strafing any AAA sites that fired up on the gunships, as well as keeping a lookout for the occasional MiGs that ventured across the border. But the North Vietnamese knew the jets lacked enough fuel to remain in the area as long as the gunships. The gunners would bide their time, tracking the planes with radar and monitoring their communications, holding their fire until the Phantoms peeled off to fly home or refuel from an aerial tanker.

Gunship pilots usually flew at altitudes of 7,500 to 9,500 feet, which kept them out of the range of smaller-caliber AA guns and still allowed their guns to be effective. Probably the gunship's best protection against AAA came from the illuminator operator (IO), an enlisted airman who literally hung out the rear cargo door in a harness, waiting to drop flares once a target was located. As soon as he spotted the muzzle flashes of AA guns he warned the pilot. Knowing it took a little over six seconds for a 37MM or a 57MM round to reach the gunship's altitude, the IO tracked the tracers to see if they appeared to be on target. At the last second he would shout to the pilot to break right or left to avoid the burst. Early in 1972, a number of the newer "E" model AC-130s were fitted with a 105MM howitzer in place of one of the 40MM cannon. Capable of firing a forty-four-pound shell 12,000 meters, it allowed AC-130Es to fire

on a heavily defended target while staying out of the range of AA fire.

Gunships working close to the North Vietnamese border, particularly around the mountain passes at Nape and Mu Gia, faced an even deadlier enemy—SA-2 surface-to-air missiles. By late 1971, the enemy had moved a number of SAM batteries into Laos along the trail itself. When AA fire drove the gunships above 9,000 feet into the SAM's prime tracking range, the electronic warfare officer often picked up a beeping signal from his equipment that indicated the plane was being "painted" by SAM radar operators. Once the beeping signal changed to a burring noise that sounded like an angry rattlesnake, he knew the SAM had locked on and was ready to be launched. There was little a gunship's crew or pilot could do to defend their bulky planes from the supersonic missiles.

Stephen J. Opitz, who served as a fire control officer aboard an AC-130, earned the nickname "magnet ass" from his squadron mates for the dubious honor of surviving three SAM attacks. His closest call came early in 1972 while flying in the heavily defended area around Tchepone. The crew of Spectre 15 were already nervous. A few nights before, on March 29, they had seen another gunship blasted out of the sky, the first AC-130 to be shot down by a SAM. They finished their patrol without incident and were heading home when the Black Crow operator suddenly shouted: "SAM locked on!" The beeps quickened into a rapid pulse, then a large red cross flashed on the screen indicating a missile launch. The IO hanging out the rear of the plane confirmed the launch: "It just lit off. I can see it!" The pilot racked the AC-130 into a sharp 110-degree bank and dove for the deck.

As the gunship plummeted toward the ground, Opitz warned the TV operator to check for any mountains below. "They are about 6,000 feet," the navigator shouted. "Watch it!" The pilot eased the ship out of the dive but the missile was still on their tail. "Holy Christ, here it comes," exclaimed one of the scanner operators. "It's a big orange flame and it's coming at us!" He screamed at the pilot: "Break again!" Just as the ship began to bank, the missile exploded overhead.

"It was like a freight train and a thump," said Opitz. The men in the sensor booth stared at each other in shock. "The TV operator got very pale and he quickly got out of his seat. I was worried he was going to bail out," recalled Opitz. "I grabbed a hold of him and he put his hand up to his mouth and threw up."

The North Vietnamese were not through with Spectre 15 yet. Dropping low to avoid the SAM had put them back in the range of the AA guns. The IO reported heavy fire on the way. Just then the Black Crow operator picked up a swarm of trucks below. Opitz ordered the gunners to zero in on the coordinates provided by the Black Crow. As fire control officer, either he or the aircraft commander decided whether to attack. Nobody in the plane seemed anx-

Above. *A stateside cousin of the Spectre gunships used in Laos, an AC–130A based at Eglin Air Force Base fires its 20MM Gatling gun.*

Left. *The Gatling guns fire so rapidly that crew members are obliged to shovel shell casings out of the gunner's way.*

Below. *AC–130 crewmen monitor the aircraft's sophisticated system of sensors and radar.*

ious to do so. The gunners reported the guns were "down." "Well arm them again," Opitz said. "We've got two good movers." Still they hesitated until the pilot came over the intercom and repeated the order: "Arm the guns!"

Following the Black Crow operator's directions, Spectre 15 rolled in above two trucks and opened fire. Still rattled by the near miss of the SAM, both the pilot's and the gunners' hands were a bit shaky. "We shot at Truck A and we hit Truck B," said Opitz. "We shot at Truck B just to really put the coup de grâce on him and we hit Truck A." Both trucks began to burn and a cheer went up from the crew. Just then, persistent enemy antiaircraft fire began hammering the gunship. "Christ, we're getting hosed," said the IO. "I can't see the muzzle flashes." Opitz looked out the door to find it was now daylight, making the black gunship a perfect target in the bright sky. Not wanting to press their luck, the crew of Spectre 15 headed home.

During 1971, gunships accounted for more than 6,000 of the trucks claimed to be destroyed or damaged along the trail. The criteria for claiming a truck "kill" had been tightened considerably. Previously, a truck was considered destroyed if hit by a single 40MM shell and damaged if a round hit within ten feet. Now gunship crews had actually to see the truck burn or explode in order to claim a kill. "We were destroying about 40 percent of the targets that we hit," Lt. Col. King said. "If you, in other words, find ten trucks, you could reasonably expect to destroy four of them and damage six of them."

Gunships normally found their own targets, but sometimes they received advisories from Task Force Alpha, the computerized center at Nakhon Phanom whose sensors monitored Communist movements along the trail. Alpha's readings usually proved accurate. "I recall one mission they gave me a string of trucks at a certain position," said King. "I drove over there and there were ten trucks just as pretty as you please within a five or ten mile road segment up there. We got all of them."

The technological counterpart to the gunship's weaponry was the Igloo White sensor program, which, from its modest beginning in 1968, had evolved into a multimillion-dollar enterprise. Task Force Alpha deployed more than 20,000 highly sophisticated seismic and acoustic sensors disguised as weeds and plants along infiltration routes in Laos. "We wired the Ho Chi Minh Trail like a drugstore pinball machine," said one air force officer. The system was officially credited with detecting and making possible the destruction of 12,000 enemy trucks in 1971 alone, though some questioned the validity of the statistics.

A number of critics claimed that the North Vietnamese played clever tricks—driving herds of elephants over the trails or playing recordings of truck sounds to deceive the Americans into dropping their bombs on empty jungle. But David R. Israel, the deputy director of the Pentagon's Defense Communications Planning Group which oversaw the sensor project, denied that was the case. "Sure they shot some, burned others and, in what was perhaps the ultimate act of contempt, we actually heard them pissing on one of our acoustic sensors," he said. "But they never really played games with us."

The fact that the North Vietnamese were ignoring the sensors left the question of their effectiveness open to doubt. According to Lieutenant Colonel R. R. Darron, a marine officer who worked closely with the sensor project, "the only logical conclusions you could come to are that either the enemy didn't understand what they were and how much damage they were doing or that they weren't hurting the enemy as much as we thought they were."

U.S. air commanders also complained that the costly electronic detection system was not able to deliver all the results that had been anticipated. "Sensors never accomplished what they were supposed to do. They did not locate targets," according to air force chief of intelligence, Major General George Keegan. Unlike the sensors used aboard the gunships, which could pinpoint and follow a moving target below, sensors along the trail gave the Americans only a fleeting glimpse of activity on those portions of the trail that had been identified and seeded with the devices.

The sensors were usually planted in rows alongside known Communist infiltration routes, so that passing vehicles triggered a series of signals that could be analyzed to determine the direction of movement and the number and speed of the convoy. But the data still had to be interpreted by the analysts, who could only guess whether the signals were generated by a convoy of trucks, a column of tanks, or merely a few bulldozers. The vehicles sometimes "disappeared" due to gaps in sensor coverage, or by turning off onto newly built bypasses or hidden trails that had not been seeded with sensors, leaving the analysts to guess where they were headed.

Analysts at the Nakhon Phanom center passed on the coordinates of a suspected target to a strike force of jet fighter-bombers, usually F-4 Phantoms. But since they were usually moving vehicles, by the time the jets arrived over the area the targets might no longer be there. Lacking any true radar bombing systems of their own, the high-flying, fast-moving jets dropped their bombs as best as they could on the assigned coordinates in the darkness. The air force equipped a few F-4s with long-range-airborne navigation (LORAN) systems similar to those used by B-52s to improve accuracy. Acting as radar controllers, they led the strike force to the target and provided them with the precise time of bomb release. But only the navy's A-6 Intruders, with their internal radar bombing systems, were capable of picking up moving targets in the dark.

Gunship pilots resented what they considered an undue emphasis on strikes coordinated by Task Force Alpha. They were often ordered to withdraw from an area for an hour or more, sometimes when they had a target in sight, to allow the fighter-bombers to come in and bomb computerized coordinates in the dark. "They didn't know what they hit and what they didn't hit, so there's no way of them knowing whether their strike accomplished anything or not," one AC-130 pilot complained. "It was an educated guess whether there was a target there to start with."

The F-4s were more effective when they worked with AC-130s or OV-10 Bronco observation planes equipped with detection sensors and Pave system laser range designators. Once the planes had picked up a target with their sensors, they marked it for the F-4s with a laser beam. The Phantom flew in and released a laser-guided bomb which homed in on the spot of light superimposed on the target by the laser beam. Coordination was essential since the AC-130s and OV-10s had to provide the F-4 with an exact description of the target so the pilot could release the bomb within the range of its limited guidance capabilities. The AC-130s and OV-10s also had to maintain a steady course to keep their lasers trained on a target; this left them vulnerable to ground fire. Later a project called Pave Sword eliminated this risk by introducing laser-seeking pods aboard the F-4s themselves.

All this technology was useless, of course, unless it produced results. To many critics, it did not. One disgruntled air force officer, who had resigned after serving as an intelligence specialist in Laos, commented: "What it amounts to is that the reconnaissance stuff was developed by nuclear-minded generals and they tried to adapt it to a guerrilla situation. So, millions of dollars of equipment and effort were tied down to find a little fellow running through the woods, and it didn't work."

By 1971, U.S. aircraft had dropped 2.2 million tons of bombs on infiltration routes in Laos. Washington was spending an estimated $10 billion a year on its aerial interdiction campaign. Yet North Vietnamese trucks and troops were still getting through. According to its own estimates, the air force was destroying only 20 percent of the trucks sighted; a full 80 percent were slipping through the electronic net. The air force chief of staff, General John D. Ryan, later said he was very skeptical of the claims made by the proponents of the electronic anti-infiltration system. "I wasn't convinced we were killing the trucks," he said. "I was never in favor of it because I didn't think it was effective." In 1972, the North Vietnamese would dramatically prove just how ineffective it had been.

Ordnance men load a dispenser with seismic sensors designed to detect enemy movements. The sensors will be dropped by aircraft over the Ho Chi Minh Trail as part of Operation Igloo White.

Air Power to the Rescue

While Washington was busy training and equipping the South Vietnamese to fight their own war, Hanoi was preparing to put the new Nixon doctrine to the test. Seven years after American forces were committed to the battle, the North Vietnamese could finally look forward to the last U.S. combat troop leaving Vietnam, and they were determined to be ready for that day. Communist leaders embarked on a new strategy, one that they hoped would seal the victory they had been seeking for so long.

In 1971, North Vietnam was finally recovering from the effects of nearly four years of bombing. Industries that had been dispersed into the countryside began returning to the major cities. Bombed-out factories and power stations were rebuilt. Roads, rail lines, and bridges were repaired. Life was slowly returning to normal, though the nation was still very much at war.

North Vietnamese troops underwent extensive training exercises while Soviet and Chinese

military supplies continued to pour into the country. Nearly 8,000 trucks were massed in truck parks and supply depots brimming with arms and ammunition. At the end of October, as the dry season began, these forces moved south in increasing numbers. American pilots reported seeing an average of 1,000 trucks on the Ho Chi Minh Trail every night—and those were only the ones they could see. Intelligence estimated that the number of troops moving south during the dry season was 25 percent higher than in the previous year. Even more alarming was a major massing of men and supplies in the southern panhandle of North Vietnam itself.

The transportation network in the southern provinces, which had been virtually destroyed by U.S. bombers during Rolling Thunder, was painstakingly reconstituted. Bridges were rebuilt and rail lines and roads repaired and expanded. Trucks carrying tons of supplies and hauling large artillery pieces poured down the revitalized transportation network. Two new fuel pipelines stretched from Haiphong south through the panhandle. American sensors began picking up activity in the DMZ itself. Three roads were being built across the thirty-mile neutral zone, and Soviet-built tanks were massing around Bat Lake in the eastern border area. The signs were unmistakable: Hanoi was preparing for battle on a much broader and grander scale than it had ever ventured previously.

Protective reaction

Washington was well aware of the Communist build-up above the DMZ. The North was under constant surveillance by U.S. "spy" satellites orbiting 100 miles or more above the earth and by U-2 and supersonic SR-71 photo jets of the Strategic Air Command which patrolled the stratosphere just below. Although these high-flying aircraft provided valuable information, they were neutralized when clouds blanketed North Vietnam. The real aerial reconnaissance workhorses were U.S. tactical photo jets, air force RF-4Cs and RF-101s, and navy RF-8 Crusaders and RA-5C Vigilantes, which had provided the bulk of aerial intelligence during the Rolling Thunder campaign.

The unarmed jets were sitting ducks for enemy gunners during their low-level photo runs, however, since they had to fly straight and stably directly over a target. There was little a pilot could do except to get in and out as fast as possible. Many times speed was not enough. Photo jets sustained a higher percentage of losses than any other type of aircraft, leading recon pilots jokingly to alter their motto of "alone, unarmed, and unafraid" to "alone, unarmed, and scared shitless."

Photo jets continued to fly over North Vietnam following the 1968 bombing halt; theoretically they were guaranteed safe passage by agreements made between Washington and Hanoi at the talks in Paris. In less than a month, however, NVA gunners had shot down one of the U.S. jets. When another was fired on in February 1970, President Nixon ordered armed escorts to accompany the photo reconnaissance jets and authorized what he termed "protective reaction" strikes against the offending enemy gun sites.

The result was an escalating series of tit-for-tat reprisals by both sides. By the end of 1970, American fighter-bombers had flown more than sixty protective reaction strikes. That number nearly doubled in 1971 as the North Vietnamese shifted their air defenses southward to cover the build-up in the panhandle and to harass American air operations along the DMZ and in Laos. SAM sites clustered along the border began firing on F-4s and B-52s over the Ho Chi Minh Trail. MiGs operating from four airfields that had recently been constructed south of Vinh launched sporadic hit-and-run raids across the border under the direction of ground radar controllers. During the last three weeks of 1971 alone, ten American aircraft were shot down over North Vietnam and Laos, with the loss of thirteen crewmen.

In order to keep a closer watch on enemy MiGs and SAMs and gather more intelligence on the North Vietnamese build-up along the DMZ, U.S. air commanders increased the number of photo reconnaissance missions. This, in turn, created more opportunities for protective reaction strikes. There were more than 90 strikes during the first three months of 1972, compared to 108 in all of 1971. The number of fighters escorting the photo planes increased from two to eight and sometimes to sixteen, carrying increasingly heavy ordnance loads. Some in the military and the press began questioning whether the photo missions were merely being used as a cover for increased bombing in the North. One pilot from the U.S.S. *Hancock* wrote his congressman early in 1972:

Last year reconnaissance flights were flown by Crusaders into the north with some Skyhawks as protection. The photo planes were unarmed and the briefing of pilots consisted of emphasis on photo intelligence. Occasionally they were fired upon which precipitated a protective reaction. The picture is now changed considerably. The concentration in the briefing room is on the strikes—the recon pilot sits in the back of the room hardly noticed. The Skyhawks are armed with our most sophisticated weapons and launched with the Crusader. Now, however, the Crusader is giving the Skyhawk protection, not from the SAMs but from the press.

Convinced that the North Vietnamese were planning to attack South Vietnam sometime in 1972, President Nixon hoped an aggressive military and diplomatic posture would deter Hanoi. At the end of 1971, he authorized Operation Proud Deep, the largest series of air strikes against North Vietnam since the 1968 bombing halt. American aircraft flew 1,025 sorties during the five-day campaign, which began the day after Christmas, hitting enemy airfields, SAM sites, POL storage areas, supply bases, and truck parks below the twentieth parallel. But the North Vietnamese continued to harass their southern neighbors. Early in 1972, they began shelling ARVN outposts across the DMZ with long-range artillery. On February 17, Nixon authorized two days of air strikes against the offending gun positions.

At the same time Nixon and Kissinger put pressure on Hanoi's allies in Moscow and Peking, hinting that any move Hanoi made against South Vietnam would be met by a resumption of full-scale bombing of the North. A few days after the bombing raids in February, Nixon made his historic trip to meet with Chinese leaders in Peking, the first visit by an American president to the Communist capital, and an event viewed with concern by Hanoi.

When the North Vietnamese failed to make the anticipated move during the Tet holidays, Washington relaxed. Nixon and Kissinger began to think that their dual strategy of isolating Hanoi diplomatically and threatening fierce retaliation had paid off. The North Vietnamese thought otherwise.

Hanoi believed the time was ripe to put America's Vietnamization program to the test. Since 1969, U.S. troop levels had shrunk from 500,000 men to fewer than 100,000. If the NVA could defeat ARVN in several pitched battles and seize large portions of territory, it would severely undermine the Saigon regime. Although they knew Nixon would react, the North Vietnamese believed antiwar sentiment in the U.S. would limit the response. If not, Nixon would expose himself to increased domestic unrest that could jeopardize his upcoming reelection bid. Deputy Foreign Minister Nguyen Co Thach said after the war: "We knew this would get Nixon very angry, because it will spoil his election, and he will return to his threats. But we also knew this one element must be considered: Big bombing [of the North] could not save Nixon in South Vietnam."

The Easter invasion

On March 30, the North Vietnamese made their move. NVA regulars, supported by tanks and heavy artillery, swept across the DMZ into South Vietnam to attack the string of fire support bases below the border. Although they had been expecting an offensive, the South Vietnamese and Americans were stunned by the size and force of the onslaught. Large-scale infantry attacks by NVA regulars, spearheaded by Soviet-built tanks, advanced under the cover of 122MM and 130MM heavy artillery fire. ARVN troops, whose training and equipment had been geared primarily toward counterinsurgency, buckled under the impact of this conventional assault. Within a week, 40,000 Communist troops had smashed their way through the

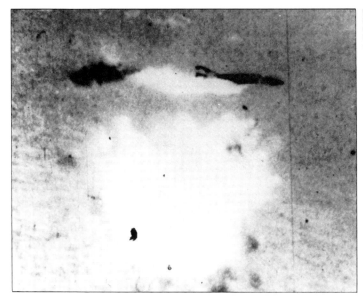

In a rare photographic sequence, an SA-2 missile explodes beneath an unarmed USAF RF-4C near Hanoi and destroys the reconnaissance craft. Such attacks provoked the U.S. to strike against enemy gun sites beginning in 1970.

border outposts and begun driving south down Route 1 toward Quang Tri City.

In Washington, Nixon's reaction was predictably pugnacious. On April 4, as the extent and force of the invasion became evident, he told his advisers: "The bastards have never been bombed like they're going to be bombed this time." Two days later he met with General John W. Vogt, who had been selected to replace General John D. Lavelle as commander of the 7th Air Force. In a thirty-minute meeting, Nixon harangued Vogt about his predecessor's lack of aggressiveness, a bizarre accusation considering the fact that Lavelle had been removed for exceeding his authority in launching protective reaction strikes over the North (see sidebar, p. 104). "I expect you to turn back the invasion and we will emerge with a victory," the president told Vogt. "We will not abandon Vietnam."

There was no question that major air support was needed if the South Vietnamese were to halt the Communist drive. The defensive line below the DMZ was crumbling rapidly. Continuous shelling by North Vietnamese tanks and long-range 122MM and 130MM howitzers fired from caves in and around the DMZ created havoc among the green troops of the 3d ARVN Division, which manned the line. Battered ground commanders called in air strikes

against anything that moved in their direction. "The number of requests submitted by the 3d ARVN during the first days was astronomical," said their U.S. adviser.

But when the invasion broke, the number of U.S. aircraft in Vietnam was at a low ebb. Just a few days before, the U.S.S. *Constellation* had been ordered home, leaving only two carriers with approximately 170 aircraft on station in the Gulf of Tonkin. The last marine aircraft had left the country nearly a year before and most air bases had been turned over to the VNAF. Only eighty-eight combat aircraft of the U.S. Air Force remained in South Vietnam—a single squadron of A–37s at Bien Hoa and three squadrons of F–4s and a detachment of five AC–119 gunships at Da Nang—and all were preparing to leave. The initial burden for air support thus fell heavily on the VNAF's 200 combat aircraft, including A–1s, A–37s, a single squadron of F–5s, and several AC–47 and AC–119 gunships.

During the first few weeks of the invasion air power could do little. The Communists had attacked at the tail end of the northeast monsoon. For twelve days the region was blanketed by thick clouds and fog which kept many aircraft grounded. Low-flying FACs who ventured underneath the clouds to observe enemy troop movements soon found out the extent of the enemy's mobile air defenses.

Seven AAA regiments had been deployed in South Vietnam, and another eight were positioned along the DMZ. Besides the usual 23MM, 37MM, and 57MM guns, the enemy had moved in large-caliber 85MM and 100MM guns. Mobile SAM sites also appeared in the South in increasing numbers. Some veteran pilots claimed the flak was as bad, if not worse, as what they had encountered over Hanoi during Rolling Thunder.

Pilots also found themselves up against a new threat—Soviet-built SA-7 Strela surface-to-air missiles. Only four and one-half feet long and two and three-fourths inches in diameter, the SA-7 could be fired from the shoulder like a bazooka. It contained an infrared heat-seeking warhead that was highly accurate within a range of 8,000 feet. Since the Strela was not particularly fast or maneuverable, pilots could outmaneuver the missile. "When they're fired, SA-7s leave a pretty good patch of smoke," said Captain Al Moore, an A-37 pilot with the 8th Special Operations Squadron. "If you can see it, you can out turn it." But the North Vietnamese waited until a plane had passed by overhead before firing the heat-seeking missile to get a clear shot at the engine exhaust. Struck from behind, pilots never knew what hit them.

Hardest hit by the newly introduced Strelas were OV-10 and O-2 observation planes which flew at low altitudes and at slow speeds. FACs were now forced to operate from higher altitudes, which severely hampered their ability to locate and identify targets for air strikes. Slower fighter-bombers, such as the A-1 Skyraiders and A-37 Dragonflies that formed the bulk of the VNAF's combat inventory, also proved vulnerable to the radar-directed AA guns and SA-7s when they flew in low enough to bomb enemy troops and tanks near to friendly forces.

It quickly became apparent that more U.S. aircraft, with their higher speeds and electronic countermeasures support, were needed. The 225 USAF fighter-bombers, mainly F-4 Phantoms, and the 52 B-52s that remained at bases in Thailand were quickly diverted from their normal operations in Cambodia and Laos, but were unable to be of much help during the first few weeks of the NVA offensive. The poor weather and heavy ground fire forced them to drop their bombs from high altitudes and rely on radar-bombing techniques, neither of which were conducive to close air suppport. High-flying B-52s struck enemy supply

---

The 155MM howitzers and ammunition shown here became the booty of the NVA when ARVN soldiers abandoned this northern firebase during the 1972 NVA offensive.

The Lavelle Affair

By the end of 1971, North Vietnam's expanded air defense system had become a serious threat not only to American reconnaissance flights but to air operations in neighboring Laos as well. SA-2 sites positioned close to the border began firing on American aircraft operating over the Ho Chi Minh Trail with increasing regularity. Occasionally, MiGs were sent to one of the four newly constructed airfields in the panhandle to launch hit-and-run raids across the border under the direction of radar controllers. During the last three weeks of 1971 alone, ten American aircraft and thirteen crewmen were lost to the enemy's defenses over southern Laos.

The Joint Chiefs began bombarding air commanders with messages to be more aggressive in countering the new threat. At a meeting in Hawaii in December, representatives from the JCS told CINCPAC and 7th Air Force staffers that "field commanders have not been flexible enough in using existing authorities." The JCS authorized air commanders to increase the number of fighter-escort reconnaissance missions to eight or even sixteen "to insure adequate damage" to enemy defenses during protective reaction strikes.

The "existing authorities" the JCS referred to were the rules of engagement established by the Defense Department that spelled out the conditions under which pilots could engage the enemy in combat over North Vietnam. Since 1965, civilian officials in Washington had exercised strict controls on the conduct of the air war in North Vietnam in an effort to regulate the level of combat to match the limited goals and political considerations inherent in a limited war. But the rules were not a simple set of guidelines that a pilot could memorize or carry with him on a card. Instead, they were a lengthy and complicated set of directives that were constantly being revised and updated. Pi-

lots used to joke that there were two crewmen in the F-4 Phantom because one had to fly the plane while the other figured out the rules of engagement.

Although the rules were fairly specific, their semantics left much room for interpretation. American fighter-pilots escorting reconnaisance jets over North Vietnam were basically allowed to react to any "hostile" actions directed at U.S. aircraft by enemy defenses and their supporting facilities. Did that mean that pilots could hit enemy SAM radars that locked onto their aircraft, or did they have to wait until the missiles were actually launched? If a MiG attacked U.S. planes, were the airfields they launched from and the ground control radar sites that directed them fair game?

Partly in response to the JCS's urging, the commander of the 7th Air Force, General John D. Lavelle, decided on "a very liberal interpretation" of the rules of engagement. He ordered protective reaction strikes against not only the specific offenders but also against associated airfields, radar sites, and the trucks that transported SA-2 missiles and their supporting fuel and ammo dumps. Lavelle believed the raids were necessary to counter the increased intensity of the enemy's defensive network in the southern panhandle. He later said: "We went in after these targets, the ones that would hurt the enemy's defensive system, so that we could operate."

According to Major General Alton D. Slay, Lavelle's deputy chief of staff for operations, Lavelle "was under the impression that you could press these rules a long way as long as you stayed within the bounds of reasonableness." But Lavelle apparently went too far. Early in March, Senator Harold Hughes received a letter from Sergeant Lonnie D. Franks, a twenty-three-year-old air force intelligence specialist of the 432d Tactical Reconnaissance Wing stationed at Udorn

Air Base in Thailand. Franks claimed he and other officers had spent hundreds of hours falsifying reports for higher headquarters. "We were reporting that our aircraft were receiving AAA reactions whether they had received them or not," wrote Franks.

The letter was forwarded to General John D. Ryan, chief of staff of the air force. The inspector general sent to investigate Franks's claims confirmed that mission reports had been falsified on at least twenty-seven occasions. Ryan summoned Lavelle to Washington on March 23. Two weeks later, the Pentagon issued a brief statement announcing that Lavelle had retired from the air force for "personal and health reasons." News reporters sensed there was more to the story than what the Pentagon was telling them. A month would pass before a Congressional investigation confirmed the rumors. Lavelle had been removed from his command for exceeding his authority in launching protective reaction strikes in North Vietnam.

According to Colonel Charles A. Gabriel, commander of the 432d Tactical Reconnaissance Wing at Udorn, Thailand, "on a number of occasions ... my wing was given instructions from 7th Air Force headquarters to conduct a planned strike against specific targets regardless of whether or not there was a reaction from the air defenses in North Vietnam." General Slay, who passed the orders on to Gabriel, confirmed that they came directly from General Lavelle.

Lavelle monitored these missions personally from his command post in Saigon. On one occasion, when the wing reported no enemy reaction during the strike, he told Slay: "God damn it; we can't have that. It's got to be 'reaction.' You have got to show 'hostile reaction.'" Lavelle explained lamely to the wing commander that pilots often never saw rounds fired at them from small-caliber weapons. "No

one can fly over North Vietnam without being fired at," he claimed. "... Just by definition people are going to shoot at you so you must report that you have been [fired] upon."

General John D. Lavelle, commander of the 7th Air Force, in 1969, before the incidents that would lead to his recall and demotion.

Believing that Lavelle "would not be such a damn fool to go about this on his own," Slay and the wing commanders in Thailand carried out Lavelle's orders. Indeed, Lavelle later claimed that his superiors were well aware of the nature of the operations under question and had informally indicated their support. Both General Ryan and the chairman of the Joint Chiefs of Staff, Admiral Thomas Moorer, however, testified that they were unaware of the falsification of reports and that they had not encouraged Lavelle to stretch the rules of engagement, either officially or unofficially. Lavelle was allowed to retire at the rank of major general, two grades below his wartime rank of four-star general.

While there was no question about Lavelle's guilt, some felt that a variety of extenuating circumstances explained his actions. Although the press played up the surface similarities with the breakdown in command that led to the massacre at My Lai, Lavelle's defenders pointed out that the air strikes ordered by him were directed not against civilians but legitimate military targets—enemy antiaircraft defenses that were shooting down U.S. planes. New Jersey Representative John E. Hunt, who served in the army air corps with General Ryan in Italy during World War II, reminded the air force chief of staff that they had occasionally "digressed" from the established rules as the battlefield situation warranted.

Alabama Representative William L. Dickson thought the root cause of the Lavelle affair was the "crazy rules for this crazy war." He and many others were critical of the way civilian leaders tried to run the war from Washington, saddling commanders in the field with complicated operational guidelines and restrictions that occasionally endangered the lives of American pilots. Whether or not these arguments provide any justification for Lavelle's having flagrantly disobeyed orders, the entire episode ended up being tinged with irony. Within a few weeks of Lavelle's recall, the long-awaited Communist offensive was in full swing, and American bombers were soon pounding the same targets Lavelle had been demoted for hitting.

lines and artillery positions around the DMZ, while F–4s equipped with LORAN radar gear worked the edges of the battlefield. But the results were questionable since neither aircraft had the accuracy to hit moving targets even when they were able to locate them through the few gaps in the cloud cover.

Although American pilots had trouble locating targets, the enemy's radar-guided defenses had little difficulty tracking the bombers through the clouds. Even the high-flying B–52s were not immune from attack. On April 8, a B–52 on a bombing mission over the demilitarized zone was hit by an SA–2 missile. The explosion damaged the plane's left wing and fuselage, but the pilot managed to land safely at Da Nang.

Others were not so fortunate. On April 2, an EB–66 sent to jam enemy radar during a B–52 mission just south of the DMZ was shot down by an SA–2 fired from inside South

Vietnam. Of the six-man crew, only the navigator, Lieutenant Colonel Iceal E. Hambleton, managed to escape from the burning plane; but he parachuted into enemy-held territory. For eleven days, the 7th Air Force tried to get him out in one of the most controversial rescue operations of the war.

To avoid their interference with rescue attempts, artillery and air strikes within seventeen miles of Hambleton's position were prohibited unless they had been cleared by higher authorities. This had a devastating effect on the ground battle since the "no fire" zone encompassed the area in which the 3d ARVN Division was desperately trying to hold off the Communists. For eleven days, the South Vietnamese found themselves unable to return fire or call in air strikes without the approval of headquarters.

Meanwhile, U.S. Air Force planes flew an average of ninety sorties per day in support of Hambleton to prevent

Two wounded U.S. advisers awaiting evacuation aboard a medevac helicopter after the fall of Loc Ninh in April 1972.

his discovery and capture. A-1 "Sandies" blasted enemy AA guns in the vicinity while rescue choppers orbited nearby, waiting to dart in and pluck Hambleton from the jungle. But after one HH-53 rescue chopper, two OV-10s, and two army helicopters were lost to enemy ground fire, along with eleven crewmen, aerial rescue attempts were abandoned. Hambleton was instructed via an ingenious code to work his way through enemy lines directed by airborne FACs while a squad of marines worked their way up the Cam Lo River to meet him.

Since Hambleton was an avid golfer, they laid out his escape route in the form of an imaginary golf course based on holes from different golf courses he had played. Instructed by the FAC orbiting overhead to "play the 14th hole at the Augusta National," for example, Hambleton knew that meant heading east by northeast and a slight dogleg to the left to reach the "green" 420 yards away. Under the watchful guidance of his FAC "caddy," Hambleton "played" his way through enemy lines to the Cam Lo River where he met the waiting marines who carried him to safety.

Vietnamese ground commanders believed the elaborate effort to save one American flier had jeopardized their efforts to contain the enemy offensive. They resented the fact that Americans seemed willing to devote more effort to saving the life of one of their own than the lives of an entire ARVN division. The USAF adviser to the 3d ARVN Division, Major David A. Brookbank, agreed. "The operation cost the 3d ARVN dearly," he claimed, depriving the South Vietnamese of artillery and air support when it was most vitally needed. During the eleven-day effort, NVA troops had moved southward through the "no fire" zone virtually unopposed.

Not until the second week of April, when the weather finally began to break, did American air power check the Communist advance long enough to give battered ARVN forces a chance to regroup north of Quang Tri. Reinforcements of fresh Vietnamese rangers and marines helped stiffen the line, but it was around-the-clock air strikes that really made the difference.

Meanwhile, air support was also desperately needed in Military Region III where the Communists had driven across the border from their Cambodian bases and opened a second front. The 5th VC/NVA Division kicked off the drive on April 5 by hitting Loc Ninh, a key position ten miles north of An Loc on Highway 13 held by 2,000 ARVN troops and a handful of U.S. advisers. Like the assault across the DMZ, the Communists' attack came under cover of a heavy artillery barrage and with tank support. For two days the garrison managed to hold on. But on the seventh, the town fell and the 700 survivors who managed to escape joined other units retreating toward An Loc.

While the 5th Division continued the drive south along Highway 13, two more Communist divisions converged on An Loc, cutting off any attempts to reinforce or resupply the city by land from Saigon. With the trap set, the enemy struck on April 13 after a withering artillery barrage. Led by six T54 tanks, the Communists overran the airstrip and pushed into the northern portion of the city. Three U.S. Army Cobra gunships, equipped with TOW antitank rockets, teamed up with ARVN troops using M72 light antitank weapons to knock out four of the tanks and blunt the armored drive. VNAF and U.S. Air Force and Navy fighter-bombers carrying "snake and nape"—low-level delivery Snake Eye bombs and napalm—decimated the ranks of onrushing attackers. One B-52 strike caught an entire column before it even reached the city, destroying three tanks and killing an estimated 100 enemy soldiers.

The following day, the Communists continued to batter An Loc with mortar and artillery fire, but their momentum had been blunted. Major General James Hollingsworth, the senior U.S. Army adviser in III Corps, reported to General Abrams that "massive air support of all types tipped the scales in our favor yesterday." A second attack on the fifteenth penetrated the city but was again repulsed with the help of heavy close air support. Failing to achieve a quick victory, the Communists settled down with the intention of starving the city into submission.

At the same time, a third prong of the Communist offensive stabbed into the central highlands. By mid-April, two North Vietnamese divisions had converged around the government outposts at Dak To and Tan Canh, as well as the string of fire support bases along Rocket Ridge on the west side of Highway 14 leading south to Kontum. Lieutenant Terry Pfaff, a forward air controller working the area around Dak To, reported finding tanks "just about everywhere" and NVA troops "walking down the roads like they owned the place." At that time there were no American strike aircraft at any bases in II Corps, so the burden again fell on the VNAF, carrier-based navy jets, and air force F-4s, AC-130s, and B-52s from Thailand. They managed to knock out half of the Communists' tank force, but those tanks that remained demoralized the ARVN defenders. Tan Canh fell on the twenty-third and Dak To the following night.

Quick to capitalize on their success, the Communists drove down Highway 14 toward Kontum, taking over the ARVN outposts along the route in rapid succession. The road was packed with fleeing troops and civilian refugees, which made close air support a tricky business. ARVN troops fled south to the safety of Kontum, abandoning large amounts of supplies and ammunition, even 105MM guns. U.S. F-4s had to be called in to destroy the abandoned equipment to prevent its capture by the enemy. One senior air force adviser bitterly remarked that during "the first two weeks of this offensive at least 80 percent of our [tactical air strikes] destroyed our own stuff which ARVN left when they broke and ran." Kontum was soon surrounded. Like An Loc, the city was entirely dependent on aerial resupply for food and ammunition.

Looking like half-caged sharks, F-4 Phantoms sit at ready alert in rocket-proof steel and concrete hangars at Da Nang in spring 1972. These and other aircraft were to be used in retaliation for the NVA offensive.

As the invasion entered its fourth week, the situation looked grim on all three fronts. South Vietnamese troops were unable to halt the heavily armed North Vietnamese regulars. U.S. and South Vietnamese air superiority appeared to be the only thing preventing total defeat. The VNAF had performed valiantly during the first month of the offensive. Its transports had moved more than 40,000 troops and delivered nearly 4,000 tons of supplies throughout the country, while VNAF fighter-bombers flew more than 150 close air support sorties per day. But the VNAF was in over its head. It lacked sufficient resources to cope with a large-scale invasion on three fronts, and the enemy's high-tech air defenses were too much for its combat fleet of slow-moving A-1 and A-37 fighter-bombers. Thirty-six aircraft had fallen to North Vietnamese AAA and SAMs by the end of April.

The burden of the defense fell heavily on U.S. air units based in Thailand. To quicken their reaction time, F-4s from Thailand used Da Nang and Bien Hoa as forward staging bases. After their first strike, pilots landed at these airfields to rearm and refuel, launched a second strike, and then repeated the process before returning home. Thailand-based gunships, employing the same technique,

were flying up to four five-hour missions in succession from Da Nang or Bien Hoa before returning to home base. Ground crews at the two bases worked in twelve-hour shifts at fever pitch, sometimes preparing planes for new missions in fifty minutes rather than the normal ninety minutes. By the end of the month, U.S. aircraft were flying 137 sorties per day in support of ARVN troops around Kontum, nearly 185 in defense of An Loc, and another 207 in the battle for Quang Tri. Even this was not enough. After urgent requests from Gen. Abrams for additional aircraft, American planes began pouring into bases in South Vietnam and Thailand. For some, it meant returning to a war they thought they had left behind. For younger pilots it brought combat in a war they thought they would miss.

Constant Guard and Freedom Train

The first to arrive were the U.S. Air Force's 35th Tactical Fighter Squadron from Kunsan, Korea, and two U.S. Marine F-4 squadrons from Iwakuni Station, Japan. The navy dispatched four additional carriers, bringing the total number stationed off the Vietnamese coast to six, more than had ever been deployed in the war at any given

time. The majority of reinforcing aircraft came directly from air force bases in the U.S. under an emergency program called Operation Constant Guard which began on April 11 when three F-4 squadrons took off for the 10,000-mile flight across the Pacific, along with Military Airlift Command transports carrying their equipment and ground support personnel. Within a mere seventy-two to ninety-six hours of their initial alert in the United States, those pilots were flying combat missions in Vietnam. Another 108 F-4 Phantoms and two squadrons of C-130 transports arrived early in May.

SAC increased its B-52 forces at Guam and U-Tapao to nearly 200 bombers. In little more than three weeks, by mid-May, the number of U.S. aircraft in Southeast Asia more than tripled, from 300 to 1,000. The air force alone eventually deployed the equivalent of fifteen squadrons and 70,000 men to Southeast Asia. The primary objective of the rapid deployment was to provide close air support for beleaguered ARVN forces in South Vietnam. However, U.S. pilots soon found themselves flying deeper and deeper into enemy territory because on April 6, President Nixon, true to his word, had authorized the resumption of bombing in North Vietnam in retaliation for the invasion.

The new bombing operation, given the code name Freedom Train, was a limited effort. American planes were sent only as far north as the twentieth parallel against enemy supply lines and storage areas that were supporting the NVA invasion force. Although Nixon preferred a major attack on the enemy's heartland, Kissinger had urged moderation, worried that such an action might endanger the chances of enlisting Soviet support for a negotiated settlement of the war as well as the prospects for strategic arms limitation talks, which were scheduled for May 22 in Moscow. Then, while Kissinger was in Moscow laying the groundwork for the upcoming summit meeting and arranging for another secret meeting with North Vietnamese negotiators in Paris, Nixon authorized a series of air strikes over Hanoi and Haiphong, principally against POL (petroleum, oil, and lubricants) facilities that provided the fuel for the trucks and tanks supporting the invasion. To emphasize the consequences in store for the North Vietnamese if they did not halt the invasion, he personally ordered SAC B-52s to land the opening blow, the first time that the powerful bombers would strike at targets in the Red River Delta.

The strike plan called for seventeen B-52s to launch a midnight raid on April 16 against a POL storage area on the outskirts of Haiphong. Six hours later, air force F-4s were to hit POL facilities ten miles northeast of Hanoi while navy aircraft hit both a warehouse complex in Haiphong and Kien An airfield southwest of the city. The mission was so secret that the F-4 pilots assigned to escort the B-52s did not receive their orders until a few hours before the scheduled takeoff time. Lieutenant Colonel Paul Craw, commander of the 4th Tactical Fighter Squadron, had just returned to Da Nang from a mission against a barracks area near Thanh Hoa when he got the word that his squadron was to provide fighter escort for the B-52s.

Flying at 24,000 feet, 10,000 feet below and slightly behind the B-52s, Craw's F-4s escorted the first wave of bombers over Haiphong. SA-2 missiles started coming up at the planes before they had even crossed the coast. Craw shouted a warning as three shot past his F-4 toward the B-52s flying 10,000 feet above. One exploded dangerously close to one of the B-52s, knocking out one of its engines and peppering the craft with shrapnel. The pilot turned back toward Da Nang where he landed on five engines. Although more than 200 missiles were fired at the bombers, the damaged B-52 was the only casualty that night. EB-66s and F-105Gs that preceded the B-52s over Haiphong had done a good job of jamming the SAMs' target acquisition radars. Additional ECM equipment aboard the B-52s helped blank out the enemy's Fan Song guidance radars. Enemy AA guns lit up the sky with a steady stream of tracer shells, but most of the guns could not reach the range of the high-flying B-52s, and most of the rounds burst harmlessly below the bombers.

Guided by their internal radar systems, the B-52s unleashed their bombs over the city. From his vantage point, Craw could see the bombers had "left the target area in flames, and secondary explosions lit up the sky." The reflections of the fires could be seen from the bridge of the U.S.S. *Kitty Hawk* 110 miles out to sea. Photo jets later confirmed that the strike had wiped out seventeen POL storage tanks, as well as destroying nearby warehouses, rail lines, and thirty pieces of rolling stock.

Six hours later, thirty-two air force Phantoms hit POL storage areas in Hanoi. Alerted by the earlier attack, the North Vietnamese managed to scramble an intercept force. Four MiG-21s engaged F-4 fighter escorts from the 432d Tactical Reconnaissance Wing, which shot down three of the North Vietnamese jets. The fourth crashed while trying to land. During the second raid on Haiphong, navy jets destroyed three more MiG-17s on the ground at Kien An airfield. An air force F-105G and a navy A-7, whose pilot was later rescued, were lost to SAMs. The word went back to Washington that heavy damage had been inflicted on all the target areas. Informed of the results, Nixon remarked to his adviser, H. R. Haldeman: "Well, we really left them our calling card this weekend."

The fall of Quang Tri

The raids on Hanoi and Haiphong did not dissuade the North Vietnamese from their offensive in South Vietnam. On April 27 columns of tanks and infantry, backed by ar-

tillery and mortar fire, broke through the South Vietnamese defensive line and advanced on Quang Tri City. For the next two days outnumbered ARVN units fought desperately to hold on to the city. With the help of American and VNAF tactical air strikes, they managed to repel repeated infantry and tank assaults. But they could not turn off the continual barrages from camouflaged North Vietnamese artillery guns which poured 4,500 rounds into the city on the thirtieth alone. Orders to evacuate Quang Tri were issued on the following day, but by then the ARVN command structure had fallen into disarray and the withdrawal turned into a rout.

In the confusion more than 100 men, including the 3d Division's headquarters staff and its U.S. advisers, suddenly found themselves cut off in the walled-in section of the city known as the Citadel. North Vietnamese troops, following on the heels of retreating ARVN forces, had blocked off Route 1 south of the city, the only escape route. The 37th Aerospace Rescue and Recovery Squadron based at Da Nang was ordered to try and evacuate the trapped men by helicopter. The squadron commander, Lieutenant Colonel William M. Harris IV, knew it would be a tricky mission.

Getting the slow-moving HH-53 Super Jolly Green Giants in and out of Quang Tri, which was now nearly surrounded by the enemy, would be risky. "If we sent the birds in low, they would be subject to intense ground fire," said Harris. "On the other hand, if we sent them in high, they would be fair game for the SAMs. There simply was no 'safe' altitude for the Jolly Greens." In addition, the tiny landing zone inside the Citadel could hold only one chopper at a time, and as with everything else of military significance in the city, North Vietnamese gunners had zeroed in on its position.

While four helicopters hovered off the coast, air force Phantoms directed by three airborne FACs worked over the area. One of the advisers trapped on the ground inside the Citadel assisted the F-4s until a direct artillery hit on the power station knocked out his radio. Finally the FACs advised the Jolly Greens to start their runs. Major Jackson R. Scott, piloting the lead chopper, asked the FAC where to expect the most ground fire. "Mainly from the two o'clock position," replied the FAC, "but after you're over the city, it will come from all over."

Preceded by six A-1 "Sandies," which laid down a smoke screen around the landing zone and strafed Communist positions, the helicopters wove through heavy ground fire toward the Citadel. First one, then a second, then a third Jolly Green landed on the postage-stamp-sized landing pad at five-minute intervals and loaded the trapped South Vietnamese and American soldiers while door gunners nervously scanned the surrounding walls and rooftops for enemy snipers. Minutes after the third chopper struggled into the air with the last forty-five survivors, Captain Donald A. Sutton, orbiting nearby in the fourth HH-53, picked up a radio message from inside the Citadel. "Hey," said the voice, "we've got more people down here!" Sutton made another trip back to the smoking LZ. Sutton and his crew waited for almost a minute with the rear ramp down but no one appeared.

Sergeant William J. Thompson stuck his head out the back door to see what was going on. The startled door gunner saw a North Vietnamese soldier lift his AK47 and fire at the idling chopper. The Americans had flown into a

After a strike on April 16, 1972, by U.S. B-52s and fighter-bombers, flames threaten docks and a freighter in Haiphong. The planes had hit a POL site in order to stem the flow of fuel to the southern battlefield.

trap. Jumping to his minigun, Thompson dropped the soldier dead in his tracks. The other door gunner began firing as snipers opened fire on the Jolly Green. Sutton immediately poured on the power, lifting the Jolly Green out of the LZ.

The rescue had cost an A-1 Sandy and one of the FAC planes, but both pilots were rescued. Incredibly, there were no casualties among the chopper crews or the 132 evacuees. One of the grateful American survivors was heard to exclaim: "Thank God for the U.S. Air Force." Ironically, the speaker was Major David Brookbank, the adviser who had criticized the extensive rescue effort to save Iceal Hambleton.

As the rescue drama played itself out, demoralized ARVN troops and thousands of civilian refugees fled in panic from Quang Tri south on Highway 1 toward Hue. American aircraft tried to cover the retreat, but they found themselves dropping more bombs on abandoned equip-

---

An ARVN soldier tends to a comrade wounded while defending Fire Support Base Bastogne in the path of the NVA's drive toward Hue.

ment and bridges that ARVN had failed to destroy to prevent their capture than they did on the enemy. "It was an appalling sight," said Lieutenant Colonel Ray E. Stratton, who surveyed the scene from the cockpit of his OV-10. "There was just a complete litter of U.S.-built armored personnel carriers, tanks, and trucks."

"SAM-7 Alley"

On May 3 Lieutenant General Ngo Quang Truong, who had distinguished himself in the battle for Hue during the 1968 Tet offensive, assumed command in Military Region I. Once again Truong organized the defense of Hue, quickly rallying South Vietnamese troops along the My Chanh River just north of the imperial city. The new ARVN defensive line held, forcing the Communists to concentrate their troops, which left them highly vulnerable to air attack. "TAC air resources were now able to attack troop concentrations and mechanized units massed in great strength," General Vogt reported.

Hoping for a quick victory, the North Vietnamese took great risks to maintain their momentum. Convoys of tanks, self-propelled artillery pieces, and trucks filled with ammunition and gasoline needed to sustain the heavily armed and mechanized Communist invasion force drove down the roads in broad daylight, exposed to American bombers which were now arriving in increasing numbers. U.S. air commanders initiated a classic interdiction campaign, destroying bridges and cutting roads to choke off the enemy's supply lines. Within three days, U.S. fighter-bombers destroyed forty-five bridges between the DMZ and the My Chanh River with laser-guided bombs and inflicted a heavy toll on enemy tanks and supply trucks strung out on the roads leading south from the DMZ.

But losses were high, particularly among low-flying OV-10 and O-2 observation planes which were extremely vulnerable to enemy SAMs and AAA that were clustered around Highway 1. SA-7s were so numerous and employed with such devastating accuracy against low-flying aircraft that U.S. pilots named the section of highway between Hue and Quang Tri "SAM-7 Alley."

Gradually, the air force began employing "fast FACs," F-4 jets in which the back seater acted as a spotter. Fast FACs were also used extensively to uncover camouflaged truck parks, storage areas, and other targets in the enemy's rear areas above the DMZ. Lieutenant Rick Bates of the 8th TFW's "Wolf Pack" fast FACs out of Ubon, remembered one mission when he directed an air strike against a storage area for hundreds of SAMs and supplies that was cleverly disguised as an orchard.

Despite their speed, the fast FACs took a lot of hits and losses. The golden rule for most pilots in a high-threat area was to stay above 4,500 feet and avoid making multiple passes over a target, but the nature of the FAC's work made this impossible. The North Vietnamese often

South Vietnamese inspect the wreckage of an 0-1 FAC plane shot down near Quang Tri during the NVA offensive.

hid guns around a truck or tank fixed up as lures. Lieutenant Bates and his pilot Captain Jim Latham eventually fell victim to one of these "flak traps." The tail section of their F-4 smashed by a 57MM shell, the two men were forced to eject and spent the rest of the war as POWs.

Fast FACs were instrumental in silencing the enemy's 130MM howitzers which had so demoralized ARVN troops at Quang Tri. The mobile guns, when camouflaged or hidden, were hard to spot from the air unless they fired and gave away their location with a muzzle flash. Once the guns were pinpointed, destroying them was a simple matter. Explained Gen. Vogt: "We'd put a laser bomb right where that gun was and blow it out." By the end of May, U.S. pilots reported seeing many of the heavy guns being withdrawn further north.

While the concentrated air campaign against North Vietnamese artillery and supply lines had helped to stabilize the Quang Tri front by mid-May, the battles at An Loc

and Kontum were still in doubt. Both of the cities and the few remaining outposts in the surrounding areas were totally isolated. Ground forces sent to relieve the garrisons could not break through enemy lines. Aerial resupply efforts provided the South Vietnamese with the only means to hold their ground while around-the-clock bombing kept the Communists at bay.

Holding in the highlands

By the end of April, U.S. Air Force, Navy, Marine, and VNAF units had flown more than 3,400 attack sorties against enemy forces in the central highlands of Military Region II. But this heavy application of air power had only blunted, not halted, the Communist advance. North Vietnamese troops overran the few remaining fire support bases and Special Forces camps to the north and west of Kontum along Highway 14.

Initially, ground troops and FACs had relied heavily on F-4 Phantoms which could respond quickly to requests for close air support. A few OV-10s with "Pave Nail" laser designator equipment were sent from Da Nang to Pleiku to work with F-4Ds carrying laser-guided bombs against enemy tanks at Kontum. Their accuracy was vividly demonstrated during an attack on a Special Forces camp early in May. One of the camp's Green Beret advisers radioed the FAC directing air support that a tank had broken through the wire and was rolling toward the command bunker. The FAC quickly called in a nearby Pave Nail OV-10 and asked for a flight of F-4s with laser-guided bombs. Guided by the forward air controller, the OV-10 illuminated the tank with its laser beam. A trailing F-4 rolled in and released a single 2,000-pound laser-guided bomb which exploded right next to the tank, blowing it back onto the wire.

The majority of the F-4s employed in the central highlands and around An Loc carried conventional "iron" bombs which lacked the pinpoint accuracy necessary to hit moving targets such as tanks or trucks. As a result, FACs and ground troops alike came to rely increasingly on AC-130 Spectres diverted from their usual missions over the Ho Chi Minh Trail. They had initially been skeptical of the gunship's capabilities, which were to them of unknown quality. After showing what their 105MM cannons loaded with World War II-vintage ammunition could do, gunship crews found themselves with more work than they could handle. One of the more effective missions occurred on May 6 in support of the small outpost at Polei Kleng, a few miles west of Kontum.

A single AC-130E from the 16th Special Operations Squadron at Ubon arrived on the scene just after dark. "You could look down and see tracers and flashes everywhere within a three- or four-mile radius of the compound," recalled Lieutenant Colonel Loyd J. King, the squadron's operations officer, who was aboard the aircraft. Since no one on the ground spoke English, King had to contact the ground controller at Kontum to get the exact coordinates of the compound and find out where he was authorized to fire. "You can fire anywhere up to the fence of the compound," was the reply.

King had the AC-130's sensor operators concentrate on picking out individual muzzle flashes and marking them for the 105MM gunner. "We fired off all ninety-six rounds at flashes like that," said King. "Before we got through ... probably in the neighborhood of an hour, there was no activity on the ground at all." The outpost's defenders then passed on a message through the controller at Kontum for the gunship to lay down a ring of fire with their 20MM and 40MM miniguns within 100 yards of the compound. After

exhausting its supply of ammunition, King's AC-130 headed back to Ubon.

Although King and his crewmen felt they had accomplished something that night, they did not know how effective they had been. One of the biggest frustrations for air crews throughout the war was their inability to find out what they had done. Weeks later King accidentally discovered that the gunship had been credited with turning back an entire regiment. Although the AC-130 saved Polei Kleng that night, the outpost later fell to the NVA.

Similar success stories about the devastating accuracy and firepower of the AC-130 Spectre gunships enhanced their reputation among forward air controllers and ground troops. "It got so that if you came down and mentioned your call sign was Spectre, everybody wanted to know if you had the Big Gun," said one AC-130 crewman.

An aircraft flying overhead captured this view of an NVA ambush of an ARVN convoy on Highway 14 near the village of Xa Vo Dinh north of Kontum.

By midmonth, Spectre gunships were flying up to fourteen sorties a day around Kontum and An Loc, using Bien Hoa and Pleiku as forward staging bases.

On May 14, the North Vietnamese finally made their move against Kontum, attacking simultaneously from the north and south with infantry and two columns of tanks after an intensive artillery barrage. For sixteen days the Communists pounded at the gates of the city. With enemy units blocking the highway south to Pleiku, the city and its defenders became entirely dependent upon aerial resupply. C-130s of the 50th Tactical Airlift Squadron and VNAF C-123s flew an average of fifteen missions a day to the besieged city, delivering tons of ammunition, fuel, and rice. When Communist troops gained a foothold at the east end of the runway the C-130s continued to sustain the city, dropping 2,000 tons of supplies by parachute.

The final attack came on May 25 as three enemy regiments fought their way into the city. "I bombed for two days inside the city," said one OV-10 FAC. "The ARVN would sit in their bunkers and call for more air, closer and closer." While B-52s pounded enemy troop concentrations and supply lines, gunships and fighters took on enemy armor. Air force crews claimed more than fifteen tanks destroyed and fifty-nine damaged. UH-1B gunships equipped with TOW antitank missiles claimed eleven more kills. Even more heartening for the Americans was the performance of VNAF A-37s. The South Vietnamese planes accounted for a higher percentage of tank kills than all U.S. aircraft combined. Once air power had broken the backs of the North Vietnamese armored units and B-52s had quieted their heavy artillery, ARVN troops were able to begin their counterattack. By mid-June, little more

Breaking a Siege

ARVN troops inside An Loc defended the city against North Vietnamese tanks, artillery, and troops who besieged the provincial capital for ninety-five days. Surrounded by Communist artillery and AAA batteries, An Loc's lifeline consisted of parachute drops from transports flown by VNAF and USAF crews—missions so hazardous they were sometimes restricted to nighttime flights. Ultimately, the stunning aerial bombardment of NVA positions around An Loc allowed ARVN to repulse the North Vietnamese and break the siege in July 1972.

Above. Lietenant Colonel Gordon Weed wheels his A-37 fighter-bomber in over An Loc to strike enemy troops. Right. Supplies fall beneath parachutes to An Loc. Left. An NVA T54 tank lies immobilized in the ruins of An Loc. It is emblazoned with ARVN propaganda slogans.

than two weeks after they came close to taking Pleiku, the North Vietnamese began withdrawing toward their border retreats in Cambodia and Laos.

Battle for An Loc

At An Loc, the situation appeared even more desperate for the South Vietnamese than it had seemed at Kontum. During the last half of April, continuous enemy shelling had pounded the city into virtual rubble. The plight of the 20,000 soldiers and civilians trapped inside the city became unbearable as sanitary conditions broke down and food stocks dwindled. Communist artillery and AAA batteries surrounding the city made it impossible to land safely at the airstrip. The beleaguered garrison relied solely on supplies paradropped by VNAF and U.S. Air Force transports. At first, the transports used low-level delivery methods, but the soccer field used as a drop zone was so small that the slow-moving C-130s were sitting ducks for North Vietnamese gunners.

The results were deadly. Between April 18 and 26, two C-130s were lost over An Loc. During the last three days of that week, every transport flying over the city was damaged. The 374th Tactical Airlift Wing canceled all daylight missions and the C-130s began flying only at night, dropping their supplies from between 6,000 and 9,000 feet. Accuracy plummeted, the besieged force recovering less than 30 percent of the supplies dropped in to them. One captured VC officer demoralized his ARVN interrogators, who were living on brackish water, canned fish, and rice, when he asked for a can of fruit cocktail. He said he had grown accustomed to eating it since his unit had retrieved cases of the stuff dropped by the Americans. More of the supplies began to reach friendly hands early in May when special equipment arrived from the U.S. that allowed the transports to initiate high-altitude, radar-guided drops.

On the morning of May 11, Communist infantry and tanks slashed their way into An Loc behind an intensive artillery barrage. The assault was covered by 23MM and 37MM AA guns and mobile ZSU-57/2 twin 57MM guns mounted on tank chassis. Five defending aircraft fell victim to ground fire, including an A-1 and A-37 of the VNAF, a U.S. Army Cobra gunship, and two USAF O-2s. But enemy air defenses could do little against U.S. B-52s. "The 52s caught the first NVA battalion in the open as it was charging on An Loc," Gen. Vogt reported. "We wiped it out."

Still, the Communists kept coming. Nearly 300 fighter-bomber sorties were flown in defense of An Loc on the

---

ARVN troops have grand stand seats in their M48 tank and M113 APC to watch bomb bursts from a U.S. B-52 Stratofortress attack ripple along Route 9 just below the DMZ during the Easter offensive.

eleventh. Phantom pilots of the 49th TFW, who had just arrived at Bien Hoa the day before after a grueling trip across the Pacific from their home base in New Mexico, were even sent into the battle without any familiarization or safety check flights. By the following day, most of the forty Communist tanks committed to the assault had been knocked out of action by fighter-bombers and Cobra gunships. But the battle continued to rage for three more days as the enemy gained control of portions of the city.

In the street fighting that broke out, air force gunships worked with ground forward air controllers to help ferret out pockets of enemy resistance. The FAC marked his position by putting out a reflector panel or a white bedsheet, which the gunship's sensor operators could pick up with their low-light-level televisions or infrared gear. Once the gunship crew established a "lock" on his position, the FAC could direct them to the target by communicating its

distance and direction from his location. Working in this fashion the AC-130 gunships were extremely effective, using their 105mm guns to blast enemy gunners barricaded in buildings inside the city.

On May 12, the enemy again began firing SA-7 Strelas, severely damaging an AC-130 working over the city. Although the SA-7s made life difficult for the gunships, whose effective operating altitude was well within the SA-7's range, the crews developed innovative ways to nullify the heat-seeking missiles. Once a crewman hanging out the cargo ramp at the rear of the plane spotted the SA-7's spiraling smoke trail he fired a flare right at the oncoming missile to confuse its infrared tracking gear by giving it another "hot" target. Another method was for the pilot to bank the gunship so that its wing shielded its engines' heat from an oncoming missile.

According to Master Sergeant Arthur W. Humphrey, an AC-130 crewman, "there were so many airplanes in the sky around An Loc you had to be cautious of not only the enemy, but your own people who were out there with you." The airspace over An Loc was a mass of confusion as VNAF, U.S. Air Force, Marine, and Navy fighter-bombers flew an average of 260 missions a day over the city, and transports and helicopters performed their jobs as well. "It was a wonder we didn't shoot some of them down," Humphrey said, "because we would be concentrating on our target and all of a sudden here comes another airplane through our orbit." But it was just this cascade of air power that broke the enemy's grip on An Loc. By late May, the Communist attack began to taper off, and by June 12 ARVN troops had mopped up the last pockets of resistance in the city. When reinforcements arrived six days later, the siege was over. At the same time, the enemy drive on Hue was also withering.

The final push

Although continuous air strikes had decimated their heavy artillery and dried up their supplies of ammunition and gasoline, the North Vietnamese made one last effort to break through the ARVN line north of Hue. During the night of May 20, about thirty amphibious PT76 tanks drove across the My Chanh River. At dawn they moved across the plain toward ARVN positions. Gen. Vogt quickly called in F-4 Phantoms with laser-guided bombs in what was to be one of the largest tank-versus-bomber engagements of the war. "The laser bombs were scoring direct hits on those damn things and blowing them to bits," said Vogt. "By the end of at most a two-hour battle, there wasn't a tank able to continue." Tactical bombers were credited with knocking out eighteen tanks and 300 ground troops during the engagement.

The North Vietnamese tried to capture Hue again on May 25, launching human wave assaults across the entire front. After four days of intense fighting, the South Vietnamese with the help of close air support forced the Communists back across the My Chanh River. Buoyed by that success, the ARVN went on the offensive. U.S. and South Vietnamese commanders planned a coordinated air and land attack to recapture Quang Tri. Until then air power had been used like a fire hose, reacting to isolated calls for help. "After somebody got in trouble on the ground, air was called in to bail them out," recalled Vogt. "All this changed at this point in time and we were now working very closely with the little guy on the ground."

On June 28, ARVN counterattacked. Following a wave of B-52 strikes, ground troops advanced against enemy positions under the cover of tactical aircraft. Within a week they had rolled the North Vietnamese back to within a mile of Quang Tri. Instead of isolating the Communist force holed up in the Citadel, the South Vietnamese decided to take the fortress by force. As a matter of pride and to avoid unnecessary damage to the city, President Thieu initially ordered ARVN to retake the city without the help of American air power. But after two and a half months of bloody and inconclusive fighting, the Communists still held Quang Tri. General Truong, now commanding the counterattack, reluctantly requested that American fighter-bombers and B-52s strike the city itself. The bombing made the difference. The North Vietnamese withdrew from the battered city on September 16.

The Communists had failed to achieve the major objectives of their Easter offensive, but they had uncovered serious weaknesses in the U.S.–South Vietnamese strategy. The unexpected size and scope of the Communist invasion exposed the futility of the Americans' high-tech campaign against infiltration down the Ho Chi Minh Trail. Despite continuous bombing and the use of electronic sensors to monitor and target enemy activities in Laos, Hanoi had managed to assemble and launch a large, heavily armed and mechanized invasion force more powerful than the force that undertook the 1968 Tet offensive. The initial collapse of ARVN units also called into question the viability of the Vietnamization program. According to General Frederick C. Weyand, who succeeded Gen. Abrams as MACV commander on June 29, it was "unlikely that the South Vietnamese could have stopped the invasion without the tremendous effectiveness of air power."

One American adviser claimed the VNAF's performance was "better than we had any right to expect" after only two years of the Vietnamization program. With a paper strength of 150 combat aircraft, the South Vietnamese averaged close to 200 sorties per day throughout the offensive, nearly double the rate of sorties six months earlier. Their transports moved 40,484 troops and delivered 3,388 tons of supplies. But the size and force of the invasion proved too much for the VNAF to handle alone.

Like the ARVN, the VNAF had been trained and equipped for low-level operations against lightly armed guerrilla units. Most of their combat aircraft were comparatively low-performance A-1s, A-37s, and F-5s, which were highly vulnerable to radar-directed AA fire and surface-to-air missiles. Lacking any ECM capabilities or support aircraft to neutralize the air defenses employed by the North, the VNAF could not operate effectively in high-threat areas. Their small fleet of C-123s did not have the capability to maintain the level of resupply needed to sustain both An Loc and Kontum.

While the VNAF was unable to cope with the conventional-style assault by the North Vietnamese, the new-look NVA force with its armor was tailor-made for American air attacks. "The change . . . permitted air to put . . . firepower in on good, worthwhile targets instead of little huts in the jungle and a few scattered guerrilla bands," said Gen. Vogt. "As the enemy massed its forces and moved into these objective areas, we simply hit them with fighter-bombers and of course massive use of B-52s. It was strictly an application of firepower. . . . After a good dose of this for several months, the enemy ranks were so badly decimated that they lost all their offensive punch and the offensive petered out in each one of those major areas."

In the first month of the offensive alone, U.S. aircraft flew 10,659 close air support and airlift sorties through the country. By August, American transports had dropped 6,385 tons of supplies into An Loc and 2,030 tons into Kontum, and nearly another 3,000 tons were delivered to isolated outposts and troops in the field. Air force, navy, and marine combat planes flew a total of 30,906 sorties from the beginning of April to the end of June in support of ARVN forces throughout the country. SAC B-52s provided an additional 6,038 sorties during the same period. This display of force was remarkable considering that the limited number of aircraft in Southeast Asia was also needed to carry out the renewed bombing campaign in the North which President Nixon had initiated on May 10.

An Evolution in Air Power

F-111

The 80,000-pound F-111 was, by the end of the war, the most sophisticated fighter-bomber in the USAF's inventory. Fitted with pivoting wings, the jet could reach speeds two-and-a-half times the speed of sound. Its terrain-following radar allowed it to fly at a continuous altitude as low as 200 feet, hugging the contour of the terrain below to mask its approach to enemy radar. Never assigned an official nickname, the seventy-three-foot-long aircraft could carry up to 30,000 pounds of ordnance, which was dropped automatically by a radar-guided computerized bomb-delivery system.

OV-10 Bronco

The OV-10, used primarily for visual recon or FAC duty, became one of the most versatile light strike and counterinsurgency aircraft in Vietnam. It could reach a top speed of 281 mph, or could loiter over an area at 55 mph, and its bubblelike canopy provided the crew with a superb view during forward air control missions. Five stations underneath and on either side of the fuselage could carry up to 3,600 pounds of bombs, rockets, guns, or cannons.

F-8 Crusader

The F-8 Crusader was the navy's primary jet fighter until 1969. The single-seat, carrier-based jet was armed with four 20MM cannons and up to four air-to-air missiles. Capable of carrying 4,000 pounds of ordnance, the Crusader was also employed in a ground attack role in South Vietnam. A photo reconnaissance version of the supersonic jet, the RF-8, was used extensively over North Vietnam throughout the war.

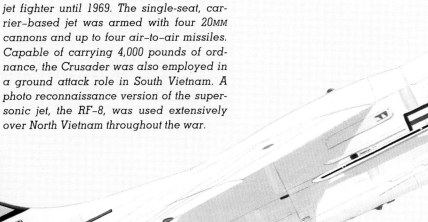

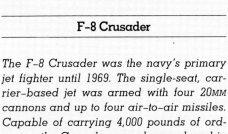

HH-53

"Super Jolly Green Giant"

The HH-53 was the USAF's largest, fastest, and most powerful heavy-lift helicopter. In 1967, it succeeded the smaller HH-3 "Jolly Green Giant" as the primary helicopter of the USAF's Aerospace Rescue and Recovery Service. Twice the size of the HH-3, the "Super Jolly Green Giant" weighed 36,000 pounds and could carry a 13,000-pound load, including thirty-three passengers or twenty-four patients on litters in addition to its crew of five.

RF-4C Phantom II

An unarmed reconnaissance version of the versatile F-4 Phantom II, the RF-4C became the air force's primary photo reconnaissance aircraft for use over North Vietnam and Laos. Navy pilots flew the "B" model for their own photo recon work. Replacing the slower RF-101, whose top speed of 1,000 miles per hour made it more vulnerable to enemy AA guns, the RF-4 could fly at twice the speed of sound. At right, ground crewmen at Udorn Air Base, Thailand, pull film from an RF-4C that has just returned from a mission over the North in May 1968.

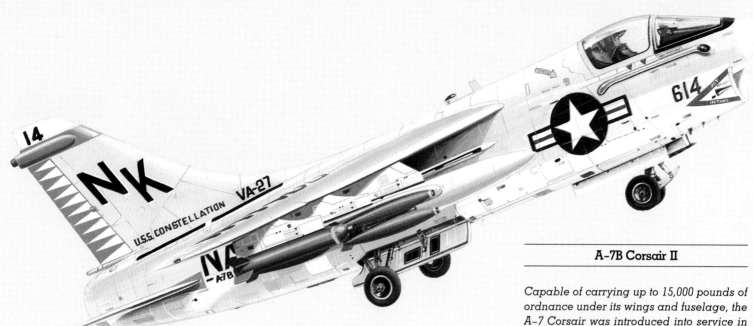

A-7B Corsair II

Capable of carrying up to 15,000 pounds of ordnance under its wings and fuselage, the A-7 Corsair was introduced into service in 1967. The A-7 replaced the smaller A-4 Skyhawk as the navy's primary attack aircraft late in the war, when it saw extensive action during the Linebacker campaign. By then two sophisticated, all-weather models of the Corsair had been introduced, one purchased by the air force, the other by the navy.

MiG-21 "Fishbed"

Produced by the Soviet design bureau named for Mikoyan and Gurevich, the MiG-21 was the fastest and most sophisticated aircraft in North Vietnam's air force and was capable of challenging all but the most modern U.S. fighters. Its light frame and swept-back wings enabled the MiG-21 to fly at Mach 2 speeds and gave it increased maneuverability without sacrificing firepower. MiG-21s usually packed a twin-barreled 23MM gun and up to four radar-guided Atoll air-to-air missiles.

A-37 Dragonfly

The twin-seated A-37 Dragonfly, an American trainer converted for VNAF counterinsurgency missions, could carry double its own weight of 5,820 pounds in bombs, in addition to a 7.62MM minigun installed in the forward fuselage. Provided to the South Vietnamese in 1969, the A-37 eventually replaced the A-1 Skyraider as the VNAF's principal strike aircraft. While the A-37's jet engine gave it a maximum cruising speed of nearly 500 knots, far faster than the A-1, its maximum range was only 1,020 miles, a third of the Skyraider's.

AC-119K Stinger

The AC-119, actually a C-119 "Flying Boxcar" converted into a gunship, was a successor to the AC-47 "Puff the Magic Dragon" gunships used so effectively in South Vietnam. The AC-119G Shadow, introduced in 1969, carried four 7.62MM Gatling guns and was used primarily for nighttime base defense in the South. A more heavily armed version, the AC-119K Stinger, added two 20MM cannons to the Gatling guns as well as radar and infrared sensors for night operations and auxiliary jet engines mounted under each wing. AC-119Ks flew against truck convoys on the Ho Chi Minh Trail, but were outmoded for that use in 1970 by the faster, more powerful AC-130 Spectres.

F-5 Freedom Fighter

Originally the T-38, an American jet trainer, the supersonic F-5 became the first jet in the VNAF's arsenal. Its versatility, simple design, and low cost made it a good choice for the VNAF; it was also easy to maintain and repair. It could carry two Sidewinder missiles on wing-tip launchers (although it never did in Vietnam) in its air-to-air role and was armed with two 20MM guns in the fuselage nose. As an air-to-ground attack plane, however, it was handicapped by a relatively small ordnance payload—a maximum of 5,200 pounds.

127

Linebacker

From the moment the Communists launched their offensive in early April 1972, President Nixon's instinct told him that it was the time to counter Hanoi's renewed aggression in the South with a ferocious bombing assault on the North, the source of that aggression. But except for limited Freedom Train bombing operations against North Vietnamese supply lines and staging areas below the twentieth parallel and raids against Hanoi and Haiphong on the weekend of April 16, the president's reaction was strangely restrained. Like President Johnson before him, this president had to carefully analyze the global implications of a major escalation of the war in Vietnam.

Just as the North's Easter invasion struck in South Vietnam, the president was preparing for a historic summit meeting in Moscow to discuss trade negotiations and complete a strategic arms limitation agreement that had been years in the making. Nixon worried that if he retaliated against North Vietnam, the Soviets might back

out of the meeting in protest. The president's concern was reinforced by his national security adviser, Henry Kissinger, who feared events in Vietnam threatened to paralyze American foreign policy, eroding his vision of a triangular balance between Moscow, Peking, and Washington that might encourage international equilibrium and at the same time foster a negotiated settlement of the war. He urged a more balanced approach of limited bombing and intensified negotiating efforts. Nixon reluctantly agreed.

But by early May, Kissinger's shuttle diplomacy between Moscow and Paris was getting him nowhere. The Communists stonily told Kissinger that they had no intention of pulling back from their offensive in the South. So, the president began listening to the inner-circle advisers who shared his hard-line views.

Gambling that Moscow was not willing to risk jeopardizing détente with the U.S. over North Vietnam, Nixon decided to act on his initial impulse. "We have the power to destroy the enemy's war-making capacity," he wrote in a memorandum to Kissinger. "The only question is whether we have the will to use that power. What distinguishes me from Johnson is that I have the will in spades."

There was already a plan for the actions Nixon contemplated—Operation Duck Hook—which the NSC had worked out with the staff of the chief of naval operations in 1969. The most controversial element of the plan, which envisioned a quick, hard-hitting bombing campaign against the North, called for aerial mining operations against Haiphong Harbor.

For years, military men had argued that the most effective way to cripple Hanoi's war effort was to cut off its external sources of supply from the Soviet Union and China. Nearly four years of bombing Communist supply lines in North Vietnam during Rolling Thunder and more than seven years of the same along the Ho Chi Minh Trail had failed to reduce significantly the number of men and amount of materiel Hanoi was able to infiltrate into the South.

North Vietnam depended heavily on Chinese and Soviet aid to sustain both its domestic economy and the war in the South. Peking shipped an average of 22,000 metric tons of supplies a month over the two rail lines and eight major roads that linked it with North Vietnam. Nearly 85 percent of its imports, however, came by sea from the Soviet Union and Eastern European nations. A full 90 percent of that, including virtually all of North Vietnam's most sophisticated military hardware—SAMs, MiG aircraft, radar equipment, tanks, heavy artillery, and radar-directed AA guns—came through the port of Haiphong.

As early as 1965, naval commanders of Task Force 77 had been authorized to prepare contingency plans to mine Haiphong Harbor, but the orders never came. President Johnson and his advisers were not willing to risk a direct confrontation with Moscow that might escalate the war beyond Southeast Asia. President Nixon had been impressed by the mining proposal when it was included in the overall plan for Operation Duck Hook, but when the interagency survey by Kissinger and his NSC staff known as NSSM-1 reemphasized the high risks, the plan was shelved. On May 5, Nixon ordered the JCS to prepare to execute mining operations against Haiphong Harbor within three days.

Mining Haiphong Harbor

At 8:10 A.M. on May 8, just eight days after the fall of Quang Tri to the NVA, six A-7 Corsairs of U.S. Navy Attack Squadrons 22 and 94 and three A-6 Intruders of U.S. Marine Attack Squadron 224 shrieked off the deck of the U.S.S. *Coral Sea.*

The plan called for the A-6s to approach the harbor from the east while the A-7s came in from the north on a path perpendicular to the Intruders. For reasons unknown to them, the pilots were instructed to make their drops precisely at 9:00 A.M., and Commander Roger Sheets, who led the strike from his A-6, was under orders to report back by radio to the carrier as soon as the last plane had cleared the harbor. Sheets set the approach altitude at fifty feet, low enough to mask the jets from enemy radar, and, to gain an element of surprise, instructed his pilots to maintain strict radio silence. Once they appeared in the open over Haiphong Harbor, there would be little they could do to protect themselves from the enemy's formidable air defenses. Each jet carried four mines of about 2,000 pounds apiece on its wing racks, a load that would greatly limit their ability to maneuver if attacked by enemy SAMs or MiGs.

ECM aircraft were ordered to neutralize radar-guided defenses. A number of diversionary strikes by other navy aircraft and offshore naval bombardments were designed to keep the enemy guessing. Despite all the protection, the JCS frankly estimated that 30 percent of the strike force would not make it back.

To help even the odds, the navy employed its guided-missile cruisers for the first time in the war, along with F-4 fighter escorts to defend the strike force against enemy MiGs. Intelligence photos indicated the two MiG bases south of Haiphong at Cat Bi and Kien An were unoccupied, so planners assumed that any threat would come from either the Kep or the Phuc Yen airfield north of Hanoi. The U.S.S. *Chicago* and the U.S.S. *Long Beach,* equipped with radar-guided, long-range surface-to-air Talos missiles, took up positions within forty miles of the coast where their radars could "look" up the Red River Valley. Fighter escorts would precede Sheets's strike force and set up screening positions near the MiG bases outside the range of the cruisers' missiles. All other support aircraft operating within the cruisers' fields of fire were to remain below 500 feet, so that any unidentified aircraft above the altitude woud be fair game.

The tactic quickly paid off. Just as the mine-laden jets streaked over the *Chicago*, eight minutes from their target, radar operators aboard the cruiser picked up four "bogies" rapidly heading southeast from Hanoi. The ship's fire control radars locked onto the enemy aircraft and a salvo of Talos missiles roared off the cruiser's deck. The lead enemy plane disappeared from the scopes, and the remaining three quickly turned back to the northeast. The MiGs posed no threat after that. Each time they ventured toward Haiphong, navy gunners merely scanned them with their fire control radars and watched them turn tail.

During the strike force's final approach, three SAMs passed harmlessly overhead. Flying below the SA-2's effective range and with the MiG threat neutralized, the navy pilots' major concern was the AAA batteries in Haiphong Harbor itself. Sheets had planned the mission so that each plane would make only one pass, minimizing the amount of time each was exposed to ground fire. The entire exercise took only two minutes. "We had our first mine in the water at 8:59 and our last one at 9:01," Sheets recalled. "We came out of it without even a scratch."

As soon as the jets were clear, the navy commander radioed the results back to the *Coral Sea*. The message was relayed through CINCPAC headquarters in Hawaii directly to the White House. The reason Sheets and his men had been ordered to drop their mines precisely at 9:00 A.M. soon became clear. President Nixon was at that moment delivering a televised speech, informing the world of the action and others that would follow.

Pointing to Hanoi's continued offensive in South Vietnam and its refusal to accept U.S. terms for a cease-fire and mutual withdrawal as evidence of the Communists' true intentions, Nixon claimed the "only way to stop the killing is to take the weapons of war out of the hands of the international outlaws of North Vietnam." He announced his decision to impose an air and naval blockade on North Vietnam by bombing and mining operations. Nixon noted that the mines in Haiphong Harbor would not be activated for three days, allowing time for any ships to leave port without harm. Of the thirty-six Soviet, Eastern European, and Chinese ships in the harbor, only five left during the three-day grace period.

Hanoi predictably condemned the mining and refused to negotiate on Nixon's terms. At home, Democratic presidential candidate George McGovern labeled the action a "flirtation with World War III," but Nixon's "silent majority" apparently approved of his decision. Subsequent public opinion polls showed support for the president had gone up. But Washington was more concerned about the reaction in the Kremlin.

Moscow publicly condemned the mining, as was to be expected. But the following day U.S. newspapers carried pictures of Nixon shaking hands with Soviet Foreign Trade Minister Nikolai Patolichev at the White House. It seemed that the Soviets were not willing to allow events in Vietnam to poison their relations with Washington. As far as they were concerned the summit meeting was still on. Kissinger would later describe the event as "the finest hour of Nixon's Presidency." It was indeed a major triumph of international diplomacy, but it was yet to be determined how effective the mining and subsequent bombing would be in achieving American strategy objectives in Vietnam.

Opening day

On May 10, three and a half years after Lyndon Johnson called a halt to the Rolling Thunder campaign, Richard Nixon authorized the full-scale resumption of bombing operations against North Vietnam. The new bombing campaign, appropriately code named Linebacker, had three major objectives: Attacking the roads and rail lines from China to cut off North Vietnam's overland supply routes as the mining operations would cut off the sea routes; destroying stockpiles of military supplies and equipment already stored inside the country; and preventing those supplies and reinforcements from reaching the North Vietnamese invasion force in the South.

On the morning of May 10, thirty-two F-4 Phantoms from the 8th Tactical Fighter Wing lifted off the runway at Ubon, Thailand. Half of the strike force carried conventional "dumb" bombs targeted for the railroad switching yard at Yen Vien, just north of Hanoi. The remaining sixteen were loaded with so-called "smart" bombs—seven TV-guided and twenty-two laser-guided bombs, weighing 2,000 pounds apiece. Their target was the Paul Doumer Bridge located a few miles south of Yen Vien on the northern outskirts of Hanoi.

The Doumer Bridge, the main entry into Hanoi for road and rail traffic, had been hit by U.S. pilots during the Rolling Thunder campaign. This time, nearly five years after it was first bombed in August 1967, the F-4s knocked out the 5,532-foot bridge over the Red River without the loss of a single plane, despite heavy AAA fire and having an estimated 160 SAMs fired at them. The pilots celebrated their victory back at the officers' club at Ubon.

It was a different story for the F-4 pilots from the 555th "Triple Nickel" Tactical Fighter Squadron flying MiG Combat Air Patrol. The four Phantoms of "Oyster" flight, led by Major Robert Lodge, took off from Udorn, Thailand, ahead of the strike force to act as a defensive screen between the bombers and the two airfields north of Hanoi. Once they crossed the North Vietnamese border, the F-4s descended to 3,000 feet and accelerated to 500 knots. The pilots knew they would need to maintain high air speed from now on if they were to evade the supersonic SAMs and outmaneuver the lighter and quicker-turning MiGs.

Lodge and his back seater, Captain Roger C. Locher, were well versed in the MiG's capabilities and weaknesses. They had downed a MiG-21 over northeast Laos in February, the air force's first air-to-air victory since the 1968 bombing halt, and had just scored their second MiG-21 kill only two days before on a mission near Hanoi.

Oyster flight had closed to within thirty miles of the Yen Bai airfield when several blips appeared on Locher's radar scope. Two pairs of MiGs, operating at altitudes of 13,000 and 16,000 feet some forty-five miles away, were heading straight for them at full throttle. Lodge ordered his flight to begin climbing to intercept them. He would aim for the leader of the first pair of MiGs while his wingman took on the leader of the second pair. As the planes converged at a speed of 1,000 knots, Locher locked the F-4's radar-guided Sparrow missiles onto the oncoming jet. Lodge launched one of the Sparrows, but the missile exploded in midflight. He quickly punched off a second one that guided perfectly, exploding in a huge reddish orange fireball. When the smoke subsided, they saw a MiG-21, its left wing missing, plunging earthward out of control. Lodge and Locher had scored their third MiG kill. Simultaneously, Lodge's wingman, Lieutenant John Markle, downed the lead MiG with two more Sparrows.

Jockeying his F-4 through the swirling smoke, Lodge managed to cut in 220 feet behind one of the remaining two MiGs. At such close range, however, his long-range Sparrows would not have time enough to guide or arm themselves. Since his F-4 was not equipped with a cannon, all he could do was hang on to the MiG's tail but try to lengthen the distance between them. Meanwhile, Captain Richard S. "Steve" Ritchie and his back seater, Captain Charles B. DeBellevue, established a radar lock on in an ideal position 1,000 feet below and 6,000 feet behind the last MiG. Ritchie quickly "ripple fired" two Sparrows. The MiG evaded the first missile, but the second exploded on target. DeBellevue saw a yellow parachute open as the North Vietnamese pilot abandoned his crippled MiG-21.

Lodge was still stalking his prey when four more MiG-19s appeared out of nowhere and converged unseen on his tail. Just as Lodge fired a Sparrow, the MiG-19s opened up with their cannon. A stream of tracer fire raked across the Phantom, which caught fire and started to lose altitude. Locher could see flames licking from behind his head and bubbles spreading throughout the Plexiglas canopy as it began to melt under the intense heat. Locher told Lodge he was getting out and yanked the ejection handle. "The next thing I heard was a big blast," he said. "When I opened my eyes, I was in my parachute and just about then I could see the airplane hit the ground right below."

Lodge never made it out. The other airmen in Oyster

flight thought Locher had perished with Lodge in the crash, but the back seater was very much alive. Landing deep in enemy territory, Locher constantly moved to evade enemy patrols. The twenty-eight-year-old captain lived on water from banana trees, berries, nuts, and chives from a peasant's garden. He often heard U.S. planes bombing targets nearby but was not able to raise anyone over his emergency radio until June 1. The next day, an HH-53 rescue chopper, escorted by A-1 Skyraiders, plucked a haggard-looking Locher from his jungle hiding place just eight miles from the MiG base at Yen Bai.

Another F-4 escorting the strike force against the Doumer Bridge that day was also shot down by MiG-19s using the same tactics. That brought the air force's kill ratio to three MiGs for two Phantoms, not particularly encouraging results. On that same opening day of Operation Linebacker, navy fliers scored their biggest aerial victory of the war. While air force Phantoms were leveling the Doumer Bridge, carrier-based A-6 Intruders and A-7 Corsairs hit the Hai Duong railroad yard halfway between Hanoi and Haiphong. No fewer than twenty-two MiGs engaged the navy jets and their F-4 Phantom escorts. Seven of the MiGs were shot down, three of them by a single F-4J from the U.S.S. *Constellation*'s Fighter Squadron 96, crewed by Lieutenant Randy Cunningham and his radar intercept officer, Lieutenant (j.g.) Willie

Driscoll. One of the MiGs they "splashed" was flown by Colonel Toon, one of North Vietnam's top fighter pilots (see sidebar, p. 134). With two previous MiG kills under their belt, Cunningham and Driscoll thus became America's first "aces" of the Vietnam War.

Closing the vise

Much to the surprise of American pilots, who were accustomed to the sporadic and highly restricted targeting authorizations of the Rolling Thunder era, 7th Air Force Headquarters ordered a second strike on the Doumer Bridge the following day. Unlike President Johnson, Nixon left the tactics and day-to-day running of the bombing campaign to air force and navy commanders in the field. While civilian officials in the Johnson administration had selected the targets and the time period in which they could be hit, Nixon gave his air commanders carte blanche in determining the timing and strength of each attack. This allowed for an element of surprise and a continued intensity that was lacking during Rolling Thunder.

On the afternoon of May 11, Captain Mike Messett, who

American bombing raids on the seventh, eighth, and ninth of June 1972 leveled the Bach Dang area of the important coal-mining and port city of Hon Gai.

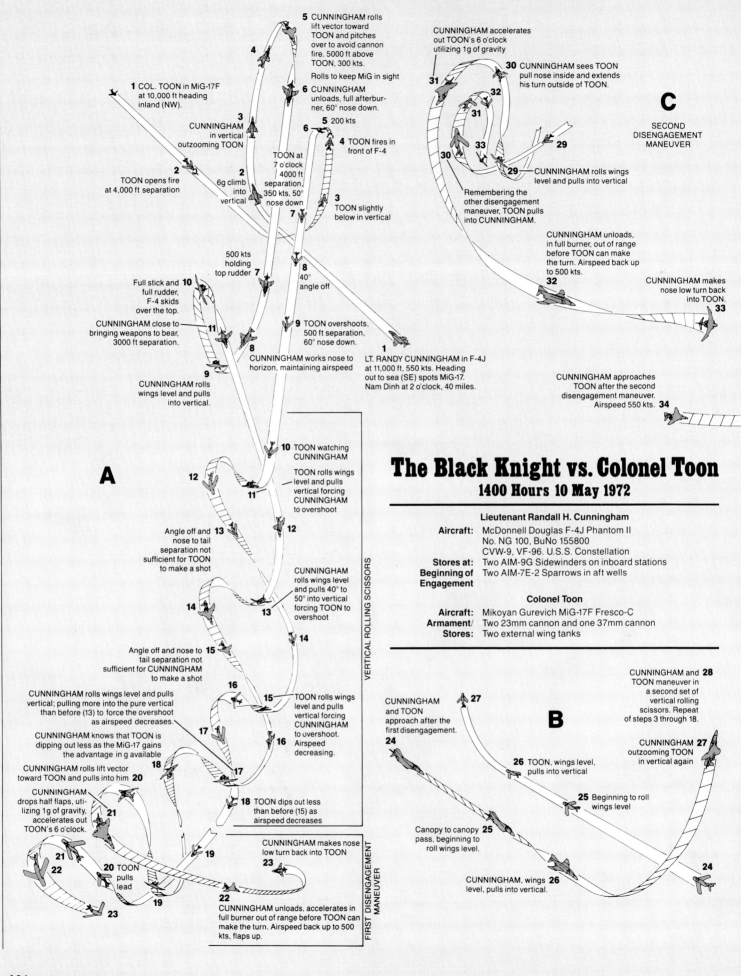

5 CUNNINGHAM rolls lift vector toward TOON and pitches over to avoid cannon fire. 5000 ft above TOON, 300 kts.

Rolls to keep MiG in sight

6 CUNNINGHAM unloads, full afterburner, 60° nose down.

1 COL. TOON in MiG-17F at 10,000 ft heading inland (NW).

3 CUNNINGHAM in vertical outzooming TOON

5 200 kts

TOON at 7 o'clock 4000 ft separation, 350 kts, 50° nose down

4 TOON fires in front of F-4

2 TOON opens fire at 4,000 ft separation

2 6g climb into vertical

3 TOON slightly below in vertical

500 kts holding top rudder **7**

7

8 40° angle off

Full stick and full rudder, F-4 skids over the top. **10**

CUNNINGHAM close to bringing weapons to bear, 3000 ft separation.

11

9 TOON overshoots, 500 ft separation, 60° nose down.

CUNNINGHAM works nose to horizon, maintaining airspeed

8

9

CUNNINGHAM rolls wings level and pulls into vertical.

1 LT. RANDY CUNNINGHAM in F-4J at 11,000 ft, 550 kts. Heading out to sea (SE) spots MiG-17. Nam Dinh at 2 o'clock, 40 miles.

A

12

10 TOON watching CUNNINGHAM

TOON rolls wings level and pulls vertical forcing CUNNINGHAM to overshoot

11

12

Angle off and nose to tail separation not sufficient for TOON to make a shot

13

CUNNINGHAM rolls wings level and pulls 40° to 50° into vertical forcing TOON to overshoot

14

13

Angle off and nose to tail separation not sufficient for CUNNINGHAM to make a shot

15

CUNNINGHAM rolls wings level and pulls vertical; pulling more into the pure vertical than before (13) to force the overshoot as airspeed decreases.

16

15 TOON rolls wings level and pulls vertical forcing CUNNINGHAM to overshoot. Airspeed decreasing.

CUNNINGHAM knows that TOON is dipping out less as the MiG-17 gains the advantage in g available

17

14

16

CUNNINGHAM rolls lift vector toward TOON and pulls into him **20**

18

CUNNINGHAM drops half flaps, utilizing 1g of gravity, accelerates out TOON's 6 o'clock.

21

17

18 TOON dips out less than before (15) as airspeed decreases

21

22

20 TOON pulls lead

19

23

19

CUNNINGHAM makes nose low turn back into TOON

23

22

CUNNINGHAM unloads, accelerates in full burner out of range before TOON can make the turn. Airspeed back up to 500 kts, flaps up.

VERTICAL ROLLING SCISSORS

FIRST DISENGAGEMENT MANEUVER

CUNNINGHAM accelerates out TOON's 6 o'clock utilizing 1g of gravity

31

30 CUNNINGHAM sees TOON pull nose inside and extends his turn outside of TOON.

32

31

33

29

30

29 CUNNINGHAM rolls wings level and pulls into vertical

Remembering the other disengagement maneuver, TOON pulls into CUNNINGHAM.

C

SECOND DISENGAGEMENT MANEUVER

CUNNINGHAM unloads, in full burner, out of range before TOON can make the turn. Airspeed back up to 500 kts.

32

CUNNINGHAM makes nose low turn back into TOON.

33

CUNNINGHAM approaches TOON after the second disengagement maneuver. Airspeed 550 kts. **34**

The Black Knight vs. Colonel Toon
1400 Hours 10 May 1972

Lieutenant Randall H. Cunningham

Aircraft:	McDonnell Douglas F-4J Phantom II No. NG 100, BuNo 155800 CVW-9, VF-96. U.S.S. Constellation
Stores at: **Beginning of Engagement**	Two AIM-9G Sidewinders on inboard stations Two AIM-7E-2 Sparrows in aft wells

Colonel Toon

Aircraft:	Mikoyan Gurevich MiG-17F Fresco-C
Armament/ **Stores:**	Two 23mm cannon and one 37mm cannon Two external wing tanks

CUNNINGHAM and TOON approach after the first disengagement.

24

25 Beginning to roll wings level

26 TOON, wings level, pulls into vertical

Canopy to canopy pass, beginning to roll wings level. **25**

CUNNINGHAM, wings **26** level, pulls into vertical.

CUNNINGHAM and **28** TOON maneuver in a second set of vertical rolling scissors. Repeat of steps 3 through 18.

B

CUNNINGHAM **27** outzooming TOON in vertical again

27

24

134

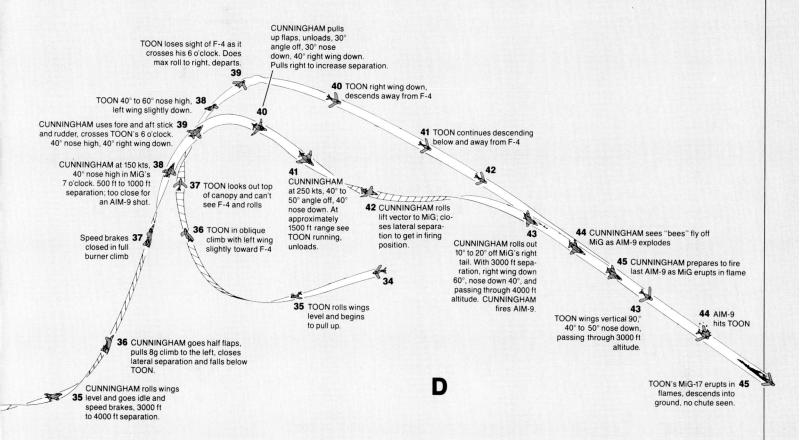

D

Seven years after Americans first encountered MiG fighters over North Vietnam, the ranks of U.S. airmen in Vietnam had yet to produce an ace, a pilot or copilot with five MiG "kills." That was to change on May 10, 1972. Pilot Randy Cunningham, nicknamed "the Black Knight," and his backseater, Willie Driscoll, both of them navy lieutenants, had previously downed two MiGs. On May 10, flying against the Hai Duong railroad yard east of Hanoi, in their F-4, they dropped their bombs only to encounter a swarm of MiGs. Knocking two of them out of the air, Cunningham turned to sea. He did not get far before meeting another enemy aircraft, a MiG-17 piloted by Colonel Toon, the top North Vietnamese ace with thirteen U.S. aircraft to his credit. Over Nam Dinh, the two pilots became locked in the duel of their lives. The diagram on these pages reenacts their aerial battle.

Spotting Toon (1), Cunningham headed toward him until Toon opened fire (2). Climbing to avoid the cannon fire, Cunningham expected Toon to "run" for home; Cunningham would then use his plane's superior speed to chase and shoot down Toon. Instead, Toon zoomed upward (3) next to the F-4, firing in front of Cunningham (4). Cunningham pitched

over (5), ignited his afterburners, and dove (6) past Toon, who gave chase. Executing a high-G vertical turn, Cunningham then forced Toon to overshoot him. But as soon as Cunningham began to maneuver into position to fire a missile, Toon (10–11) went into a "vertical rolling scissors," a dangerous defensive maneuver, causing Cunningham to overshoot. Locked in the scissors (12–18) until Toon slowed (19) trying to fly in behind Cunningham and fire, neither pilot could take more than a fleeting advantage and they eventually disengaged (20–23).

Approaching each other again (24), Cunningham and Toon passed canopy-to-canopy (25), pulled into the vertical, and again maneuvered in a rolling scissors.

After coming out of the second scissors (29–33), Cunningham and Toon turned to meet in what was to be their last encounter. As the two pilots climbed toward each other (34–38), Toon turned away from the F-4 and started to run (39–42) because his fuel was running low. Rolling in behind, Cunningham unleashed one of his heat-seeking Sidewinder missiles (43). It was the beginning of the end for Toon. Cunningham later described what happened.

The missile hit him ... it looked like a bunch of bees flew off. I thought I just wounded him [but] ... a big flame erupted. I never saw him get out of the airplane. There were rumors that he got out with extensive damage, but survived. ... I never saw a chute.

Cunningham had just defeated "the best pilot I ever encountered, American or otherwise," and he and Driscoll had already that day accomplished the first (and only) triple kill of the war. But with three missiles and plenty of fuel remaining, he and Driscoll wanted to stay in the fight. Encountering another MiG, they began to give chase when four more MiG-17s appeared on their tail. Luckily for the two airmen, another F-4 in the area scared off the MiGs by firing a Sidewinder in their midst. With that, Cunningham and Driscoll headed for the U.S.S. *Constellation* only to be downed by a SAM at the mouth of the Red River. Plucked from the water by rescue helicopters, they reached the *Constellation* to find most of its crew of 5,000 topside to greet them. As they strode toward the huge crowd, Randy Cunningham and Willie Driscoll walked into the annals of aerial warfare as the first U.S. aces of the Vietnam War.

had flown in the previous day's mission against the Doumer Bridge, found himself back in the cockpit of his F-4 leading a flight of four toward Hanoi to put the finishing touches on the bridge. Three planes carried six MK84 2,000-pound laser-guided bombs, and the fourth toted two MK118s each weighing 3,000 pounds. To neutralize the MiG threat, Messett's roommate, Captain Dave Smith, led another flight of four Phantoms against the North Vietnamese Air Defense Command complex at the Bac Mai airfield on the southern outskirts of the capital.

Messett's flight did not encounter any MiGs that afternoon, but SAMs were flying fast and furious. A few passed directly through his formation but failed to detonate. Strangely enough, the SAMs stopped firing when the Americans reached Hanoi. Messett guessed the North Vietnamese did not expect the bombers to return so soon and were not prepared. The flight rolled in over the bridge and unleashed its LGBs, sending three more spans of the bridge into the Red River. The four Phantoms flew back to Thailand unopposed.

While Messett's flight did not encounter any MiGs, their fighter escorts and the F-105 Wild Weasels flying anti-SAM support had their hands full. Despite the raid led by Capt. Smith on the North Vietnamese Air Defense Command Post at Bac Mai, radar controllers at the underground center who directed the MiGs that were airborne that afternoon did their job well. A flight of MiG-21s downed an F-105 and an F-4 screening the strike force. One of the Phantom escorts managed to bag one of the attacking MiGs. But the North Vietnamese Air Force had evened its score with the USAF at four jets apiece.

On May 13, F-4 Phantoms from the 8th Fighter Wing at Ubon flew against the biggest prize of them all, the 560-foot reinforced concrete and steel girder bridge that spanned the Song Ma River near Thanh Hoa: the Dragon's Jaw. Between 1965 and 1968, U.S. Air Force and Navy bombers had pounded the bridge with more than 12,500 tons of explosives without bringing it down.

This time, the Americans used deadly accurate 2,000- and 3,000-pound laser-guided bombs against their old nemesis. Fourteen Phantoms unleashed a total of sixty-nine tons of explosives over the bridge that morning. Smoke and debris belched into the air around the Dragon's Jaw. When the dust settled, an RF-4C zoomed in to take pictures of the damage. The western end of the bridge had been completely knocked off its forty-foot concrete abutment on the riverbank. The twisted and disfigured bridge had finally gone down. The North Vietnamese tried to repair the damage, but periodic strikes by navy and air force bombers kept the Dragon's Jaw out of commission until the end of the war.

By the end of the month, American bombers had destroyed thirteen bridges along the two rail lines from Hanoi to the Chinese border. Another four were down on the line between the capital and Haiphong. Several more

on the rail line leading south to the DMZ, including the Dragon's Jaw, had also been felled. By June 30, the 8th TFW alone had destroyed 106 bridges. Intelligence analysts estimated that there was no uncut stretch of the North Vietnamese rail system longer than fifty miles, forcing the enemy to divert trucks needed for the offensive in the South to carry supplies around the bombed-out choke points in the North. The crippling of its transportation network, coupled with the mining of Haiphong, severely weakened Hanoi's ability to support its invasion force in South Vietnam.

By June, North Vietnam's imports, according to American estimates, had been reduced from 160,000 tons to a mere 30,000 tons a month, and intelligence analysts guessed that the North Vietnamese were left with only two months' worth of supplies. The most serious shortage was in precious POL stocks needed to fuel the trucks and tanks committed to the offensive in the South. The mining of Haiphong Harbor had cut off North Vietnam's major source of supply—oil tankers from the Soviet Union. A few Soviet tankers anchored offshore and unloaded their oil onto shallow-draft barges which made a run for the coast under the cover of darkness. But navy jets maintained a continuous patrol overhead, waiting to pounce on the barges as soon as they cleared the safety of the neutral tankers. The only other source of supply was cut off when American bombers destroyed the POL pipeline running south from China.

Its external sources of supply gone, North Vietnam had to rely on the estimated 160,000 metric tons stored at sites scattered around the country. But by the end of June, air strikes were believed to have destroyed all the large POL tank farms holding a quarter of these supplies. More than 100,000 tons still remained in smaller dispersed sites, but distributing the oil from them put an even greater strain on North Vietnam's transportation network. Navy bombers also destroyed the pipeline running south to the DMZ, forcing the Communists to transport the POL stores by truck. Analyzing the effects of renewed U.S. bombing, Major General Robert N. Ginsburgh, of the Office of the Secretary of the Air Force, who had served as an aide to the NSC during the Johnson administration, remarked that Linebacker had "a greater impact in its first four months of operation than Rolling Thunder had in 3½ years."

"Smart bombs"

Linebacker succeeded in large part because of the widespread use of "smart bombs," such as the laser-guided bomb (LGB) used primarily by the air force and the electro-optically guided bomb (EOGB) preferred by the navy. Both were extremely accurate and packed a heavy punch. A handful of these smart bombs were now demolishing the same targets previously splattered by tons of conventional ordnance during the Rolling Thunder campaign.

The decisive role smart bombs played in the campaign was remarkable considering the fact that there were only about a dozen "Paveway One" laser-designator pods in the 7th Air Force's inventory. Nicknamed "Zot" by pilots, the system relied on the F-4 back seater visually acquiring a target through a high-powered telescope that was mounted on the canopy rail. Once he had the target lined up in the telescope's cross hairs, he would turn on the laser pod slung underneath the plane's wing. The pod moved with the movement of the telescope and shot a pulsating beam of energy from the plane to the target. Trailing aircraft then released their laser bombs within a prescribed area surrounding the beam known as the "laser basket," which enabled the bomb's optical seeker to "see"

and home in on the spot of laser light where the designator beam hit the target.

A more sophisticated laser package, known as Pave Knife, was actually built into a number of F-4 Phantoms. These planes were equipped with a TV screen in the back seat that transmitted a picture directly from a movable television camera mounted in the laser pod itself. Besides being more accurate than planes using the Paveway One system, Pave Knife aircraft could deliver their own laser bombs as well as designate targets for other aircraft. But Pave Knives were even more rare; there were only six in existence. Two were lost over North Vietnam in the opening stages of the campaign, leaving the 7th Air Force with only four to shoulder the bulk of the work.

The Dragon's Jaw

The famed Dragon's Jaw Bridge, a key link in the supply line stretching from the Hanoi-Haiphong area to the DMZ and a symbol of North Vietnamese determination, was finally destroyed by laser-guided bombs on May 13, 1972, (above), after years of unsuccessful attempts. The combination railroad and highway bridge was reopened for rail traffic (left) one year later, in time to mark the celebration of Ho Chi Minh's birthday.

*Linebacker I severely crippled the North's electrical supply.
Above. Reporters inspect damage to the Kim Band hydraulic
works south of Hanoi. Below. Rubble strews the site of the
Cua Cam hydraulic station after strikes on July 30, 1972.*

While these laser-equipped forces hit "hard" targets such as bridges and power plants, the air force and navy sent larger strike forces of up to thirty-four aircraft to drop conventional bombs against less concentrated targets, such as supply depots, troop training centers, and rail yards. The combination allowed American bombers to hit virtually every target Washington had authorized. The only exceptions were military targets in heavily populated areas, especially Hanoi and Haiphong, which were placed off-limits to avoid creating civilian casualties. But as the surgical precision of the smart bombs became ap-

parent, many of these were opened up to air strikes.

The precision of laser-guided bombs was vividly illustrated during the campaign to cripple North Vietnam's electrical system. By early June, American bombers had knocked out six power plants that provided 70 percent of the country's electrical supply. Only the thermal power plant in Hanoi, declared off-limits because of its location in the center of the city, remained operative. Destruction of the facilities forced the North Vietnamese to rely heavily on diesel-powered generators for the bulk of their electrical power; this used up more of their precious POL stores. But the North Vietnamese were ready to flick the switch on a new hydroelectric plant located sixty-seven miles northwest of Hanoi at Lang Chi that could restore virtually all the electricity that had been lost.

General Vogt's first request to hit the power station before it became operational was rejected in Washington. The plant sat on top of a large dam. If any of the bombs missed their mark and breached the dam, the ensuing flood would wipe out a number of villages downstream, killing as many as 23,000 civilians. Washington had strictly forbidden the bombing of dams and dikes to avoid such casualties. Vogt tried again, appealing directly to the chairman of the Joint Chiefs. He was confident that his pilots could knock out the plant with laser-guided bombs without hitting the dam. "If you think you can do it without destroying the dam," said JCS Chairman Admiral Thomas Moorer, "you're authorized to proceed."

General Vogt briefed the pilots of the 8th Tactical Fighter Wing at Ubon on the importance of the mission, warning them that there was no room for error. Since the building that housed the plant's four turbine generators was protected by a blast-proof roof, one flight of F-4 Phantoms would go in first to bomb a hole through the roof; a second flight would deliver the laser-guided bombs on the turbines themselves. The time-delay detonating fuses and delivery altitudes had to be calculated exactly so the bombs would explode at the precise height and not penetrate the dam itself. The pilots carried out the plan to the letter, destroying the generators without scratching the dam.

The successful raid was highly significant in light of Hanoi's propaganda campaign to convince the world that the Americans were systematically trying to destroy North Vietnam's 2,700-mile system of dikes and dams in order to ruin the country's economy by flooding farmlands and villages. Foreign journalists and Americans sympathetic to the North who visited the country during the bombing, from former U.S. Attorney General Ramsey Clark to actress Jane Fonda, were taken to view scenes of bombed-out dikes in the Red River Delta. On August 11, in a conversation with Clark, Pham Van Dong accused the U.S. of waging "a war of genocide" and deliberately bombing North Vietnamese dikes.

An investigation by the State Department, undertaken

The Pentagon answered North Vietnam's charges that U.S. planes were bombing dikes by releasing pictures like this one, which it said shows three 37mm antiaircraft guns on a dike east of Hanoi firing at U.S. reconnaissance planes.

at the request of Congressional critics at the end of July, found evidence of damage against the dikes in only twelve specific instances. Photo reconnaissance of these areas indicated that all were located near legitimate military targets such as supply depots and highways, and that the damage was the result of a few stray bombs. Although reports suggested that flooding was greater than in previous years, it was largely a conscious decision by North Vietnamese leaders (as they later admitted) to divert workers normally engaged in repairing the natural damage done to the dikes during the previous rainy season to support the invasion in the South.

Pilots particularly resented the accusations that they were indiscriminately hitting the dikes since it was the one thing they were forbidden to do. Aware that the dikes were off-limits, the North Vietnamese often routed supply trucks along roads atop the dikes and even stockpiled supplies and positioned antiaircraft guns on them to protect them against the bombers.

Although AA guns atop the dikes were considered legitimate targets if they were firing, pilots were reluctant to hit them since such an attack would trigger an intensive investigation by higher headquarters to determine the legitimacy of the pilot's decision. It was a classic "Catch-22" situation for U.S. pilots who were asked to fly into the most heavily defended airspace in the history of aerial warfare.

Protecting the strike force

North Vietnam's air defense system had grown enormously since the bombing halt in 1968. Late in 1970, Colonel Dang Tinh, a senior officer in the NVA's Air Defense Command, warned: "If the American imperialists dare to return and fight in the North it will have new plans of action, its technical weapons will have improved, and the war will be even more violent than before." Many independent military observers agreed, labeling North Vietnam's air defense system the third best in the world, behind those of the Soviet Union and Israel.

Between 1966 and 1972, the North Vietnamese almost doubled the number of their SAM sites to nearly 300. They had 1,500 AA weapons, many of them long-range, radar-guided 85MM and 100MM antiaircraft guns. Their air force had also grown by 25 percent, to a total force of nearly 250 MiGs. The entire system was tied into a centralized air defense command network that operated nearly 200 radar sites positioned throughout the country. Ground controllers at the radar stations could identify and target incoming bombers for any one of their three weapons systems (AAA, SAMs, or MiGs) or coordinate attacks by all three simultaneously.

To increase the survival rate of strike aircraft operating in this hostile environment, the Americans relied heavily on equipment designed to neutralize the enemy's radar-guided defenses. Virtually all U.S. strike aircraft were, by

1972, equipped with radar homing and warning (RHAW) gear that warned a pilot when SAM radars were tracking his aircraft. A pulsating electronic signal sounded in the pilot's headset at different levels of pitch to indicate when a missile had locked onto or been launched at his plane. Another innovation from the Rolling Thunder campaign, pods crammed with ECM equipment which emitted radio signals that confused and jammed enemy radar frequencies, were slung under the wing of fighter-bombers.

RHAW gear and ECM pods gave individual aircraft a certain measure of protection, but neither system was foolproof. The North Vietnamese often sent out dummy radar signals to confuse RHAW gear. ECM pods had a limited range and were only effective when pilots maintained a precise flight formation that provided mutual support. To augment their jamming capabilities, a number of specialized ECM aircraft accompanied strike aircraft on each mission. The air force used EB-66s filled with electronic radar detection and jamming gear. The navy modified a number of A-6 Intruders especially for ECM work. Redesignated the EA-6, the aircraft had an additional twin-seated cockpit behind the normal side-by-side front cockpit to accommodate the pilot, his bombardier-navigator, and two ECM specialists who controlled the two jamming pods underneath the jet's wings.

Specialized F-105 Thunderchiefs, known as Wild Weasels, were sent in ahead of the strike force to search out and destroy enemy SAM sites during the mission. These twin-seated F-105Gs carried special equipment designed to detect and locate SAM radar signals and Shrike antiradiation missiles that could actually home in on the signal itself. They were usually accompanied by two F-4 Phantoms carrying cluster bomb units (CBUs), which could also hit the SAM site once it was uncovered, finishing off what the antiradiation missiles had started.

Besides heavy use of Wild Weasels and ECM support planes to neutralize enemy radar and radar-guided defenses, the Americans revived a method first employed by the British RAF in World War II during a raid on Hamburg in 1943. Aircraft preceding the strike force laid down a corridor of "chaff"—thousands of strips of metal foil or metalized Fiberglas—to mask the incoming bombers from enemy radar. The strips were cut in prescribed lengths to jam certain wavelengths used by enemy radars. Air force EB-66s and F-4s, and navy EA-6As, equipped with special dispensing pods, released the chaff in cardboard tubes designed to tear apart upon release. Once the chaff entered the plane's slipstream, it created a large corridor of radar-reflecting metal in the plane's wake.

These combined countermeasures considerably reduced the effectiveness of enemy radar-guided AA guns and SAMs. The North Vietnamese missiles were averaging only one kill for every 150 missiles fired. But the large numbers of support aircraft needed to accomplish this added substantially to the cost of each mission. Out of a total strike force of eighty aircraft, only twelve to sixteen were actual strike aircraft. The rest were ECM, Wild Weasel anti-SAM, early warning radar, and other support aircraft.

Fighter escorts now had to be provided not only for the bombers but the supporting planes as well. An average of twenty jets were assigned as a MiG Combat Air Patrol (MIGCAP) to protect each strike force from enemy fighters. Pilots particularly dreaded escorting the "chaff birds" that preceded the strike force into the target. Required to fly a predictable straight course and slowed down by the extra weight of their chaff loads, the planes could not evade attack. "Flying so slow over the North is one of the hairiest things about flying chaff," said Captain Wes Zimmerman, an F-4 pilot based at Takhli. "The chaff bombers were vulnerable and the North Vietnamese knew it so they would send MiGs up to meet them."

During a chaff mission thirty miles southwest of Hanoi, Zimmerman's F-4 was hit by shrapnel from a SAM that exploded underneath his right wing. Seconds later the flight was jumped by MiGs. Zimmerman and his back seater tried to outmaneuver a MiG-21 chasing their damaged plane. Two of the MiG's Atoll missiles detonated close on the F-4's tail, sending the warning lights on Zimmerman's instrument panel into a blinking frenzy. The timely approach of another F-4 drove off the MiG, but Zimmerman's plane was in bad shape. The F-4's rudder and stabilizers were gone and its right wing flaps shredded. Zimmerman coaxed the Phantom back to Nakhon Phanom, where he made an emergency landing just seconds after the plane's engines quit.

The enemy's ability to coordinate simultaneous attacks by SAMs and MiGs underscored the sophistication of North Vietnam's air defense system. In particular, the growing aggressiveness and effectiveness of North Vietnamese MiGs alarmed the American high command. During the Linebacker campaign they proved the greatest threat to U.S. aircraft, accounting for nearly a third of all combat losses, a significant increase over their performance during Rolling Thunder.

MiGs vs. Phantoms

In May 1972, the North Vietnamese air force consisted of 246 aircraft, 120 MiG-15s and 17s, 33 MiG-19s, and 93 MiG-21s. Against them, the Americans could field a far greater number of F-4 Phantoms, which had become the primary fighter-interceptor for both the air force and the navy, although the latter still employed a number of F-8 Crusaders. While the MiG-17s and 19s could not match the F-4s' Mach 2 speed, they were very effective at low altitudes, where their superior agility could be put to good use. The Phantom and the MiG-21 were almost evenly matched. The Soviet-built fighter was only about two-thirds the size of the F-4, but its smallness made it harder to see from a distance, and its lighter weight gave it more maneuverability and a tighter turning radius. The F-4's twin engines gave it the edge in speed and rapid acceleration, but they also left a telltale trail of black smoke, which the MiG's smaller, cleaner-burning engine did not. Both carried radar-guided missiles, and some models of each also had internally or externally mounted cannon. The real differences between the two lay in tactics, supporting facilities, and the men who flew them.

Although the younger American pilots who flew during 1972 did not have the same level of experience as those who fought the 1965-68 campaign, they were still far better trained than their North Vietnamese counterparts. Most MiG pilots were recruited directly from schools, or even rice fields. One remarked that before he became a pilot he had never been in an automobile, let alone an airplane. Some were so unskilled that American pilots were credited with "downing" a number of MiGs by simply outmaneuvering them. North Vietnam lost at least six MiGs during engagements in which U.S. pilots never fired a shot. The inexperienced pilots either were forced into making a fatal error and crashing while trying to escape from a pursuing Phantom, or they simply ejected from their planes in desperation.

As time passed, the North Vietnamese developed a solid core of veteran pilots. Many received extensive training in the Soviet Union or were tutored by Soviet and North Korean advisers in North Vietnam itself. Although they were forbidden from engaging in combat, the instructors often accompanied the recruits on training flights in the immediate vicinity of their bases. The Chinese, who supplied all of North Vietnam's MiG-19s, also provided instructors for these aircraft. During the 1968-72 bombing halt, the North Vietnamese devoted a lot of time and effort to improving their pilot training programs and refining aerial tactics. They also studied U.S. tactics carefully, searching for weaknesses and planning countermeasures. "Know the enemy when he enters and kill him when he arrives," was the watchword of North Vietnamese aviators.

MiG pilots worked very closely with ground control intercept (GCI) radar controllers who monitored virtually every American plane that crossed into North Vietnamese airspace. GCI controllers assigned specific targets to pilots and directed them on an intercept course that allowed them to close in unseen behind their victims. By concentrating the MiGs in attacks on small or isolated flights they could neutralize the American's superior numbers.

Basically, MiG pilots used hit-and-run tactics. "They wouldn't attack unless they were almost positive they had a clear advantage," said one F-4 pilot. The most common intercept tactic was to approach on a course parallel to the incoming flight at a range of twelve to fifteen miles, passing by just outside the edges of an F-4's radar range. The MiGs would then circle in behind the flight and launch a high-speed attack from either a higher or a

The MiG Pilots

As they gained experience in fighting American attack aircraft, North Vietnamese air force pilots became skillful and aggressive antagonists. Right. Soviet-trained North Vietnamese pilots discuss tactics in front of a MiG-17. Far right. A MiG-17 takes off from Gia Lam airport. This heavily armed and highly maneuverable fighter was particularly effective at low altitudes. Below. North Vietnamese air force pilots run to their supersonic MiG-21s.

lower altitude. They would engage their afterburner to gain speed, fire their missiles, and either dive low for the deck or climb and pull away before the F-4s could react.

Sometimes North Vietnamese radar controllers would send in two groups of MiGs on either side of an incoming flight to attack simultaneously. If the F-4s turned to evade or engage one group, the other would be in a perfect position to pounce on their tails. Another tactic was for a flight of MiG-21s to feign an attack on a flight of F-4s and lure them into the range of MiG-17s or MiG-19s positioned nearby at a higher or lower altitude. A favorite trick of North Vietnamese pilots was to lure the F-4s into the range of SAM missile sites on the ground. U.S. pilots, well briefed on the positions of these "SAM rings," would often break off the attack. Ground controllers picked up the formation while it was turning around and passed on the information to the MiG pilots who then turned their fighters in behind the F-4s for a quick shot with a radar-guided Atoll missile.

Destroying their airfields seemed the most logical way to reduce the MiG threat. Late in May, U.S. bombers did just that. They hit nine major air bases in the span of a few weeks, sparing only the airfield at Gia Lam, which doubled as Hanoi's international airport. But the bombers could do little more than crater the runways, which could be repaired with little difficulty. In the meantime, the North Vietnamese simply moved their MiGs to bases in southern China where the Americans were prohibited from following.

When U.S. pilots were able to engage the elusive MiGs, North Vietnamese pilots immediately moved in as close as possible where their tighter turning radius and better maneuverability could counter the F-4's superior speed. "Keep close to the enemy," North Vietnamese squadron commander Luu Huy Chieu told his pilots. "That's the only way you'll shoot him down." While most MiGs were equipped with internally mounted cannon for close-in fighting, of American planes only the F-4E had a similar capability. A few others were fitted with external 20mm cannons bolted underneath the plane's fuselage, but the majority of F-4s relied on air-to-air missiles, which were less effective at close range.

The radar-guided AIM-7 Sparrow, the primary air-to-air missile used by the air force during the war, was designed as an antibomber weapon and did not have the maneuverability needed in a fighter-versus-fighter engagement. It also required the back seater to establish a radar "lock on" before firing. "In a turning fight at five Gs, it's very difficult to get that thin pencil beam of our radar dish superimposed on a tiny MiG when the ranges and angles are changing so rapidly," said Major Henry Bielinski. At the same time, the back seater was constantly craning his neck to check the six o'clock position for other MiGs coming in behind.

While the Sparrow had only a 10 percent kill ratio, the heat-seeking AIM-9 Sidewinder was rated slightly better

at 22 percent. Navy planes employed it in almost all of their kills. Air force F-4s rarely carried Sidewinders, relying instead on their 20mm cannon, if they had them, for close-in work. But it was difficult for a pilot to switch quickly from the radar missile system to the gun mode. He had to manipulate a number of switches in the heat of battle to accomplish the transfer. Eventually, the switch panel was modified, and during Linebacker air force F-4s achieved 50 percent of their kills with 20mm cannon.

By late June, the North Vietnamese, for the first time in the war, were scoring more kills than the U.S. Air Force. The air force came under increasing pressure from the Pentagon, which pointed to the navy's far better record—a twelve to one kill ratio. The disparity was indicative of differing philosophies on air-to-air tactics and equipment and the varying combat conditions navy and air force pilots faced in their respective zones of responsibility.

When the air force withdrew its F-105 Thunderchiefs from combat in Southeast Asia in 1970, the 7th Air Force had to rely on its F-4 Phantoms as fighter-bombers as well as fighter-interceptors, and its pilots had to train for both roles. The navy, on the other hand, made a conscious effort to separate the two roles, employing its A-4s, A-6s, and A-7s as attack aircraft, while its F-4s were used mainly as fighter-interceptors. The navy had also established a combat training program in 1968, known as Top Gun, utilizing the lessons learned during the Rolling Thunder campaign to refine and improve its air-to-air tactics. In mock air battles, F-4 pilots were pitted against other navy pilots trained in MiG tactics who flew smaller A-4 Skyhawks, which resembled the MiGs in profile and performance, under the control of radar controllers using Soviet/North Vietnamese tactics.

Another reason for the navy's success was the fact that their targets were usually closer to the coast. Coming in from the sea, carrier-based jets only had to face a fighter threat in a 180-degree radius in front of them. Their opposition came mainly from slower MiG-17s, which the North Vietnamese felt were more of a match for the navy's A-6 and A-7 attack bombers than the air force's faster F-4 fighter-bombers.

Perhaps the biggest advantage for navy Phantom pilots was that they almost always operated within a friendly radar environment. The navy kept a radar ship stationed a few miles offshore that could look up the Red River Delta region as far as the MiG airfields north of Hanoi. Air controllers aboard these ships, code named Red Crown, kept a close watch on MiG activity. They warned pilots of MiG threats to the force and directed fighters to intercept them.

Air force jets did not enjoy the same luxury. Flying from bases in Thailand, the F-4s had to cross 100 miles of defended airspace to reach their targets in the Red River Delta. Operating in the enemy's backyard, constantly monitored by his radar, and far beyond the limits of their own radar sites in Thailand, they had to fight their way in and their way out. "In a way the situation is similar to the conditions during World War II," said General William Momyer, the former commander of the 7th Air Force who took over the Tactical Air Command in 1968, "when the German fighters were able to pick the place and time of engagement with our penetrating bomber forces. The North Vietnamese have the same kind of advantage because they know where our strike forces are going while we, because of the absence of radar coverage, are fighting tactically from a defensive position."

Gradually, the 7th Air Force began coordinating with the navy to integrate its pilots into the sea-based radar system. The air force also began stationing EC-121 early-warning radar planes, known by the call sign Disco, along the Laotian border and in the Gulf of Tonkin to act as airborne command and control centers for its fighters. Overall control of all aircraft operating in North Vietnam rested with the 7th Air Force's special controlling facility at Nakhon Phanom, code named Teaball, which monitored and collated reports from a variety of surveillance sources, both radar and communications intelligence, and relayed the updated information to pilots via Disco or Red Crown.

Teaball's air controllers provided valuable information that allowed American pilots to meet the North Vietnamese on their own terms. Not only could they warn a pilot of a MiG and give its location, but they could also tell whether it was a MiG-17 (Red Bandit), MiG-19 (White Bandit), or a MiG-21 (Blue Bandit). By monitoring an enemy aircraft from the moment it took off from the airfield, Teaball could also determine when the MiG was low on gas by calculating its speed and the time it had been airborne against the plane's fuel capacity and consumption rate. American pilots' eyes would light up when they heard Teaball controllers call out a Black Bandit, the code words for a MiG low on fuel.

The words "Heads up, Green Bandit" brought quite a different reaction from American pilots. It meant that their opposition was one of North Vietnam's top aviators, one of the experienced fighter pilots whose names were well

The first air force aces of the war, Capt. Steve Ritchie (left) and Capt. Charles DeBellevue, stand by their F-4. Each star signifies a downed MiG.

known to American intelligence experts who monitored enemy radio communications. Many of these Green Bandits were aces, having shot down five or more American planes. With the refinements in tactics and radar support, the American forces soon began producing more aerial aces of their own.

Between August 1 and October 15, the air force's kill ratio improved dramatically, matching the four-to-one level during the highest point of Rolling Thunder. On August 28, after seven years of combat in Southeast Asia, the air force also produced its first ace of the war when Captain Richard S. "Steve" Ritchie downed his fifth MiG-21. Twelve days later, Captain Charles B. DeBellevue, who was Ritchie's back seater during four of his five victories, teamed with another pilot to down two more MiGs, bringing his total to six kills. On October 13, Captain Jeffrey S. Feinstein became the air force's second bombardier-navigator ace of the war.

Ten days after Feinstein's fifth victory, Operation Linebacker came to an end. Thanks to the use of smart bombs, technological advances in electronic countermeasures, and improvements in air-to-air tactics, U.S. pilots had achieved their objectives. Linebacker played a crucial role in halting the enemy offensive in the South by drying up the sources of supply that were vital to sustain an invasion force armed and equipped for conventional warfare.

The stalled offensive in the South and the devastation caused by the bombing in the North had helped to bring Hanoi back to the peace table in early August. North Vietnamese negotiators dropped many of their more strident political demands, including the participation of the Vietcong in the Saigon government, and agreed to discuss terms for a cease-fire. As a gesture of good faith, Nixon had ordered a bombing halt on October 23, a week before the formal agreements worked out between Kissinger and North Vietnamese negotiators were to be signed in Paris. On October 26, Kissinger told reporters that "peace is at hand." But his prophecy was not to be fulfilled until after American bombers entered the skies of North Vietnam one last time.

The Christmas Bombings

The peace that Henry Kissinger had seemed to promise in October looked ever more distant in November. The talks in Paris between Americans and the North Vietnamese broke down, and on December 13, the talks broke off without even the semblance of agreement. The following day, an exasperated Nixon sent an ultimatum to Hanoi, advising them to return to the negotiating table within seventy-two hours. When Hanoi refused, Nixon once again played his best, perhaps his only, bargaining card—American air power. This time he was ready to open up for attack virtually every target of military and economic significance in North Vietnam. "I don't want any more of this crap about the fact that we couldn't hit this target or that one," Nixon told the chairman of the Joint Chiefs, Admiral Thomas Moorer. "This is your chance to use military power to win this war." He melodramatically added: "And if you don't, I'll hold you responsible."

Major Bob Connelly, an F-4 flight commander

with the 13th TFS at Udorn, was preparing to meet his wife in Bangkok when his squadron commander called him into his office and asked him to cancel his leave. "Why?" asked Connelly. "I can't tell you," answered his CO, "but I've got to have you fly." Since the end of Linebacker, Connelly's squadron had flown a few missions in Laos and the southern panhandle of North Vietnam, but none was of major significance. Now rumors were flying around the base that something big was brewing. No one knew what it was until a few days later, December 18, when the 13th's pilots filed into the squadron briefing room.

"We're going downtown tonight," said the briefing officer. The F-4 pilots could not believe their ears. They had rarely flown night bombing missions over Hanoi and thought such a mission was suicidal. The briefing officer quickly told them they would not be carrying any bombs. Instead, they would be flying fighter support for other aircraft. He slid back a panel on the briefing board to reveal a map marked with thick, black lines, all leading toward Hanoi. "The BUFs are going downtown," he said. BUF was the fighter pilot's euphemism for a B-52, which, in its bowdlerized version, stood for Big Ugly Fellow. The natural rivalry between fighter and bomber pilots had intensified during the war. Many fighter jocks were embittered by the fact that B-52 crews were awarded the same medals for missions over relatively peaceful South Vietnam that they earned for flying in the heavily defended airspace over the North. At the briefing in Udorn that afternoon, the consensus among the fighter pilots was: "These guys are finally going to earn their combat pay."

For the B-52s, it would indeed be a new ball game. Up to then, they had acted as a sort of long-range artillery for ground forces in South Vietnam and Laos, while the fighter-bombers took on the heavily defended targets in the North. "The crews welcomed the opportunity to use the 52 the way it was designed—as a strategic bomber," said Lieutenant General Gerald W. Johnson, commander of the Strategic Air Command's 8th Air Force at Andersen AFB, Guam. "We were finally called upon to go right into the teeth of the tiger and get the toughest targets in the toughest environment."

The decision to employ the B-52s on a large scale was motivated by both political and tactical considerations. For the first time in the war, military leaders were given the opportunity to prove their claims that unrestricted bombing could bring Hanoi to its knees. The only real constraint imposed by Washington was the desire to avoid civilian casualties. The president's intent was clearly reflected in the directive issued by the JCS to its commanders in the field. The operation, code named Line-

backer II, called for "a three-day maximum effort, repeat maximum effort, of B-52/TACAIR strikes in the Hanoi/Haiphong areas. . . . Object is maximum destruction of selected military targets." The cable also advised air commanders to be prepared to extend the bombing campaign after the third day for an indefinite duration.

Another reason for bringing the B-52s into action was the fact that the September-through-May monsoon season in North Vietnam made visual bombing strikes by fighter-bombers difficult. The B-52s, with their own radar bomb navigation systems, would hit larger targets on the outskirts of the two cities at night, while the fighter-bombers would strike smaller targets close to populated areas by day with either laser-guided bombs or LORAN radar-guided bombing techniques.

The B-52s would carry the bulk of the burden. SAC's reputation as the nation's foremost offensive weapon was now on the line. Responsibility for the success of the mission lay with General John C. Meyer and his staff at SAC headquarters in Omaha, Nebraska. They would select the specific targets and the number of bombers for each mission, determine tactics, and plot the routes in and out of the target areas. In line with the JCS directive, their plan for day one of the operation, December 18, called for a force of 129 bombers, divided into three waves spaced about four to five hours apart, to hit five targets in the Hanoi area. It would be the largest heavy bomber operation mounted by the U.S. Air Force since World War II.

The orders reached 8th Air Force headquarters on December 15, giving General Johnson and his staff only three days to prepare. To meet SAC's strike force requirement, they would have to draw on more than half of their total inventory of approximately 150 B-52s based at Andersen Air Force Base on Guam and 60 more at U-Tapao, Thailand. The need to allocate radio identification "call signs" for the B-52s required some ingenuity. Traditionally, each formation of three B-52s, known as a "cell," was assigned a color as its call sign. But for this huge flotilla, some forty-three colors were needed. "They'd gone clear down to peppermint and bronze," said one pilot.

In addition to the B-52s, other air force, navy, and marine units were called on for supporting aircraft, including F-4 fighter escorts, radar-jamming planes, chaff planes, F-105 Wild Weasels, search and rescue teams, and KC-135 refueling tankers. Coordinating all these aircraft sent in from different directions into a precisely timed schedule was no easy task. During the preflight briefing that afternoon, crews received reams of complicated instructions detailing navigational headings, aerial refueling locations and schedules, the various radio frequencies and call signs of the supporting planes, the initial point where they would turn onto their final bomb run headings, exit routes, and designated bail-out areas. The crews had only a few hours to digest all of this information before they were loaded on buses and driven to waiting planes.

The scene at Andersen AFB, known to SAC personnel as "the Rock," brought back memories of the 8th Air Force's heyday nearly forty years before when its B-17s and B-24s lined up on airstrips in England for their massive daylight raids against Germany. The entire flight ramp paralleling the runway was jammed with B-52s parked nose to tail. Ground crews and base workers, many who had been up all night preparing the bombers for the afternoon launch, lined the runway to watch the procession of bomb-laden B-52s slowly taxi past the arming area and onto the runway.

At 2:41 P.M., the first Stratofortress soared into the air. Within minutes, the first wave of twenty-seven B-52s was airborne. After assembling in cells of three, they chased the sun west across the Pacific. During the 3,000-mile flight to the Vietnamese coast, there was little to do but watch and wait. Each six-man crew checked and rechecked instrument readings. In the front cockpit, the pilot and copilot worked the eight throttles that controlled the jet's engines. Below them, in a separate compartment, were the table navigator and radar navigator who mapped headings and courses and monitored the bomb load. Behind the pilot and copilot, facing the rear of the plane, sat the electronic warfare officer who worked the equipment that detected and jammed enemy radar. Next to him sat the tail gunner, who manned the B-52's four rearward-firing .50-caliber machine guns. In the older D models, the tail gunner sat in a turret in the tail of the plane.

After refueling from KC-135 tankers over the Philippines, they headed inland across South Vietnam and into Cambodia, where they turned north and joined another group of twenty-one B-52s from the U-Tapao airfield in Thailand. Strung out in a line about seventy miles long, the forty-eight bombers made their way north, almost to the Chinese border, before they turned south along Thud Ridge and headed toward the Red River Valley and Hanoi. It was the same route that fighter-pilots had been using since the beginning of the war. But now it was the B-52s' turn to run the gauntlet of MiGs, SAMs, and AAA that defended the North Vietnamese capital.

Thirty-nine support planes flew ahead to prepare the

On November 23, 1972, Henry Kissinger and Le Duc Tho (right) confer outside Paris. Three weeks later, the negotiations broke down.

way. Air force EB-66s and navy and marine EA-6s took up their positions at a safe distance from the targets and began jamming enemy radar. F-105 Wild Weasels searched out and attacked any SAM sites that turned their radars on the strike force, while F-4s laid down corridors of chaff immediately in front of the B-52s. They were accompanied by other Phantoms flying anti-MiG escort for the entire strike force. Even with all these supporting aircraft, the B-52 pilots expected it to be a rough ride.

The biggest threat would come from the nearly thirty SAM sites with more than 200 missile launchers that ringed Hanoi and Haiphong. Cruising at an altitude of 36,000 feet, the huge bombers flew at the SA-2's optimum effective range. To ensure accuracy, the B-52s were under strict orders not to deviate from their preplanned bombing course, even to evade a SAM attack. A B-52 pilot would be hard pressed anyway to outmaneuver a SAM traveling at Mach 2 in the huge, bomb-laden planes that some pilots equated to driving "a Mack truck with four flat tires." The only thing that stood between them and the SAMs was their own radar-jamming gear, the supporting ECM aircraft, and Wild Weasels.

As the first bombers reached the outskirts of Hanoi, Captain Hal Wilson in the lead plane from U-Tapao reported "wall-to-wall SAMs" ahead. "The whole sky was lit up with the red glow of their engines," said another pilot. Crewmen counted at least fifty of the missiles. The North Vietnamese were firing them in salvos of three or more at a time. One B-52, damaged by shrapnel from an exploding SAM, was forced to head back to U-Tapao before it reached its target. Lieutenant Colonel Don Rissi was leading the last three cells of the first wave over the Yen Vien railroad yards when the North Vietnamese salvoed seventeen SAMs at once toward the cluster of nine B-52s. Two of the missiles caught Rissi's B-52 two minutes from the bomb release point, damaging the crew compartment and setting the plane on fire. Thirty seconds later, the B-52 went out of control, spinning earthward like a huge burning leaf. Three of the crew bailed out before the fuel tanks caught fire, but Rissi was not among them. The plane disintegrated into thousands of metal pieces as nearly

150,000 pounds of fuel exploded. The resulting fireball "lit the valley almost as bright as day," said a watching F-4 Phantom pilot.

Two were gone, but the B-52s kept coming. According to Lieutenant Steve Bricker, an F-4 pilot flying escort for the last two waves of B-52s that night, the scene reminded him of a World War II movie as the long lines of slow-moving bombers continued to roll in over Hanoi. "It looked like a big ballet in the sky," he said.

There were inevitable miscues and slip-ups in the carefully orchestrated plan of attack. The B-52 crews were not accustomed to flying in large formations, let alone while under attack from surface-to-air missiles which many were seeing for the first time. Some violated instructions and broke formation to avoid oncoming SAMs, while others had difficulty keeping track of the other planes in their cell. Radio frequencies were saturated with a confused clutter of voices making radio identification difficult. Two cells of B-52s with the similar-sounding call signs of "cream" and "green" had such a difficult time identifying themselves that the commander of the first cell changed his call sign to "ice cream." Communications between the B-52s and their F-4 escorts, which flew at a lower altitude, were just as confused. "We flew with every light on we could find," said Bricker, because "you had a few scared B-52 tail gunners firing at anything they thought they saw out there."

The tail gunner in Brown 3, however, made no mistake about his target. Staff Sergeant Samuel O. Turner was calling off SAM sightings after his plane had released its bombs and was turning to head home when he picked up an unidentified "bogie" on his radar. A low-flying MiG-21 was closing in on the bomber's tail in a rapid climb. Turner quickly locked his radar-guided guns onto the onrushing MiG and fired a burst as the swept-wing jet came within range. A gigantic explosion rocked the B-52 just as the blip disappeared from Turner's radar scope. Back at base, another tail gunner confirmed the kill, reporting he had seen the MiG explode in a brilliant fireball. Turner became the first B-52 tail gunner and the first noncommissioned airman since the Korean War to shoot down an enemy plane.

Few MiGs attacked that night, however. Twenty-one B-52s in the first wave had hit the three main MiG bases surrounding Hanoi. As expected, the B-52s' main antagonists were the high-flying SAMs. More than 200 were launched that night, bringing down only three of the bombers and damaging two others. Ninety-four percent of the B-52s released their bombs on their targets. By the time the last wave of bombers returned to Guam late the next day, pilots scheduled to fly in the first wave of the following night's mission were already revving up their engines.

The tactics and plan of attack for the second strike were virtually identical to those of the first night. The B-52s attacked from the same general direction, executing a ninety-degree turn over the target after releasing their bombs and exiting along a westward route (see map, page 156). The results of day two were better than they could have hoped for. All ninety-three B-52s struck their targets on schedule without any loss. One B-52 in the first wave received minor damage. Two planes in the second wave were hit harder, but both dropped their bombs on target and limped home safely.

Although some of the crews began questioning the repetitive plan of attack and recommended changes in tactics and variations in the direction of approach to avoid falling into a predictable pattern, SAC headquarters judged the lead time required to develop a new plan and make the necessary adjustments too prohibitive. Their mandate was to apply maximum pressure against North Vietnam for three days. Considering the loss-free mission on the nineteenth, they decided to continue with the same game plan the following night. It would prove to be a costly mistake.

The darkest hour

The plan for December 20 called for a total of ninety-nine B-52s to move in from the northwest and attack targets around Hanoi and Haiphong in three waves. All but two cells in the first wave of thirty-three bombers were targeted against the Yen Vien railroad yards on the northern outskirts of Hanoi. Again, the bombers flew in typical SAC fashion, strung out in a long line at 36,000 feet following in the wake of the chaff planes which laid down their protective corridors. By now, the North Vietnamese knew the pattern of attack by heart.

Pilots in the first wave of B-52s that night noticed a number of MiGs shadowing them during their approach run. "We quickly learned what the MiGs had been up to," said Captain Roland A. Scott. "Apparently the MiG-21 we saw was flying with us to report [our] heading, altitude and airspeed to the missile sites." Several SAMs were launched simultaneously from opposite directions at Scott's aircraft soon after the MiG's departure. They arrived in pairs a few seconds apart and were set to detonate at the altitude called in by the MiG pilot rather than relying on their radar guidance system, which could be jammed by American aircraft.

Scott's plane was rocked by the blast from the clusters of SAMs exploding around it. "One exploded so close and caused such a loud noise and violent shock that I told the crew I thought we had been hit." But Scott's plane made it through with only minor damage. Three other B-52s in the first seven cells over Yen Vien, however, never made it back. They were all hit by surface-to-air missiles just as they made their turns over the target after releasing their bombs. Two went down immediately, while a third reached Thailand before the crew was forced to abandon the plane.

When the news reached SAC headquarters in Omaha, Gen. Meyer had to decide whether to cancel the second two waves in light of the heavy losses. He and his staff were under pressure from higher authorities, both military and civilian, who had questioned sending the multi-million-dollar bombers in against Hanoi's defenses in the first place. "Many people in Washington were worried that the Air Force would fail," said Meyer's deputy chief of staff for intelligence, General Harry N.

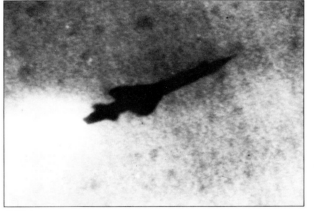

SAM missiles posed a lethal threat to the B-52s. Top. Near Hanoi, an SA-2 sits on its launcher. Above. A SAM in flight, photographed by an RF-101 Voodoo.

brunt of Hanoi's defenses. But the third wave, with three of its four targets in the Hanoi area, suffered the same fate as the first wave. Three more B-52s plunged to earth in flames, and two more were damaged. The losses prompted an outburst of criticism in Washington. Some were already labeling the strikes a "blood bath" and warned that SAC could not afford to lose many more Strato-fortresses without losing its reputation and prestige as well. Even the B-52 crews were be-

Cordes. "Many senior Air Force people were concerned that if the bombing continued, we would lose too many bombers and airpower doctrine would have proven fallacious. Or if the bombing were stopped, the same thing would occur." After polling his staff, Meyer wired 8th AF headquarters with his decision: "Press on!"

Four hours later, the second wave hit the power plant at Thai Nguyen and the supply transshipment point at Bac Giang. Since both targets were well to the north and northeast of the capital, the B-52s did not have to face the

ginning to question the wisdom of their superiors.

The tactics were basically the same as those that had been employed by SAC in Arc Light missions over South Vietnam since 1965. The three B-52s in each cell flew in a single file, maintaining a distance of at least 1,500 yards between them, and each cell followed a mile or so behind another. These bomber streams, which pilots jokingly referred to as "the baby elephant walk," proved excellent for maximizing bomb coverage in their designated target "boxes." But it did not take long for B-52 crews to realize

151

that the baby elephant walk courted disaster in the heavily defended skies over the North.

"We had a formation approximately 70 miles long of one aircraft behind the other lumbering toward North Vietnam," said Captain Robert E. Wolff, "all using the same route, altitude and heading. If 36 aircraft turned at a certain point to a certain heading, it does not require much of an educated guess to decide where to aim at number 37." The predictability of the B-52s' pattern of attack allowed SAM operators to fire their missiles without turning on their radar tracking gear, thus neutralizing American ECM and Wild Weasels. Since the B-52s were a big target and a SAM did not have to score a direct hit to inflict major damage, they merely approximated the heading, speed, and altitude of the formation, then fired off a barrage of missiles fitted with proximity fuses set to explode at the desired altitude.

While many expected the B-52s to be most vulnerable on the last leg of their bombing runs, when they had to fly straight and level to ensure accuracy, most of the bombers were hit as they were leaving the target area. The strike plans during the first three days called for the B-52s to make a 180-degree turn over the target after dropping their bombs, then head back the same way they had come under the protection of the chaff corridors. But during the banking turn the aircraft exposed its maximum profile to SAM radars, while its own ECM jamming signals, then pointed skyward from antennas underneath the plane, were rendered useless.

Crews at both bases complained about the carbon-copy-style plans of attack being sent down from SAC headquarters. "The crews were concerned over tactics that we believed injurious to our health," said Wolff, "and we were very vocal about these in our debriefings." During briefings, heated remarks passed between staff officers and crewmen, who were now openly challenging the predictable, repetitive strike plans. Some crewmen even wrote letters to higher headquarters pointing out the flaws in their tactics and suggesting changes. But SAC was an extremely centralized operation with a tightly regimented chain of command. The idea of bomber crews suggesting changes in tactics was heresy in a service whose training emphasized the strict guidelines and controls essential to their primary function as a nuclear deterrent force.

Still, SAC commanders realized something had to be done to reduce losses. They needed time to figure out a solution, but there was to be no respite in the bombing. At the end of the initial three-day maximum effort, Washington ordered the raids to continue indefinitely. SAC headquarters decided to let the B-52s at U-Tapao carry the ball for the next few days. The decision was partly due to the fact that of the six bombers lost to date, four were "G" models which were fitted with unmodified ECM equipment. G models made up two-thirds of the B-52 fleet based in Guam, while all of the B-52s at U-Tapao were

"D" models which carried larger bomb loads and were equipped with a more sophisticated and apparently more effective ECM package.

SAC commanders insisted on sticking to the same tactics however, and losses continued to mount. On December 21, thirty B-52Ds from U-Tapao were sent against three new targets—the airfield at Quang Te and the storage depots at Van Dien and Bach Mai south of Hanoi. Scarlet 1, the lead plane in the first cell targeted for Bach Mai, lost its radar just as it was making its final approach. Captain Pete Giroux tried to jockey the bomber behind one of the trailing planes so he could use its radar to drop his bombs. But in the process, Scarlet 1 drifted out of the chaff corridor and became separated from the other two bombers. Deprived of the mutually supporting ECM pattern of the cell, the isolated bomber fell to an alert SAM crew.

Four minutes later, Blue cell began its run on Bach Mai. By now the SAM firings had become so rapid that the co-pilot aboard Blue 1 remarked: "It looks like we'll walk on SAMs tonight." Blue 1 never made it to the target. Before reaching its bomb release point, the B-52 was bracketed above and below by two exploding SAMs. Shrapnel set the left wing on fire and shattered the cockpit glass, wounding the pilot. Cold air rushed through the hole, decompressing the cabin pressure and spreading the fire. The pilot pressed the alarm light signaling the crew to bail out.

Lieutenant Colonel Bill Conlee watched two SAMs skyrocket past him as he drifted earthward in his parachute. Blue 1's electronic warfare officer was bleeding from shrapnel wounds on his face and arm, but he steered the chute clear of a large river by tugging on the directional cords with his good arm and headed toward an open field. When he was within 300 feet of the ground, Conlee began to think he had made it down undetected. But a burst of gunfire that whistled past him quickly shattered Conlee's thoughts of escape.

"I touched down, dumped my chute and took off my helmet and at once was set upon by a mob of North Vietnamese, both civilian and military. They immediately took my gun, watch, and my boots. They then stripped me at gunpoint to my underwear and forced me to run for approximately a mile through a gauntlet of people with farm implements, clubs and bamboo poles. During this wild scene, several blows succeeded in breaking ribs and badly damaging my right knee. The mob scene ended when they halted me in front of a Russian truck, which was used to transport me to Hanoi."

Conlee spent the first three days in solitary confinement in the section of Hao Lo prison known as Heartbreak Hotel. The solitude was occasionally interrupted by "beating and kicking sessions by my captors in an effort to force me to my feet and to persuade me to talk to them," he said. But with his injuries, Conlee could not have stood up even if he wanted to. On Christmas Day he managed to sit in an upright position long enough to drink a pot of tea.

As the losses grew, morale among the B-52 crews plummeted, particularly at U-Tapao, where crews were assigned to fly virtually all of the missions between December 21 and 23. Stories spread of pilots exaggerating maintenance problems in order to get their planes taken off combat status. Flight surgeons found more and more crewmen lining up outside their offices during sick call. According to Dana Drenkowski, an F-4 pilot during Linebacker II who had previously served as a B-52 pilot, two doctors he talked to "specifically used the term 'mutiny' to describe what was happening."

Although the air force admitted that there was some concern expressed by B-52 crews over tactics, its spokesmen vehemently denied allegations of a near mutiny. They cited only one instance where an officer refused to fly. While critics of the war pointed to the rumors of disaffection among the crews to buttress their calls for a halt to the bombing, they were off the mark. Virtually every U.S. airman in Southeast Asia enthusiastically supported the objectives of the Linebacker II campaign. As one pilot noted: "We felt that even though we might lose a couple of people, hell, let's get this Goddamn war over with so we don't have to stay here forever."

After nearly eight frustrating years of limited and heavily restricted bombing operations against North Vietnam, pilots were finally allowed to launch the kind of strategic bombing blitz that they and their commanders had been asking for since 1965, one which they believed would destroy Hanoi's will and ability to continue the war. Even those B-52 crewmen who disagreed with the tactics employed were in agreement that Linebacker II was long overdue. According to Capt. Robert Wolff, "at last it seemed that we were going to attempt to end this war and everyone was proud to have some part in that operation."

Night and day

During the two days before Christmas, while SAC headquarters wrestled with the problem of new tactics, the B-52s were targeted increasingly against SAM sites around Hanoi and Haiphong. SAMs were still a big problem for the B-52s, but MiGs were scarce. For the first time, U.S. planes were authorized to hit North Vietnamese air bases on a continuous basis. In addition to B-52s, air force and navy fighter-bombers hit the airfields by day. But what really broke the back of the North Vietnamese air force were the preemptive strikes launched by air force F-111s against the airfields every night before the B-52s went in.

Nicknamed the Aardvark because of its long, slender nose, the F-111 was one of the most controversial and costly aircraft ever built. It was originally designed to meet both navy and air force requirements for a carrier-based interceptor and an all-weather, radar-delivery fighter-bomber. Instead of saving an estimated $1 billion in separate fighter programs, cost overruns and defects in construction more than tripled the initial price tag for each aircraft. Structural modifications added eight tons to the weight of the plane; this precluded it from taking off from carriers and caused the navy to cancel its contract. The high costs and technical problems were largely a result of the F-111's radically new design concept.

Like the navy's A-6 Intruder, the F-111 was equipped with a sophisticated attack radar system capable of around-the-clock, all-weather weapons delivery. But unlike the A-6's system, which plotted a course to the desired target and provided the crew with the precise moment of bomb delivery, the F-111's ballistics computer continuously plotted the impact point of any bomb relative to the aircraft's speed, altitude, and heading. Instead of following a predetermined path which brought the plane in straight and level on the actual bomb delivery run, an F-111 pilot could close in on a target from any direction, altitude, and speed to release his bombs.

The F-111's real edge lay in its terrain-following radar system which read the lay of the land and actually "flew" the aircraft at a constant, predetermined altitude. The F-111 could fly thousands of miles over hilly terrain in poor weather at supersonic speeds, never getting higher than 200 feet above the ground. By hugging the ground, the F-111 could use the terrain to mask itself from enemy radar. The low-level attack also kept it well below the effective altitude of any SAMs, and its Mach 1 speed made the plane almost immune to AA fire.

After a compressed schedule of testing in 1967, the air force rushed a detachment of eight F-111s to Thailand in March 1968 to participate in the last phases of the Rolling Thunder campaign. During fifty-five night missions over North Vietnam, three of the jets disappeared without a trace, presumably lost in crashes due to either equipment malfunctions or pilot error. The F-111 was quickly pulled out of combat for further testing and crew training.

The jets would not return to Southeast Asia until September 1972, when the 474th Wing was deployed to Takhli AFB, Thailand, during the last month of Linebacker I. Bill Coltman, a veteran of the earlier combat deployment, flew the wing's first mission over the North a few days after their arrival. "We never heard from him again," said one of his wing mates. It was like 1968 all over again as pilots had difficulty finding their targets, and unexplained losses continued to pile up. The commander of the 7th Air Force, General John Vogt, considered pulling the F-111s out of combat for a second time. But the end of Linebacker I in late October gave the air force time to identify and correct the problems caused by equipment malfunctions, inadequate training in the U.S., and a lack of understanding by 7th Air Force planners who were unfamiliar with the F-111's unique capabilities and sent the planes against targets that did not show up well on radar. By the time Linebacker II began, the much-maligned F-111s were rapidly winning high marks at 7th Air Force headquarters.

They were so effective in their surprise attacks on MiG airfields during the first few nights of the campaign that Gen. Vogt decided to use them against the SAM sites that were proving so troublesome to the B-52s. The F-111's low cruising altitude kept it well below the SAM's effective range while it hit the sites with 500- and 750-pound low-drag Snakeye bombs. Soon the F-111s were flying an average of twenty-four sorties per night over North Vietnam, hitting power plants, railroad yards, and other targets.

The North Vietnamese were never able to detect the supersonic, low-level intruders which they called "whispering death." No sooner would they sound the all-clear alert after a bombing raid than they would be surprised by a lone F-111 streaking toward them unannounced to drop its bombs. One of the few F-111 pilots shot down during Linebacker II recalled one of his guards approaching him and saying: "You F-111." He made a flat sweeping motion with the palm of his hand, and in an awed tone said: "Whoosh!"

While the F-111s and B-52s pounded targets by night, air force, navy, and marine fighter-bombers struck by day. TAC alone averaged nearly 100 sorties per day, and some wings in Thailand launched fifty to sixty aircraft at a time. "Sometimes it would take you an hour by the time you started your engines until you finished going through the arming area and you would be sitting nose to tail all the way out," said an F-4 pilot at Udorn. They usually were sent in against pinpoint targets such as bridges, including the Doumer and Canal Rapides bridges near Hanoi, and smaller railroad yards and spur lines.

Ninety percent of the time, the pilots were forced to fly on instruments and drop their bombs by radar. F-4s equipped with LORAN radar bombing gear acted as pathfinders for A-7 Corsairs which had limited radar capabilities of their own. During the rare periods of good weather, F-4s carrying laser bombs hit targets close to heavily populated areas, such as the Hanoi thermal power plant, and those that the B-52s had missed. One of these was Radio Hanoi, the main communications center for the North Vietnamese Army and the source of constant propaganda broadcasts by "Hanoi Hannah."

B-52s hit the radio station during the first few days, demolishing the main power supply, the nearby barracks, and several other outbuildings. They failed, however, to scratch the tiny building housing the actual transmitter and antennas which was surrounded by a thick twenty-foot-tall concrete revetment. F-111s tried again, but the radio stayed on the air with the help of diesel-powered generators. Finally, during a break in the weather, a flight of F-4s hit the transmitting station with laser-guided bombs. The 2,000- and 3,000-pound bombs landed smack in the center of the walled-in compound, which reflected the blast effect inward and leveled the structure to the ground. Hanoi Hannah remained off the air for the remainder of the campaign.

Casualties were extremely light among the fighter-bombers. Fewer than a dozen tactical aircraft were lost during the entire campaign. Strangely enough, they encountered very little opposition from the North Vietnamese air defense system during their daylight missions. "They weren't shooting a thing in the daytime," said one F-4 pilot. "It was just eerily quiet. No SAMs, no triple A, no nothing. You could put on an airshow and nobody was there to bother you. They were saving it all for at night and the B-52s."

The beginning of the end

Over Christmas the Americans observed a thirty-six-hour cease-fire; then the bombers returned in full force, a total of 120 B-52s aimed at ten targets, two in Haiphong, one at Thai Nguyen, and seven in Hanoi itself. Strategic Air Command headquarters had finally authorized the tactical changes pilots and local commanders had been urging. Ten waves of bombers would attack from seven different directions in a single, simultaneous assault in order to overwhelm North Vietnam's air defenses. The lead plane in each wave was given the same time-over-target so that all 120 B-52s would drop their bombs within a fifteen-minute time span. To confuse the enemy further, each wave would approach its target at a different altitude and exit by a different route.

The number of supporting aircraft was increased to a total of 113 planes. Chaff tactics were revised. Instead of sowing their metal strips in corridors, the chaff planes dropped large clouds directly above the targets. This prevented the North Vietnamese from learning ahead of time the route of the approaching strike force and also gave the B-52s more room to maneuver when the SAMs began arcing toward them. Electronic warfare officers aboard the B-52s had also been briefed on the results of specialized tests conducted in the U.S. that analyzed enemy radar frequencies and ECM procedures during the initial stages of the campaign. The tests confirmed the weaknesses of the B-52G model's unmodified ECM equipment, and for the remainder of the campaign the Gs were used only against less heavily defended targets outside the Hanoi area.

Pilot morale went sky-high. Although the changes in tactics had created a complicated strike plan that demanded precision timing and teamwork, the crews welcomed the challenge. Major Bill Stoker, who was selected to fly the lead B-52 from the Guam force, recalled the sight as he taxied his plane onto the runway a few minutes before takeoff. "As far as we could see there were B-52s lined up nose-to-tail. It's difficult to describe the feeling of leading such a vast array of power."

As the B-52s roared off the Rock, a Soviet intelligence-gathering trawler cruising off the coast radioed word of the launch to Hanoi. The North Vietnamese had no doubt about their destination. During the two-day pause, they

An F-111 flies toward a target in North Vietnam. Communists called the fighter-bomber "whispering death."

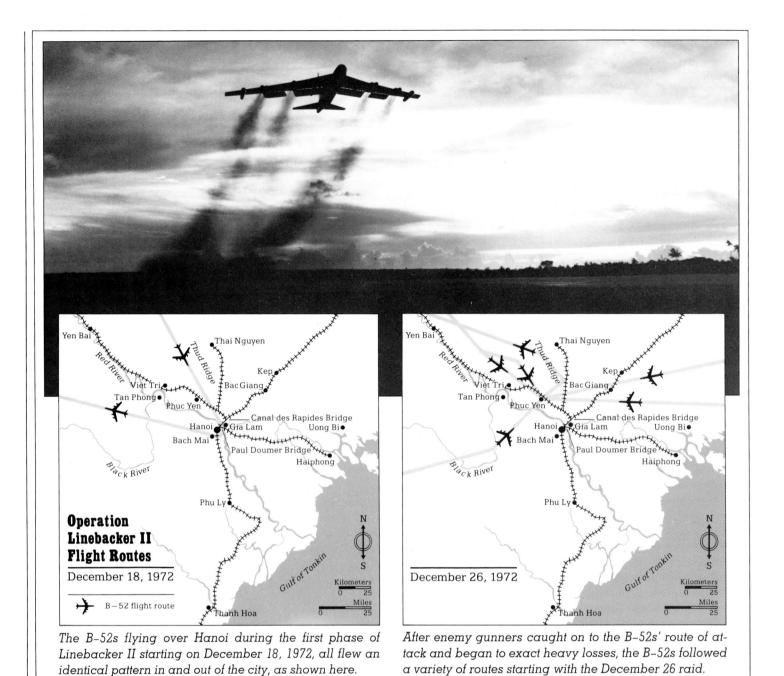

The B–52s flying over Hanoi during the first phase of Linebacker II starting on December 18, 1972, all flew an identical pattern in and out of the city, as shown here.

After enemy gunners caught on to the B–52s' route of attack and began to exact heavy losses, the B–52s followed a variety of routes starting with the December 26 raid.

had worked feverishly to shore up their battered air defenses. In the Hanoi complex itself, which had not been hit in five days, SAM sites were repositioned and restocked with missiles.

Colonel James R. McCarthy, commander of the 43d Strategic Wing, who flew in one of the eighteen bombers targeted for the Hanoi railroad yards and POL storage area, began counting the SAMs that darted toward the strike force as they turned on their final bombing run. "After 26 SAMs I stopped counting," he said. "At bombs away, it looked like we were right in the middle of a fireworks factory that was in the process of blowing up. The radio was completely saturated with SAM calls and MiG warnings. ... It was apparent that the North Vietnamese had loaded up plenty of missiles and were using them."

As McCarthy's cell turned for home, one of the SAM

missiles scored a direct hit on a B–52 bomber behind it. The plane disintegrated in an explosion that "lit up the whole sky for miles around," according to McCarthy. "The radios went silent. Everyone was listening for the emergency beepers that are automatically activated when a parachute opens. We could make out two, or possibly three, different beepers going off." Now all McCarthy and the other wave leaders could do was wait until the rest of the Stratofortresses completed their runs and the cell leaders reported in.

The new tactics helped protect the B–52s but could not make them immune to the enemy missiles. The incessant barrages of North Vietnamese SAMs brought down two of the bombers—Ebony 2, which McCarthy had seen go down, and Ash 1, which had been hit over Hanoi and crashed while trying to make an emergency landing at U–

Tapao, Thailand. Two more sustained minor damage. The B-52s had unleashed more than 4,000 tons of bombs on their ten targets, leaving heaps of smoking rubble, all within the span of just fifteen minutes.

The following night, sixty B-52s hit six more targets around Hanoi. Again they were met by a continuous stream of SAMs, and two more B-52s went down. But this was the last gasp for Hanoi's defenses. The North Vietnamese had virtually exhausted their limited supply of SAMs, and there were no replacements since the mining of Haiphong had cut them off from their Soviet suppliers. During the last two strikes, on December 28 and 29, the B-52s faced only a few missiles, most of which flew erratically and detonated harmlessly, away from the planes.

On December 30, President Nixon announced that the North Vietnamese had agreed to return to the negotiating table, so Linebacker II came to an end. During the eleven-day campaign, SAC B-52s flew a total of 729 sorties in which they unleashed more than 15,000 tons of ordnance on thirty-four targets in the heavily defended Red River Delta region. Bomb damage assessment photos from reconnaissance aircraft revealed how immense the destructive power of the Stratofortresses had been. By U.S. count, nearly 1,600 military structures were damaged or destroyed, along with 372 pieces of rolling stock. An estimated 80 percent of the country's electrical power production capacity had been wiped out, as well as more than a quarter of its POL stores. Airfields, roads, and rail lines were rendered unusable by the continual strikes.

Hanoi's defenses, while deadly at their peak effectiveness, had proven unable to maintain the high level of pressure necessary to stop the bombers. None of the B-52s were lost to MiGs, and only one was slightly damaged by AA fire. All fifteen B-52 losses resulted from SAM missiles, but the ratio of kills to missiles fired revealed that the SAMs' effectiveness was far lower than expected. Estimates of the number of SAMs actually fired ranged from 884 to as many as 1,242. Even taking the more conservative figure, the North Vietnamese were capable of only a 1.7 percent kill rate, almost half their 3 percent kill ratio when defending against strikes by large numbers of fighter-bombers. SAC commanders pointed to the statistics as proof that the B-52 could successfully penetrate a hostile air defense environment and hit large targets with devastating effect and accuracy. But the low loss rate would not have been possible without the support of air force, navy, and marine tactical forces, which provided chaff and ECM, Wild Weasel, and fighter-escort protection to the B-52s.

The view from Hanoi

The Christmas bombings, as Linebacker II came to be known, constituted both the largest and the most controversial air campaign of the entire war. The first major

escalation of the war on the part of the U.S. since the invasion of Cambodia in 1970, it was widely condemned at home and abroad. The criticism was fueled by Hanoi's charges of indiscriminate bombing of civilians which were backed by eyewitness reports from foreign diplomats and reporters. The most damning evidence presented by the North Vietnamese was the bombed-out rubble of a large section of the hospital at Bach Mai in the southern suburbs of Hanoi. Among those who were taken to view the scene was an Indian diplomat who reported that the hospital had been "razed to the ground."

At first, Pentagon officials denied that U.S. planes were bombing civilian areas or that the hospital had been hit, claiming that such damage was probably the result of stray SAMs and badly fused antiaircraft shells, which often landed in inhabited areas. Later, they conceded that there would inevitably have been "collateral" damage in heavily populated areas near military targets. The hospital at Bach Mai was a case in point. It was located on the edge of a North Vietnamese airfield and air defense command center, and a major POL storage facility was only 200 yards away. Reconnaissance photos later showed that the bombs that had landed on the hospital were from a single B-52 which had released its load, intended for the airfield, prematurely. The photos also confirmed that one wing of the sprawling medical complex was actually hit, not the entire complex as Hanoi claimed.

Although most targets in highly populated areas were reserved for strikes by more precise F-111s or F-4s carrying highly accurate laser-guided bombs, B-52s were employed against a few of the more strategic installations on the outskirts of Hanoi, and inevitably some of the bombs went astray. It was estimated that in up to 90 percent of all B-52 missions, one or more bombs would land outside the designated target box because of damaged or bent tail fins. Occasional navigational errors and radar and bomb-release-mechanism malfunctions also impaired the bombs' accuracy.

While there is no question that American bombs resulted in civilian deaths, accusations by Hanoi and numerous antiwar groups that the U.S. was engaged in terror bombing were unfounded. Telford Taylor, an American jurist who was in North Vietnam during the bombings, saw no evidence to persuade him that American bombers were deliberately attacking civilian targets in Hanoi. A prosecutor at the Nuremberg war crimes trials after World War II and a critic of the Vietnam War, Taylor remarked: "Despite the enormous weight of bombs that were dropped, I rapidly became convinced that we were making no effort to destroy Hanoi. The city remained largely intact and it seemed quite apparent that if there were an effort to destroy Hanoi it could have been done very readily in two or three nights."

Still, the image persisted in the U.S. where American media reports tended to equate the massive B-52 raids

The Hospital at Bach Mai

American planners and pilots exercised extreme caution to avoid hitting civilians during the Christmas 1972 bombings. Even at that, they could not avoid killing innocent citizens and destroying non-military targets. The razing of part of the Bach Mai hospital was the most publicized case in point. A B–52 aiming for Bach Mai airfield (right) missed its target by 1,000 meters and dropped several bombs on one wing of the hospital. The resultant destruction, including twenty-eight deaths, became a symbol for those who claimed that Linebacker II had been a terror bombing.

Right. *Bombs hit the airfield at Bach Mai, three kilometers south of the center of Hanoi.* Below. *On January 9, 1973, the hospital holds a funeral for the victims of the B–52 bombs. The poster at left blames President Nixon for the deaths.*

158

A crew works to clear rubble that once was part of the Bach Mai hospital.

with the saturation bombing raids launched against Germany and Japan during World War II. The B-52, the largest bomber in the world, was widely known for its heavy ordnance load (twenty tons or more) and its carpet-bombing delivery pattern that could obliterate an area a half-mile wide by a mile long. In light of this perception, and the admission by U.S. officials that the B-52s were being used over the heavily populated areas of Hanoi and Haiphong, some newspapers argued, as did the *Washington Post*, that the administration's insistence that the U.S. was only bombing "military targets" was a "cruel deception." "Even if the 'targets' were strictly military," the *New York Times* noted in an editorial on December 22, "a great deal more than military would inevitably be caught up in such sweeping devastation."

Indeed, in terms of the total number of bombs dropped, Linebacker II could be compared to some of the heaviest and most destructive bombing raids in World War II. During the eleven-day campaign, more than 20,000 tons of bombs fell on North Vietnamese territory. But despite the magnitude of the effort, the level of civilian casualties was surprisingly low. According to official North Vietnamese sources, 1,318 civilians were killed in Hanoi as a result of the bombing, and another 306 in Haiphong. By comparison, the nine-day bombing campaign against Hamburg in 1944, during which Allied bombers expended less than 10,000 tons of ordnance, caused more than 30,000 civilian deaths. A two-day raid on Dresden in 1945 with a smaller number of incendiary bombs left nearly 200,000 civilian dead.

Although the targets were military in nature, there was no question that President Nixon intended the bombings to have psychological shock value. He wanted to illustrate vividly to Hanoi's leaders the lengths to which he was willing to go if they did not agree to a negotiated settlement of the war. He also wanted to demonstrate America's toughness to President Thieu, who had objected to the initial cease-fire agreement ironed out the previous fall, accusing Kissinger of negotiating a "separate peace" with Hanoi behind his back. At the same time, Nixon did not speak publicly about the political objectives of the bombing. "Silence," commented Kissinger, "enabled him to avoid giving our actions the character of an ultimatum and thus permit Hanoi to return to the conference table without loss of face."

When the North Vietnamese did return to the bargaining table, they claimed a victory over the American bombers. According to Ha Van Lau, who later became North Vietnam's ambassador to the United Nations, "it was a decisive victory—an aerial equivalent to Dien Bien Phu—which obliged Nixon to sign the accords." Even after the cease-fire agreement was signed, Nixon and Kissinger remained evasive about the cause-and-effect relationship of the bombings and negotiations. When asked to comment on the question at a press conference on January 24,

Kissinger noted: "I will say that there was a deadlock in the middle of December and there was rapid movement when the negotiations resumed on January 8. These facts have to be analyzed by each person for himself." There were some Americans who had very definite views on the subject—the 591 prisoners of war, nearly 90 percent of them airmen, who were then still in North Vietnamese prisons and could now look forward to returning to the United States.

From the moment they heard the unmistakable sounds of the B-52 bombers overhead, the POWs finally began to believe the war would soon be over. Colonel Robinson Risner, who had spent more than seven years in North Vietnamese prison camps, later recalled the surge of hope

that spread among the prisoners of war when they heard the bombs exploding. "We knew that they were B-52s and that President Nixon was keeping his word," Risner said. "We saw a reaction in the Vietnamese that we had never seen under the attacks from fighters. They at last knew that we had some weapons they had not felt, and that President Nixon was willing to use those weapons to get us out."

Another long-timer, Colonel Jon A. Reynolds, said he could see the difference the bombings made in the guards' faces. "There was no joking, no laughing, no acts of defiance or reprisal," he remembered. "They simply headed for their shelters—individual manholes—and pulled concrete lids over their heads. For the first time, the United States meant business. We knew it, the guards knew it, and it seems clear that the leaders of North Vietnam knew it. Some, perhaps most, will suggest that the negotiations did not result from the B-52 strikes," said Reynolds. "From my vantage point, however, the reason the North Vietnamese negotiated was obvious."

The remains of a B-52 Stratofortress downed during Operation Linebacker II litter turf near the Hanoi Botanical Garden. The North Vietnamese downed fifteen B-52s during the Christmas bombings in 1972.

POWs

The treatment of American prisoners by their North Vietnamese captors remained a mystery to the outside world throughout the war. Since there was no declaration of war, Hanoi maintained the prisoners were not entitled to the rights accorded to POWs by the Geneva Convention. Only at the war's end did the world learn of their harrowing experience. For the 591 American POWs still alive, 472 of them airmen, the cease-fire agreement signed on January 27, 1973, meant freedom from squalid conditions in cramped cells and torture. The glimpses of prison life shown here were conditioned by the Communist captors, who determined who could photograph and what they could depict.

Left. American prisoners in 1967 are escorted across the compound at an improvised prison in Hanoi nicknamed "The Plantation." Below. Air force Colonel Robinson Risner (left) and navy Captain James Stockdale in their cell at the "Hanoi Hilton" in February 1973, just before their release. Captured in September 1965, the pilots led the POWs' organized resistance.

The Americans were held in several different prison camps in North Vietnam. The most widely known was Hao Lo, the main prison in downtown Hanoi which the POWs called the "Hanoi Hilton." The nicknames of other camps, the "Zoo," "Alcatraz," and the "Rockpile," more accurately attested to the stark living conditions of the POWs. Most prisoners spent years in the same tiny cell, sometimes with a second prisoner, with little more than a concrete slab for a bed and a bucket for a toilet. While they were occasionally allowed out of their cells to exercise or use the common showers, the high points of a POW's day were the meager twice-a-day meals that usually consisted of watery soup and a slice of bread or a bowl of rice.

At the Hanoi Hilton. Right. On February 10, 1973, POWs receive fresh clothing. In the upper left, the hand of a prisoner grips the cell bars. Below. A basketball game involves (left to right) Norman Daniels, Jerry Coffee (behind Daniels), Dave Corey, Gary Anderson, Bill Robinson, Tom Browning, and Dean Woods. A few days after photographers left, guards took away the prisoners' basketball and sneakers. Inset. In 1971, for the first time, instead of being isolated singly or in pairs, prisoners were placed together in large cell blocks like this one.

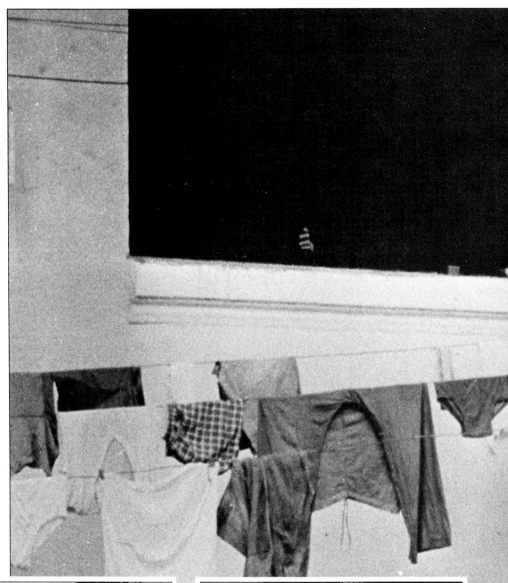

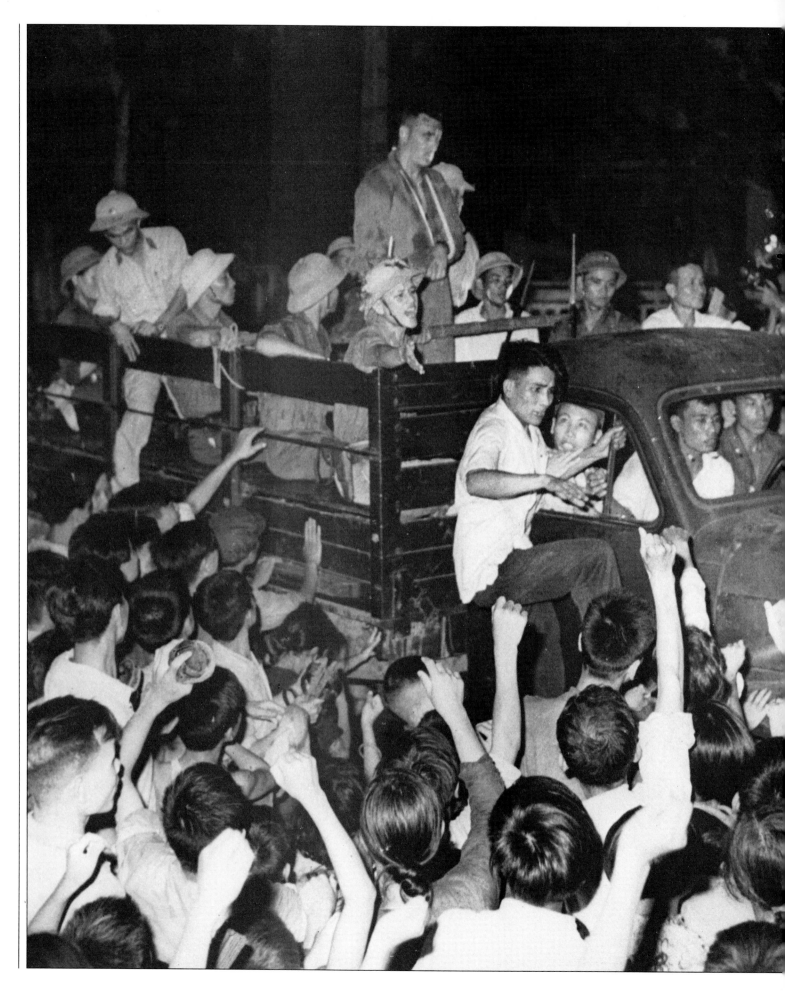

Throughout the war, the North Vietnamese attempted to use the POWs for propaganda purposes. Captured pilots were paraded before angry citizens, who were goaded into a partriotic frenzy by party officials to strengthen support for the war effort at home. Hanoi staged photos of the prisoners intended to show the "humane" treatment they received and invited U.S. antiwar activists and foreign journalists sympathetic to the North's cause to meet with the POWs. Many prisoners signed statements and taped broadcasts condemning the war and confessing to their "crimes" against the North Vietnamese people. But what the world did not know until later was that these "confessions" were the result of dehumanizing psychological mind games and brutal torture sessions intended to "break" the POWs.

Left. *Captain Neal Murphy Jones, an air force F-105 pilot shot down on June 29, 1966, is paraded through the streets of downtown Hanoi.* Above. *Christmas services for POWs in Hanoi, December 1970.* Right. *The docile appearance of Lieutenant Commander Richard Stratton in this photo released by Hanoi in 1967, which was accompanied by a "confession" of his "crimes," led many Americans to believe that the North Vietnamese were using mental or physical pressure on the POWs.*

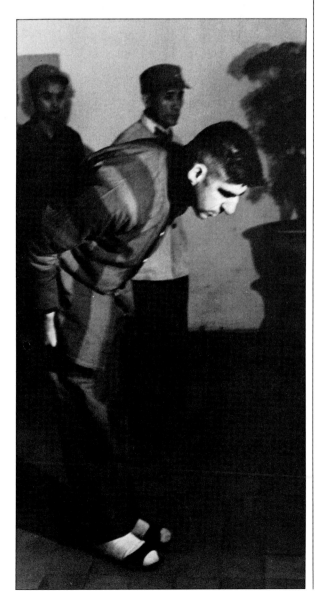

These drawings by John McGrath, who spent six years in Hao Lo prison, convey the grim details of the POWs' treatment. Adhering strictly to the military code, some refused to divulge anything more than their name, rank, and serial number until their jailers' punishments broke them. Others' strategy was to give in to trivial requests and questions. But demands for answers with military and propagandistic value were met with made-up responses, the POW holding out as long as he could resist the pain. Whatever the price, POWs would rally behind each other, reaching to the man being tortured with shouted words of encouragement.

Above. *Torture methods forcing a man to bend cause extreme pain in the back and legs and leave no telltale scars.*

Right. *Men at Hao Lo prison in summer 1969 reported beatings by rubber hoses and straps. One man received 100 strokes daily for nine days, which nearly killed him. Another was tortured to death after an escape attempt.*

Below. *Dreaded manacles of two flat steel bands. The tight-fitting bands would cut into the prisoner's wrists if he relaxed enough to let his elbows separate.*

168

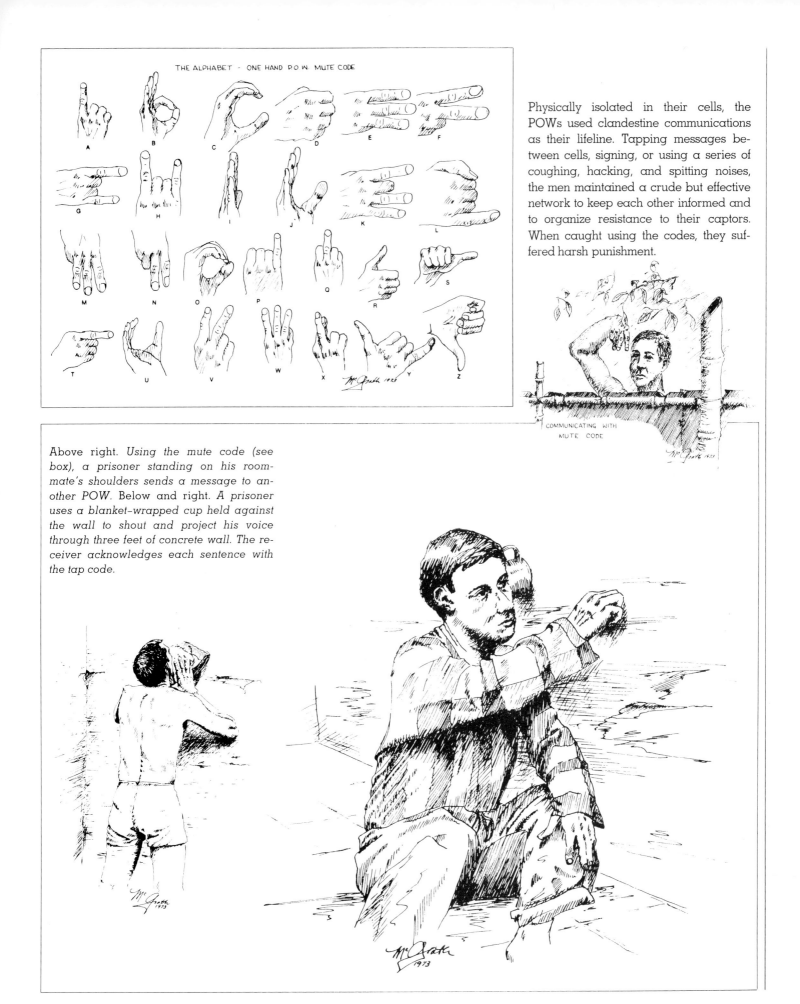

THE ALPHABET - ONE HAND P.O.W. MUTE CODE

Physically isolated in their cells, the POWs used clandestine communications as their lifeline. Tapping messages between cells, signing, or using a series of coughing, hacking, and spitting noises, the men maintained a crude but effective network to keep each other informed and to organize resistance to their captors. When caught using the codes, they suffered harsh punishment.

COMMUNICATING WITH MUTE CODE

Above right. *Using the mute code (see box), a prisoner standing on his roommate's shoulders sends a message to another POW. Below and right. A prisoner uses a blanket-wrapped cup held against the wall to shout and project his voice through three feet of concrete wall. The receiver acknowledges each sentence with the tap code.*

The Legacy of Air Power

By March 28, 1973, 591 American POWs at last were home. The only U.S. military personnel officially on duty in Vietnam were fifty advisers attached to the newly created Defense Attaché's Office in Saigon—a mere remnant of the nearly 3 million Americans who had traveled 10,000 miles from their homeland to fight or otherwise serve in that small beleaguered country. What now passed for U.S. military headquarters was at Nakhon Phanom Air Base in Thailand, where the U.S. Support Activities Group/7th Air Force directed continuing combat operations in Laos and Cambodia that still involved American airmen.

Although U.S. bombing operations in Laos had slackened during the Easter offensive, American B-52s and F-111s had been instrumental in beating back a major Pathet Lao offensive in November. The air force again shifted its attention to Laos after the cease-fire, flying nearly 1,850 combat sorties during the first two months of 1973. Although negotiations resulted in a tenuous cease-

fire on February 21, American bombers continued to mount sporadic strikes at the request of the Laotian government in response to Communist truce violations until mid–April.

In Cambodia the war ground on with no end in sight. North Vietnamese and Khmer Rouge forces drew an ever-tighter ring around the capital of Phnom Penh. Between January 27 and the end of April, U.S. B–52s, F–111s, A–7s, and AC–130s flew more than 12,000 bombing sorties and dropped 82,000 tons of bombs in support of Lon Nol's beleaguered forces. This sharp escalation of bombing in Cambodia stirred renewed Congressional criticism. In July, President Nixon reluctantly signed a bill that set August 15 as the cutoff date for all funds "to finance, directly or indirectly, combat activities by U.S. military forces in or over or from off the shores of South Vietnam, Laos or Cambodia." That morning, Captain Lonnie O. Ratley landed his A–7 at his base in Thailand after flying what many considered to be the last U.S. bombing mission of the war.

The final act

While Congress prohibited any further American combat operations in Southeast Asia, the 7th Air Force continued to maintain a strong presence in Thailand. The Strategic Air Command's B–52s remained on ready alert, and tactical fighter-bombers conducted training exercises known as Commando Scrimmage as a pointed reminder to Hanoi of Nixon's warning that any violation of the cease-fire agreement would bring a "strong reaction." Washington hoped that, by maintaining a credible threat of resumed bombing in the event of a large-scale invasion, it could keep the conflict limited to a level within the capabilities of the South Vietnamese military.

For the first year and a half, the strategy appeared to be working as both sides concentrated on consolidating the areas under their control. The Communists tried to isolate and capture remote ARVN outposts. Saigon relied heavily on air power to protect them and keep the enemy off balance. On paper, the Vietnamese Air Force appeared to be more than equal to the task. In January 1973, the South Vietnamese possessed the fourth largest air force in the world with 2,075 aircraft of twenty-five different types and 61,147 officers and men. But according to General William Momyer, "only the most optimistic thought it likely that [the] VNAF could manage such a force in the next few years."

The VNAF's limited maintenance and logistics system was unable to keep all these aircraft in flying condition,

and at least 224 aircraft had to be placed in storage. This relieved some of the strain and allowed the VNAF to maintain a 70 percent operational readiness rate for its fighters. But transport maintenance suffered as a result. Only nine out of a total of thirty-two C–130s were in flyable condition on any given day. This severely limited South Vietnam's ability to airlift forces and supplies to critical areas and far-flung outposts.

There were growing shortages of spare parts, fuel, and munitions, the latter partly due to the VNAF's tendency to expend vast amounts of ammunition against minimal targets. Stocks took weeks to be delivered due to inadequate accounting procedures and to frequent delays and slip-ups in processing orders and shipping the supplies from warehouses to air units in the field.

Communist air defenses also were taking their toll. The enemy moved large numbers of radar-directed AAA and SA–7 units into the area immediately below the DMZ and along the western border regions. Five SA–2 battalions deployed around Khe Sanh provided SAM coverage in Military Region I as far south as Quang Tri. Lacking ECM equipment to counteract these radar-guided weapons, the relatively low-performance VNAF planes suffered heavy losses when they tried to operate in highly defended areas. In less than two years of the cease-fire, nearly 300 fixed-wing aircraft were lost along with nearly 200 helicopters, almost a fifth of South Vietnam's inventory.

Saigon looked to Washington to replace these aircraft, as well as its dwindling stocks of spare parts, aviation fuel, and ammunition. This was allowed by the cease-fire agreements, but no replacements came. Instead, Congress sought to reduce American aid commitments to South Vietnam. Late in July 1974, Congress imposed a ceiling of $1 billion on U.S. military aid to Saigon during the next year. A few days later, the House trimmed the figure even further, to $700,000.

On August 9, President Nixon was forced to resign as a result of the Watergate affair. This left in doubt the credibility of Nixon's personal pledge to President Nguyen Van Thieu that the United States would undertake "swift and severe retaliation" against the North if it violated the cease-fire accords.

Although the continued presence of air force B–52s and fighter-bombers at bases in Thailand kept alive the hope that American planes would return in the event of an all-out offensive, the South Vietnamese sensed the worst and began preparing for it. In light of U.S. aid cutbacks, Saigon's strategy of holding on at its border outposts was no longer possible. Early that fall, ARVN began pulling back to more defensible positions in the central highlands to conserve remaining planes and ammunition. The VNAF cut in half the maximum number of flying hours for combat aircraft, and planes now carried only two bombs instead of four. Requests for air support came under increased scrutiny as ARVN commanders were pressured to stop requesting air strikes against ill-defined targets such as "suspected" enemy troop locations. Combat missions in the heavily defended areas north of Hue and west of Highway 1 became severely restricted. FACs and recon aircraft were withheld from these high-threat areas, or flew at 20,000 feet, an altitude that reduced their effectiveness. By employing their air assets in a defensive role rather than trying to carry the war behind the enemy's lines to hit his base camps and disrupt his supply lines, the South Vietnamese relinquished their air superiority and left the Communists with a secure sanctuary in which to stage, prepare, and launch attacks.

While the cuts in American aid demoralized and weakened Saigon's forces, the North Vietnamese were constantly growing in strength. The Ho Chi Minh Trail, now immune to attack, became a virtual superhighway for moving large quantities of supplies and troops into position along the South Vietnamese border. Convoys of 300 or more trucks were photographed by American reconnaissance planes, which continued to fly over Laos until mid-1974.

By December, Hanoi's leaders sensed that the balance of strength had fundamentally changed in their favor. They began planning a major offensive for the spring of 1975, with General Giap's protégé, army Chief of Staff General Van Tieng Dung, in command. The only unanswered question was how the U.S. would react. Many of Hanoi's leaders were convinced that the U.S. withdrawal and Nixon's resignation had turned America inward. Others were more cautious. If Washington chose to intervene on Saigon's behalf with U.S. air power it could be a replay of the failed 1972 Easter offensive all over again.

Dung launched a limited thrust across the Cambodian border at the end of the year to test ARVN and gauge the American response. The results surpassed Hanoi's most optimistic expectations. By mid-January, the North Vietnamese controlled the entire province of Phuoc Long. The loss of an entire province so close to Saigon—the first to be captured by the Communists since the 1972 invasion—was a major military and psychological setback for the South Vietnamese. Even more ominous was Washington's mild reaction, a verbal protest and nothing more. The limited response confirmed Hanoi's assessment of America's unwillingness to reinvolve itself in Vietnam. Preparations for the final push went into high gear.

Late in February, the North Vietnamese air force began sending its aircraft farther south, and for the first time it began regular helicopter supply runs across the border into Quang Tri Province. By early March, thirteen NVA divisions, supported by tanks and heavy artillery, were poised to strike, and another seven were in reserve. The first blow fell on March 9, when the North Vietnamese attacked Ban Me Thuot in the central highlands. The VNAF 6th Air Division flew more than 200 sorties in support of ARVN troops holding the town. But it was not enough.

While the U.S. pumped huge amounts of military equipment into South Vietnam, American pilots in Vietnam made training their VNAF counterparts top priority. Here, on November 20, 1972, a U.S. Marine Corps pilot (with pistol) checks out his A-7 Corsair II in the presence of two fledgling South Vietnamese pilots.

Other army corps commanders, who continued to exercise de facto control of the air units in their corps areas, refused to release their planes during the critical stages of the battle. Ban Me Thuot fell five days later.

The setback triggered a wholesale reorganization of South Vietnam's defenses. Thieu decided to abandon Kontum and Pleiku in the central highlands and establish what he considered to be more defensible positions farther south and east. He also withdrew units from Military Region I to shore up the defense around Saigon itself. This forced the regional commander to withdraw from his positions around Quang Tri and Hue and to fall back on Da Nang. Poor communications between field commanders and the failure to plan for adequate air cover turned the orderly withdrawal into a disorganized rout.

Neither the commander of the VNAF nor any of his field commanders was involved in the consultations. The commander of the 6th Air Division at Pleiku had only forty-eight hours' notice to evacuate his aircraft and personnel from the city. There was barely any close air support during the withdrawal because VNAF airmen became involved in evacuation operations and in arranging for their families to reach safety. In the confusion, 100 planes were abandoned to the advancing North Vietnamese.

The scene was repeated in Military Region I as ARVN troops began withdrawing from the cities of Quang Tri and Hue. Instead of sending his aircraft to slow the progress of the advancing North Vietnamese, the ARVN commander ordered his air units to conserve their planes for a stand at Da Nang. Lacking sufficient air support, the retreating troops panicked. Columns of dazed soldiers and refugees poured into the city with Communist troops close on their heels. On March 28, the North Vietnamese began shelling the Da Nang airfield. With the runway under heavy attack and the growing breakdown in command, it was now impossible to defend the city. The 1st Air Division was ordered to withdraw. VNAF security forces were unable to contain ARVN soldiers who tried to force their way aboard the planes. Another 180 aircraft and large stocks of supplies were abandoned in the hasty and disorganized evacuation.

The day that Da Nang fell, U.S. Army Chief of Staff General Frederick Weyand arrived in Saigon to determine if there were any options open to the U.S. to help reverse the declining situation. Many, including U.S. Ambassador Graham Martin and Major General Homer D. Smith, who headed the Defense Attaché's Office, clung to the belief that with a rapid and massive infusion of military aid the South Vietnamese could hold out. Others were less optimistic. Colonel William Le Gro, chief intelligence officer for the U.S. Defense Attaché's Office in Saigon, told Weyand: "Defeat is all but certain within 90 days." Only "U.S. strategic airpower" could help South Vietnam avert total defeat, and even that was "questionable," according to Le Gro. But neither alternative was likely. Congress remained unwilling to loosen its purse strings and Washington had ruled out any direct U.S. intervention. When, during a meeting with Weyand and Martin on April 3, Thieu inquired about using American B-52s to help defend Saigon he was informed it was out of the question.

Washington's decision not to come to their rescue with massive air power was a shattering blow to South Vietnamese morale. With their backs to the wall, South Vietnamese commanders lifted all restrictions on VNAF units, and they began hitting the enemy with everything they had. But the effort was too little and too late: Instead of striking at the enemy's supply lines in the rear, where North Vietnamese tanks and artillery pieces were lined up bumper-to-bumper along the highways, VNAF planes had their hands full hitting enemy troops threatening ARVN units in the immediate battlefield.

The South Vietnamese tried to regroup and hold the coastal cities, but they fell in rapid succession, leaving only isolated pockets of stiff resistance. When NVA forces captured the airfield at Nha Trang on April 1, two A-37 units based at Phu Cat and Phan Rang were all that was left of the VNAF's fighting force in Military Region II. They put up a spirited fight. At Phu Cat, VNAF security forces protected the airfield after ARVN pulled out, while pilots flew mission after mission against advancing enemy troops. They struck targets so close to the airfield that they barely had time to pull up their landing gear before they dropped their bombs. But by the fifteenth, both air bases had to be evacuated.

Since March 10, the VNAF had flown nearly 3,500 close air support sorties and expended more than 5,000 tons of ordnance. Although it was close to the level of effort the VNAF had managed during the 1972 Easter offensive, without additional U.S. support it was nowhere near enough. The VNAF's relatively slow A-37s and lightweight F-5s just could not stand up to the Communists' mobile air defenses. The VNAF's operational strength had been reduced by more than half due to combat losses, maintenance problems, and abandoned aircraft. Although it had always prided itself on being an elite fighting force, the VNAF became afflicted by the mood of defeatism that swept through the country. As resistance crumbled, pilots began deserting with their aircraft, flying themselves and their families to safety.

On April 8, a VNAF A-37 appeared over Saigon without warning and bombed the presidential palace. President Thieu, the obvious target of the attack, was unhurt. A VC radio broadcast claimed the pilot, Nguyen Thanh Trung, was a Communist agent. Others believed the attack was part of a coup effort by Nguyen Cao Ky and other VNAF officers to depose Thieu. Although Ky vehemently denied the charge, the incident heightened Thieu's distrust of the air force, which he knew was still extremely loyal to former Air Vice Marshal Ky. The bitter rivalry between the two men had long been considered a major reason for the VNAF's debilitating "second sister" status within the Vietnamese military.

While speculation raged over the actual reason for the attack on the presidential palace, its real significance was described by CIA analyst Frank Snepp: "For all the sophisticated weaponry and warning systems the Americans had installed around the city, the government had been unable to prevent one determined pilot from going for the jugular."

By midmonth, the Communists appeared to be on their way to a total victory throughout Southeast Asia. Across the border in Cambodia, Khmer Rouge forces had penetrated the defenses surrounding Phnom Penh. On April 12, U.S. Marine and Air Force helicopters evacuated all American personnel from the capital. Five days later, Communist troops occupied the city. It appeared to be only a matter of time before Saigon met a similar fate, as NVA troops continued their relentless drive toward the South Vietnamese capital.

The South Vietnamese dug in for a last-ditch stand at Xuan Loc, thirty-five miles northeast of Saigon. VNAF planes flew more than 600 sorties in support of ARVN troops defending the city. Even a few C-130s, loaded with 15,000-pound "Daisy Cutter" bombs and crude fire bombs fashioned out of fifty-five-gallon drums filled with gasoline and oil which crewmen rolled out the rear cargo doors, joined the fray. But the North Vietnamese outflanked the defensive line and closed within artillery range of Bien Hoa airfield. All operational aircraft had to be moved farther south to Tan Son Nhut and Binh Thuy. When Xuan Loc fell on April 22, the battle was all but over.

As the outcome became apparent, Washington set in motion its emergency evacuation plan, Operation Frequent Wind. On April 20, U.S. Air Force C-130s and C-141s began airlifting Americans and South Vietnamese refugees out of Tan Son Nhut airport. For the next eight days pandemonium reigned. As the North Vietnamese tightened the noose around Saigon, thousands of Vietnamese converged on the base demanding to be evacuated. Heavy fighting broke out on the outskirts of the capital. On the twenty-seventh the first rockets landed in downtown Saigon. The airlift was now seriously threatened as the Communists encircled the city with a net of antiaircraft weapons. Fred Fine, one of thirty-one Air America pilots ferrying evacuees from outlying areas into Tan Son Nhut by helicopter, noted in his diary that "there's a constant threat of SA-7 Strela missiles when flying and many new, unplotted AA positions. Reds now have a 57MM [AAA] Firecan radar position eight miles from the airport."

The airlift was temporarily halted on the twenty-eighth, after three A-37s that had been captured by the North Vietnamese and put into their service launched a midday bombing raid on Tan Son Nhut airfield. Six of the enemy's 250-pound bombs exploded on the flight line, damaging three AC-119s and several more C-47 transports. VNAF

F-5s scrambled to intercept them, but the raiders escaped unscathed. An American ex-serviceman employed by the CIA who was helping to coordinate the airlift recalled the irony of the event: "How many times in my two years as a combat officer in the delta had I called in air strikes against the VC! Now I knew what it was like to be on the receiving end and totally defenseless."

The next morning the North Vietnamese shelled the airfield, hitting a C-130 taxiing down the runway and killing two American marines who were helping supervise the evacuation. Once again the airlift ground to a halt. "Rockets were streaming all over the place," said an American at the airfield. "Vietnamese aircraft were taking off in droves." "We thought they were going to pound the Reds," said another Air America pilot, "but no such luck as they screamed out of the area bound for U-Tapao, Thailand." Others flew themselves and their families to the safety of U.S. carriers offshore.

A few die-hard VNAF pilots fought to the end. An AC-119 that had been patrolling the airfield perimeter all through the night landed to rearm and refuel and took off again just before daybreak. All eyes in the crowd of anxious civilians waiting to be evacuated were riveted on the lone gunship as it laid down a sheet of fire on North Vietnamese troops advancing on the eastern end of the airfield. But at 7 A.M. the gunship was hit by an SA-7 and plunged to the ground in flames. A few hours later an A-1 Skyraider met the same fate. Many believed that the appearance of SA-7s so close to the airfield spelled an end to further evacuation by air. "At that point," wrote Fred Fine, "we all figured that maybe we'd have to walk and swim out to the 7th Fleet."

With the airport under siege, by midafternoon Washington shifted to its plan to evacuate the remaining Americans and as many refugees as possible by helicopter. Navy and marine CH-46s and air force and marine HH-53s and CH-53s stationed on carriers offshore began shuttling evacuees from Tan Son Nhut or the U.S. Embassy compound to navy ships. They were escorted by air force and navy fighters and marine Cobra gunships by day and AC-130s at night. Though armed to the teeth, the escorts were under strict orders not to fire unless they received clearance from the C-130 airborne command post orbiting overhead or in "a dire tactical emergency involving threat of life to the helicopter crews and/or their passengers," recalled one A-7 pilot.

Throughout the missions, the choppers encountered heavy fire from both Communist and nervous ARVN gunners. The most serious threat came from several North Vietnamese SA-2 sites located on the outskirts of Bien Hoa just ten nautical miles northeast of the capital. Captain John Guilmartin, the senior officer in a detachment of two air force HH-53 rescue helicopters stationed aboard the U.S.S. *Midway*, recalled being scanned by no less than three SA-2 radars as his formation of three helicopters de-

During the frantic evacuation of Americans and of some South Vietnamese from Saigon on April 30, 1975, a UH-1 helicopter is ditched in the sea by its South Vietnamese pilot because there is no room for it on the U.S.S. Blue Ridge.

scended toward Tan Son Nhut. Both the choppers and their escorts were often forced to take evasive action as their onboard detection equipment warned them of impending missile launches.

Although the squalling signals coming over his headset from the SAMs' Fan Song tracking radars were so loud that Guilmartin was forced to turn his detection gear off, the missile sites never fired. But a radar-directed 57MM battery located just north of Tan Son Nhut opened fire on a flight of incoming marine choppers. An air force F-4 "Iron Hand" fighter locked onto the NVA site's radar signal and fired a Shrike antiradiation missile. The F-4's wingman followed up with a full load of CBUs, which knocked the 57MM battery out of commission. Except for sporadic covering firing by helicopter door gunners during the remainder of the evacuation, it was to be American air power's final parting shot of the war.

After a grueling around-the-clock effort by U.S. helicopters, Operation Frequent Wind, the largest evacuation by helicopter ever mounted, came to an end on April 30. Even the North Vietnamese were stunned by the scale and swiftness of the effort. In just eighteen hours, seventy-one helicopters had evacuated 1,373 Americans, 5,595 South Vietnamese, and 85 foreign nationals. Only one CH-46 was lost when it ran out of gas and crashed in the sea. All but two of the men aboard were rescued. When added to those airlifted out

Triumphant North Vietnamese take over the Tan Son Nhut airport outside Saigon.

aboard fixed-wing transports earlier in the month, U.S. aircraft had evacuated 57,507 people from South Vietnam. Air power had again exhibited its flexibility and quick-response capabilities, but in a lost cause.

Assessing the air war

From 1961 until 1972, U.S. fixed-wing aircraft flew an estimated 3.5 million combat sorties in Southeast Asia and expended more than 6.2 million tons of bombs, more than the combined total expended by Allied forces in World War II. For all this awesome display, in the final analysis American air power was unable to influence the outcome of a war against an enemy that was outclassed in almost every technically measurable way. The ultimate failure illustrated one of the inherent misconceptions of U.S. strategic thought in Vietnam—an almost blind faith in America's numerically and technologically superior military force, a faith that created an illusion of invincibility.

When America's involvement in Vietnam began on a very limited scale in the early sixties, the emphasis was on helping the South Vietnamese help themselves. But by 1965, these modest efforts had failed to achieve the desired results, and the Johnson administration decided to intervene with U.S. military forces.

Initially, American air power was committed to the battle to check the Vietcong advance in order to buy time for the arrival of U.S. combat troops and bolster sagging South Vietnamese morale. It accomplished these tasks and more. From 1965 to 1968, air power helped reverse the declining situation and turn the tide to the allies. The responsiveness of air power, together with its ability to concentrate and deliver firepower quickly, was instrumental in keeping the enemy off balance, denying him freedom of movement, preventing him from massing his forces for large attacks, and decimating his ranks when he did. U.S. transports and helicopters provided the allies with unprecedented mobility in reacting to enemy attacks, airlifting supplies and reinforcements to besieged outposts and troops in the field, and mounting search and destroy operations of their own.

When employed against enemy forces in contact with friendly troops, air power was extremely effective. According to General William Westmoreland, "never in all history has the U.S. Army received better air support than today at the hands of the 7th Air Force." While allied troops were secure in the knowledge that U.S. aircraft were ready to supply them with supporting firepower at a moment's notice, the enemy could not mount a significant ground operation without fearing an air strike. Once the Vietcong emerged from the safety of their hidden strongholds to mount an attack, they exposed themselves to a deadly array of aerial weaponry.

Air power particularly excelled when confronting North Vietnamese Main Force units. The best examples are the battles for Khe Sanh during the 1968 Tet offensive and Quang Tri and An Loc during the 1972 Easter offensive. In both cases the North Vietnamese used conventional tactics which allowed American bombers to attack highly concentrated targets with devastating results. But for the most part, the enemy fought differently, a low-intensity war in which small units blended into the population, a war of movement, marked by hit-and-run attacks by small, elusive guerrilla bands. There were no clearly defined fronts, few set battles, and no easily identifiable base camps or rear storage areas. Against this kind of guerrilla warfare, air power was far less effective.

Fewer than half of all bombing strikes in South Vietnam were in direct support of ground troops engaged with the enemy. Most strikes hit areas where reconnaissance and intelligence sources had confirmed or suspected the presence of enemy troops. When air power was employed in this fashion the results were extremely mixed. The one bright spot in this style of aerial counterinsurgency warfare was the work of airborne forward air controllers who scouted the countryside for signs of the enemy and directed fighter-bomber strikes against these targets. They were by far the best intelligence sources, providing immediate and definite targets.

On the other end of the scale were uncontrolled air strikes against targets generated by less reliable and timely means such as photo reconnaissance, interrogations of prisoners and deserters, and other intelligence sources. By the time the information passed through the chain of command and was translated into an actual order for an air strike, the guerrillas frequently had moved to other locations. There was a tendency to apply massive amounts of force against these targets to cover the widest area possible in the hopes of hitting something. B-52s, devastating when they had a concentrated target, were probably the least effective weapons when dealing with a guerrilla force.

The questionable benefits of this style of bombing, which measured success in terms of "killed by air" statistics that were of dubious accuracy, came at a high cost. The U.S. spent millions of dollars in munitions and logistical support to destroy VC camps that consisted of a few bamboo huts in the jungle. The lavish use of aerial firepower also proved to be counterproductive when used without a certain amount of caution. Since the guerrillas often blended in with the local population, the bombing sometimes killed innocent civilians or destroyed their homes and farms. Attempts to evacuate civilians from certain areas in order to create "free fire zones" generated large numbers of refugees who either became wards of the government or Communist sympathizers. Besides creating mistrust among the population and giving the enemy a huge propaganda windfall, the creation of free fire zones drew criticism both at home and abroad.

The ready availability of such a large and highly responsive aerial armada had other drawbacks as well. Ground troops came to rely heavily on air power to accomplish tasks they could have accomplished without it. The rationale was that America's overwhelming superiority in aerial firepower could achieve the results by expending ammunition rather than the lives of combat troops. Though air power did save lives in the short run, in the long run it upset the balance between ground operations and firepower. Bombing could achieve only transitory successes, which were meaningless unless exploited in conjunction with ground operations. This syndrome eventually became rooted in South Vietnamese military

strategy as well. ARVN forces came to rely on air power so much that when the U.S. planes left they expected the same level of support from their own air force, which was incapable of the task.

Bombing in a limited war

Washington policy makers at first hoped the mere presence of American aircraft in Vietnam would bring the Communists to the negotiating table. While the infusion of U.S. aircraft and combat troops did manage to deny the enemy a victory, as long as Hanoi continued to supply its forces in the South with men and materiel the Communists could continue their guerrilla war indefinitely. Civilian and military leaders eventually agreed that the only way to defeat the insurgency was to strike at its source in North Vietnam. But they were bitterly divided on how to go about convincing Hanoi to abandon its aggression in the South. These fundamental differences over U.S. bombing strategy against the North, which first arose in 1965 and are outlined in detail in the companion volume on the air war, *Thunder From Above*, would continue throughout the war.

The Joint Chiefs of Staff favored a strategic bombing campaign, arguing that the destruction of key military, industrial, and economic targets located in the Red River Delta region around Hanoi and Haiphong would cripple the war effort and bring North Vietnam to its knees. The civilian leadership rejected the idea as too extreme, fearing that a massive bombing blitz risked the possibility of Chinese or Soviet intervention which might escalate the war into an international crisis. Instead, President Johnson and his advisers developed a limited bombing campaign they hoped would contain the risks of escalation while persuading Hanoi to cease its support of the war.

From the outset, Operation Rolling Thunder was never considered to be a program of strategic bombing in the classic sense but rather a series of limited yet forceful signals coupled with diplomatic incentives to achieve a psychological and political effect. As its name suggests, it was to exhibit a "mounting crescendo" of force which would eventually bend Hanoi to accept U.S. terms. It was based on the proposition that by gradually applying additional increments of strength and threatening to go further the attacker could force a weaker adversary to the point where he would submit. It seemed a perfectly pragmatic strategy that would eventually bring a rational opponent to his senses with a limited application of force and a minimum of risk. But Hanoi's leaders were not the opponents Washington expected.

"What we didn't realize was that we were dealing with a regime in Hanoi that was bellicose beyond belief," according to a senior State Department official who served in both the Johnson and Nixon administrations. "We did not understand them to be the hard-headed sons of bitches that they turned out to be. [They were] ready to

Innocent victims, a mother and her children, wade across a river in Loc Thuong to escape bombing by American marines of a village believed to shelter Communist guerrillas, July 30, 1966.

take any amount of punishment, being fortified perhaps in the thought that we would cave in at home morally or politically. And if they held out long enough, that they could win out. And in that, of course, they were right."

Even though the Rolling Thunder campaign appeared unable to achieve either the political or the psychological objectives intended, the Johnson administration continued the bombing to make Hanoi pay a heavy price for its support of the war and limit the flow of men and materiel to the battlefield in South Vietnam. But after three years of dropping more than 850,000 tons of bombs on targets in North Vietnam at a cost of 929 aircraft lost and more than 700 airmen killed or missing or who died in captivity, Washington was no closer to realizing its objectives than before it started. It was one of the most ineffective applications of force in the history of warfare.

One of the major flaws of Rolling Thunder was its reliance on gradualism. Classic military doctrine emphasizes the importance of surprise and the concentrated application of force in any bombing campaign. The slowly rising level of the bombing, both in weight and geographic scope, handed the enemy numerous advantages

by default. It gave Hanoi time to condition its people and economy to the psychological shocks and hardships imposed by the destruction and to prepare adequate passive and active defensive measures to lessen the impact. Hanoi quickly dispersed its factories into the countryside where they would be less vulnerable to bombing. Stockpiles of vital war supplies were scattered in small caches throughout the country. The entire population was mobilized to keep the supply lines open to the South.

Gradualism also gave Hanoi time to study American strategy, tactics, and weaponry and to adjust and expand its air defenses accordingly. Within a few years North Vietnam developed a modern, sophisticated air defense system that not only inflicted a heavy toll on American planes and pilots but also forced the Americans to devote still more resources to protecting their bomber strike forces. Rapid technological advances in electronic countermeasures equipment and antiradar weaponry and aircraft, including F-105 Wild Weasels and their Shrike missiles, increased the survivability rate of American planes more than fivefold, but the price was high. The CIA estimated in 1966 that the cost of this air war to the United

States was ten times the economic and military damage it was inflicting in North Vietnam.

By forcing the enemy to divert additional manpower to maintain and defend the logistics network, the bombing did raise the cost of Hanoi's support of the war and severely strained its already impoverished economy. Agricultural and industrial production suffered, and the army lost the services of many able-bodied men diverted to transportation and labor units. But the bulk of the estimated 600,000-person labor force included large numbers of women and teen-agers who were not suitable for frontline combat duties. In the long run, the need to mobilize its population to combat the effects of the bombing was probably a boon to Hanoi. By rallying the people in a national crusade against the "Yankee air pirates," the party was able to strengthen its control over the population and create a unified home front.

The bombing also handed Hanoi a valuable propaganda edge. By maintaining that the war in the South was a purely internal conflict between a repressive regime in Saigon and a popular uprising led by the Vietcong, the

---

Some of the intensive air power that helped to contain the North Vietnamese Easter offensive of 1972 strikes enemy positions near An Loc in Military Region Three on May 20 while American advisers and 21st ARVN Division soldiers look on.

North Vietnamese portrayed the United States as the aggressor, exploiting the image of a mighty U.S. war machine ruthlessly unleashing its destructive power on a tiny, economically backward nation. The constant stream emanating from Hanoi of stories and photographs illustrating the devastation of American bombing brought international condemnation from neutrals and allies alike and nourished the antiwar movement at home.

One irony of this image was that American pilots were branded as wanton criminals, engaging in terror bombing and killing innocent women and children, when in fact they were operating under the strictest set of guidelines ever imposed in the history of aerial warfare. Every target, particularly during the Rolling Thunder campaign, was carefully scrutinized by the American president or a host of civilian advisers and analysts before it was authorized for attack. The most important criteria in the selection process were the estimates of possible civilian casualties. The military was rarely allowed to strike at targets located in or near heavily populated areas. The level of effort, types of ordnance, and even the tactics employed were often dictated by officials in Washington to lessen the chance of collateral damage to civilian homes and lives.

During his period as commander-in-chief, President Johnson, assured by the generals that America's modern and technologically advanced air force could bomb with

surgical precision, stressed that the bombing was directed solely against military targets. But in any bombing campaign, no matter how strict the guidelines, civilian casualties were inevitable. As long as accidental deaths and destruction occurred, Hanoi had ample grist for its propaganda effort. At the same time, by making it clear that American planes could not bomb in certain areas, Washington clearly indicated the limits to which it was willing to go, thereby encouraging the North Vietnamese to soldier on. The restraints also placed American pilots at a tactical disadvantage, which enhanced the effectiveness of enemy countermeasures.

American air forces were asked to do things they had not been trained or structured to do—carrying out an interdiction campaign against a target system of jungle trails, mountain passes, and thousands of small supply caches widely dispersed throughout the countryside. As the supplies scattered further into the maze of roads, mountain trails, and jungle paths, their vulnerability to bombing decreased geometrically.

The Joint Chiefs of Staff and air commanders in the field continually pressed for a more militarily effective strategy. Although they were remarkably vocal in their criticisms of the restraints and limitations placed upon the use of air power, when they failed to convince civilian policy makers to accept their way of thinking the generals tended to

lapse into the traditional "can do" attitude of professional soldiers. Only by convincing the politicians that air power could achieve the limited goals they had set could the military justify air power's effectiveness and continued use, which was in their own best interest.

The generals relied heavily on superior numbers and technology to achieve better results. All the advances in aircraft design, improved radar and navigational systems, and "black boxes" crammed with sophisticated electronic equipment provided pilots with a better edge. Advanced radar and computerized weapons systems, such as those aboard the A-6 Intruder and the F-111, enabled pilots to deliver their ordnance with pinpoint accuracy in darkness and all kinds of weather. Optically and laser-guided "smart bombs" would revolutionize air-to-ground ordnance delivery and tactics. Yet, the use of these multi-million-dollar, high-performance aircraft and expensive weapons to seek out and destroy individual trucks was extremely uneconomical.

The vast supporting structures and long-range planning necessary to maintain and employ such advanced aircraft and weapons systems created a bureaucratic monolith. Rather than admit that the aircraft and systems they had spent millions researching, developing, and producing might not be the most cost-effective means to achieve certain objectives, military leaders tried to make

the pieces fit. As civilian cost-effectiveness analysts monitored every move they made, for the officers the name of the game was "use 'em or lose 'em."

These bureaucratic impulses exacerbated the traditional rivalries between the service branches in competition for greater shares of the glory which inevitably translated into larger slices of the appropriations pie. Each tried to outshine the other in providing the glowing statistics civilian policy makers wanted to hear. According to a former commandant of the Marine Corps, David M. Shoup, "the Navy carrier people and the Air Force initiated a contest of comparative strikes, sorties, tonnages dropped, 'killed by air' claims, and target grabbing which continued up to the 1968 bombing pause. Much of the reporting on air action has consisted of misleading data or propaganda to serve Air Force and Navy purposes."

One of the most vivid examples of this numbers game mentality occurred in late 1965 and early 1966 when U.S. air units in Southeast Asia suffered a severe bomb shortage. Instead of sending up fewer aircraft with full bomb loads, air commanders felt compelled to launch the same number of planes, each carrying fewer bombs. "The truth

of the matter," air force Captain Ben Allen noted in his diary, "is that the 2d Air Division reports the number of sorties flown and not ordnance delivered. Therefore, to keep the Air Force looking as good as the Navy we must fly more sorties and report more damage. The biggest war out here must be between the Air Force wheels and the Navy wheels trying to justify their existence. This type of planning could cost us a lot of airplanes and pilots." Although losses due to this policy are impossible to calculate, the fact that it needlessly exposed pilots and planes to enemy defenses speaks badly for the numbers mentality among the brass at the Pentagon.

Interservice rivalries also complicated and fractionalized the command structure of the air war. "Vietnam was an organizational nightmare," according to air force General David C. Jones, who later became chairman of the JCS. "Each service ran its own air war." Unlike World War II or Korea, there was no unified command for control of air operations in Southeast Asia. Theoretically, the commander-in-chief, Pacific, ran air operations outside South Vietnam from his headquarters in Honolulu, while the in-country air effort was controlled by the MACV com-

President Lyndon Johnson's gradual escalation of the Rolling Thunder campaign allowed the North to emplace increasing numbers of AA guns, like these shown firing at U.S. aircraft near Hanoi in 1972.

mander through his deputy for air operations who was also commander of the 7th Air Force. In reality, the air wars in Laos, Cambodia, and North and South Vietnam were treated as separate entities, and within each the different services retained control of their own aircraft. This further fractionalized the command and control structure.

"Certainly, the command chain in Vietnam was the most fouled up thing in recent history," said former Secretary of the Air Force Harold Brown, "in part because the Joint Chiefs refused to face up to the issue of how you organize command in the field for most effective operations." This lack of organized command dramatized a flaw in the JCS system that was initiated when the U.S. armed forces were unified under a single department and secretary of defense after World War II. Comprised of the heads of all the service arms and a single chairman, the Joint Chiefs of Staff were made responsible for coordinating the various service arms for the secretary of defense. But integration of the forces gave the chairman little real authority, and the service chiefs, each responsible for training, equipping, and organizing his own branch of the service, remained constantly torn between the need to be advocates for their own services and the duty of wearing "joint hats" and putting interservice parochialism behind them.

Because America was divided and there was far from unified public support for a war that did not threaten directly the security of the U.S., there was little sense of urgency or pressure of national will, as there had been in World War II, to suppress the natural parochial interests of the services. As a result, during the Vietnam War the U.S. military often was its own worst enemy.

The limits of air power

The bombing halt in 1968 and the election of Richard Nixon turned American strategy in Vietnam into an effort to reduce America's commitment while trying to ensure South Vietnam's continued survival and seeking an honorable settlement of the war with Hanoi. The keys to success were to be Vietnamization and U.S. air power.

Between 1969 and 1972, American air efforts focused on aiding the South Vietnamese in securing the countryside and training its air force to take over the war. Air power was to substitute for departing ground troops and, at the same time, provide a shield against any external threats and cut off the Communists in the South from their sources of supply. Since North Vietnam was out-of-bounds except for sporadic bombing raids, America's interdiction campaign concentrated on Laos and Cambodia. But this escalated battle against the Ho Chi Minh Trail proved almost as fruitless as Rolling Thunder. The brief incursions into Cambodia and Laos by allied ground forces appeared to have achieved better results in disrupting Communist supply efforts than had years of bombing, but these were only short-lived and temporary successes.

In hindsight, some military men argue that the only effective way to have interdicted the Ho Chi Minh Trail would have been to introduce large numbers of ground troops in Laos. Others claim that a ground invasion of the North would have been the best way to strike at the roots of the problem. But because of a combination of military and political risks that U.S. national leaders perceived at the time, and in light of their strategic priorities and objectives, the task was given instead to air power.

While aerial interdiction operations in Cambodia and Laos proved that even with the advantages of superior numbers and technology bombing could not stop a determined enemy, air power did again confirm its value as a defensive weapon. U.S. aircraft almost single-handedly kept the pro-Western regimes in Laos and Cambodia from falling to the Communists. American close air support for loyalist forces in the field and bombing operations against enemy staging areas effectively neutralized Communist offensive operations. Still, in the long run vast expenditures in men, money, and planes did little more than maintain a stalemate.

Air power also proved to be the decisive element in turning back the 1972 North Vietnamese Easter offensive, chiefly because the Communists committed conventional military forces to battle. North Vietnam employed large infantry units equipped with tanks, heavy artillery, and trucks which were extremely vulnerable to bombing and heavily dependent on supply lines to provide the food, fuel, and ammunition needed to sustain such a large force.

Although it could not be considered a strategic bombing campaign in the strict sense, the renewed bombing of North Vietnam in Operation Linebacker I, in contrast to the earlier Rolling Thunder campaign, was a dramatic demonstration of the effective application of conventional air power. Unlike President Johnson, President Nixon ordered American bombers over the North to achieve maximum results with minimum restrictions. The sustained bombing of rail yards, highways, power plants, airfields, and military installations seriously degraded Hanoi's war-making capability, and the mining of Haiphong deprived the enemy of valuable external sources of supply.

Military men point to the success of Linebacker I to support their claims that politically imposed restrictions were the real reason for the failure of the Rolling Thunder campaign. They argue that if only the civilians had allowed them to launch the same kind of sustained and concentrated campaign earlier in the war, the outcome might have been different.

But the circumstances in 1965 and 1972 were not the same. Linebacker I was able to achieve its success because the North Vietnamese had decided to launch a major conventional offensive, which was far more vulnerable to conventional bombing than a guerrilla war of attrition.

The Linebacker II campaign offered air power advocates the chance to prove their arguments that unrestricted bombing could bend Hanoi to acquiesce to American terms for a political settlement of the war. It was the one truly strategic bombing campaign of the war, comparable in a way to the use of U.S. bombing during the latter stages of the Korean conflict. When the Communists stalled at the negotiating table in Korea after a tentative cease-fire agreement had been struck, U.S. fighter-bombers launched massive air strikes against North Korean military and economic targets. Heavy B-29 bombers were employed, just as B-52s were used against Hanoi in 1972. This bombing from the fall of 1952 to the summer of 1953 was considered to be a key factor in influencing the North Koreans and the Chinese to sign the Korean armistice.

There the parallel ends. The negotiated settlement achieved in Vietnam brought only temporary quiet, not lasting peace. If unrestricted strategic bombing did indeed renew the bargaining process in 1973, by then it was too late. The settlement gave an illusion of victory, but its terms reflected the disenchantment of the American people with the war and their unwillingness to continue. The withdrawal of all U.S. forces from South Vietnam and the decision not to retaliate with massive bombing when the North Vietnamese invaded in 1975 left the Saigon regime to face its fate alone.

Many in the military have since argued that if they had been allowed as early as 1965 to conduct a swift, strategic bombing offensive similar to the 1972 Linebacker campaign, the war would have been over in a few years, perhaps months. While such a campaign would probably have been far more effective in a military sense than the on-again, off-again pressures of Rolling Thunder, that it would have led to a lasting peace is extremely doubtful. Hanoi had much to lose by accepting America's hard-line negotiating terms and ending the fighting in 1965, but by 1972, Hanoi knew that all Washington wanted was the opportunity to withdraw gracefully.

Advocates of air power continue to maintain that the war was lost by the politicians who prevented them from achieving the military victory they believed they were capable of winning. "The experience was marked by great frustration," said General David Jones. "Frustration flowing from the lack of a clear definable objective and a means for measuring success in achieving that objective—frustration from stringent rules of engagement which tended to offset advantages in skill and technology."

While much of the blame for the ineffectiveness of air power could be laid on civilian policy makers, the Vietnam experience offered convincing evidence that it cannot alone win a war. While air power can be a decisive factor in achieving limited military and political results, it cannot compensate for a flawed strategy.

In an outdoor-museum-like setting in 1976, North Vietnam exhibits the remains of one of the American B-52 bombers shot down during the raids on the North.

184

Bibliography

I. Books and Articles

ABC News. "Vietnam Peace Accords—A Look Back." Transcript of a televised interview with Richard M. Nixon, January 27, 1983.
Allen, M-Sgt. Ken. "Cleared for Takeoff." *Airman*, August 1969.
Allman, T. D. "The Blind Bombers." *Far Eastern Economic Review* (January 29, 1972).
Anderson, William C. *BAT-21*. Bantam, 1983.

Berkowitz, Marc J. "The Christmas Bombing: A Case Study in National Security Policy Formation." Unpublished thesis, Georgetown University, December 6, 1983.
Bielinski, Maj. Henry E. "The F-4E—A Pilot's View." *Air Force*, November 1972.
Bland, Lt. Col. Ruskin M. "Special Express." *Air University Review* (July–August 1967).
Branfman, Fred. "Laos: No Place to Hide." *Bulletin of Concerned Asian Scholars* (Fall 1970).
————. *Voices from the Plain of Jars: Life Under an Air War*. Harper & Row, 1972.
————. "The Wild Blue Yonder Over Laos." *Washington Monthly*, July 1971.
Brown, David A. "U.S. Presses North Viet Air War." *Aviation Week & Space Technology*, July 3, 1972.
Brown, Harold. "Air Power in Limited War." *Air University Review* (May–June 1969).

Clark, Ramsey. "What I Saw and Heard in North Vietnam." *Life*, August 25, 1972.
Cohen, Capt. R. J. "Helicopters—Panacea or Pipedream?" *Army Quarterly* (July 1973).
Cole, Sgt. Dave. "Another Monday Morning." *Airman*, September 1972.
————. "The Connies of College Eye." *Airman*, March 1973.
————. "Time of the Tigers." *Airman*, October 1972.
————. "A Time to Teach and a Time to Learn." *Airman*, August 1972.

Davis, Larry. *Gunships*. Squadron/Signal Publications, 1982.
DeBerry, Capt. Drue L. "Vietnamese Air Force Technical Training, 1970–1971." *Air University Review* (January–February 1973).
Dommen, Arthur J. *Conflict in Laos*. Praeger, 1971.
————. "Laos: The Year of the Ho Chi Minh Trail." *Asian Survey* (February 1972).
Drendel, Lou. *Air War Over Southeast Asia. A Pictorial Record*. Vol. 2 (1967–1970); Vol. 3 (1971–1975). Squadron/Signal Publications, 1983, 1984.
Drenkowski, Dana. "Operation Linebacker II." *Soldier of Fortune*, Pt. 1, September 1977; Pt. 2, October 1977.
Drury, Richard S. *My Secret War*. Aero Publishers, 1979.
Dunn, Peter M. "F-111 Aardvark." In *Flying Combat Aircraft of the USAAF–USAF*, edited by Robin Higham and A. Siddall. Air Force Historical Foundation. Iowa State Univ. Pr., 1975.
DuPre, Flint. "Rescue at a Place Called Kham Duc." *Air Force*, March 1969.
Durham, Maj. Charles V. "I Heard It at Paris." *Airman*, April 1975.

Eade, Gen. George J. "Reflections on Airpower in Vietnam." *Air University Review* (November–December 1973).
Easterbrook, Gregg. "All Aboard Air Oblivion." *Washington Monthly*, September 1981.
Eschmann, Maj. Karl J. "Spirit and Surge." *Air Force*, July 1984.
Everett, Capt. Robert P. "Guardians of the Glidepaths." *Airman*, February 1969.
————. "Sweat and No Sweat." *Airman*, November 1969.
Ewing, Lee. "SEA Effort Goes On." *Air Force Times*, May 30, 1973.

Fellowes, Cmdr. Jack H. "Operation Homecoming." *U.S. Naval Institute Proceedings* (December 1976).
Francis, Capt. John, Jr. "F-111: A Pilot's View." *Air Force*, April 1971.
Frisbee, John L. "The Air War in Vietnam." *Air Force*, September 1972.
————. "Igloo White." *Air Force*, June 1971.
————. "Mission: Troops in Contact." *Air Force*, October 1972.
————. "VNAF Meets the Test." *Air Force*, June 1972.

Gervasi, Tom. *Arsenal of Democracy*. Grove Pr., 1977.
Ginsburgh, Maj. Gen. Robert N. "Strategy and Airpower: The Lessons of Southeast Asia." *Strategic Review* (Summer 1973).
Glister, Col. Herman L. "Air Interdiction in a Protracted War." *Air University Review* (May–June 1977).
————. "The Commando Hunt V Interdiction Campaign." *Air University Review* (January–February 1978).

Herring, George C. *America's Longest War*. John Wiley & Sons, 1979.
Hersh, Seymour M. "How We Ran the Secret Air War in Laos." *New York Times Magazine*, October 29, 1972.
————. *The Price of Power: Kissinger in the Nixon White House*. Summit Bks., 1983.
Hetz, Martin F. *The Prestige Press and the Christmas Bombing, 1972*. Ethics and Public Policy Center, Washington, D.C., 1980.
Hopkins, Charles K. "Linebacker II—A Firsthand View." *Aerospace Historian* (September 1976).

Hubbell, John G. *P.O.W.: A Definitive History of the American Prisoner-of-War Experience in Vietnam, 1964–1973*. Reader's Digest, 1976.

Karnow, Stanley. *Vietnam: A History*. Viking, 1983.
Kelly, M-Sgt. Dick. "Until the Eagle Soars." *Airman*, May 1971.
Kirk, Donald. *Wider War: The Struggle for Cambodia, Thailand, and Laos*. Praeger, 1971.
Kissinger, Henry. *White House Years*. Little, Brown, 1979.
————. *Years of Upheaval*. Little, Brown, 1982.
"The Legendary Ho Chi Minh Trail." *Vietnam Courier* 20, no. 5 (May 1974).

Littauer, Raphael, and Norman Uphoff, eds. *The Air War in Indochina*. Beacon Pr., 1972.

Maclear, Michael. *The Ten Thousand Day War*. Avon, 1981.
Malloy, Michael. "The Death Harvesters." *Far Eastern Economic Review* (January 29, 1972).
Manning, 1st Lt. Stephen O. "Something Big Coming!" *Airman*, September 1973.
McArdle, Maj. Frank H. "The KC-135 in Southeast Asia." *Air University Review* (January–February 1968).
Menaul, Air Vice Marshal S. W. B. (RAF). "The Use of Airpower in Vietnam." *Journal of the Royal United Services Institute* (June 1971).
Mersky, Peter B., and Norman Polmar. *The Naval Air War in Vietnam*. Nautical and Aviation Publishing, 1981.
Momyer, Gen. William W. "The Evolution of Fighter Tactics in SEA." *Air Force*, July 1972.
Mullane, Lt. Cmdr. Paul N. "The Smart and the Dumb." *Naval Aviation News*, January 1972.

Nalty, Bernard C., et al. *An Illustrated Guide to the Air War Over North Vietnam*. Arco, 1981.
Nihart, Brooke. "Army Reports Helicopter Success in Laos, Air Force Skeptical." *Air Force Journal*, April 5, 1971.
Nixon, Richard M. *RN: The Memoirs of Richard Nixon*. Grosset & Dunlap, 1978.

Osborne, Capt. Arthur M. "Air Defense for the Mining of Haiphong." *U.S. Naval Institute Proceedings* (September 1974).

Parks, W. Hays. "Rolling Thunder and the Law of War." *Air University Review* (January–February 1982).
Peterson, Iver. "The Bomber Pilots Like Their Work." *New York Times Magazine*, March 19, 1972.
Prouty, Fletcher. "The Secret Team." *Washington Monthly*, May 1970.

Redmond, Col. DeLyle G. "Aviator Support to a Counterinsurgency War." *U.S. Army Aviation Digest*, June 1972.
Reed, David. "Mission: Mine Haiphong Harbor!" *Reader's Digest*, February 1973.
Reynolds, Lt. Col. Jon A. "Linebacker II: The POW Perspective." *Air Force*, September 1979.
Robbins, Christopher. *Air America*. G. P. Putnam's Sons, 1979.
Rodman, Peter W. "Sideswipe: Kissinger, Shawcross and the Responsibility for Cambodia." *The American Spectator*, March 1981.
Robinson, Anthony, Antony Preston, and Ian V. Hogg. *Weapons of the Vietnam War*, Bison Bks., 1983.

Sams, Kenneth. "How the South Vietnamese Are Taking Over Their Own Air War." *Air Force*, April 1971.
Schemmer, Benjamin F. *The Raid*. Harper & Row, 1976.
Scutts, J. C. *F-105 Thunderchief*. Charles Scribner's Sons, 1981.
Shaplen, Robert. "Letter from Indochina." *New Yorker*, March 6, 1971; April 24, 1971.
————. "Our Involvement in Laos." *Foreign Affairs* (April 1970).
Sharp, Adm. U. S. Grant (Ret.). "Air Power Could Have Won in Vietnam." *Air Force*, September 1971.
Shawcross, William. *Sideshow: Kissinger, Nixon and the Destruction of Cambodia*. Simon & Schuster, 1979.
Smith, Melden E., Jr. "The Strategic Bombing Debate: World War II and Vietnam." *Journal of Contemporary History* (January 1977).
Snepp, Frank. *Decent Interval*. Random House, 1977.
Sturn, Ted R. "Flight Check to Glory." *Airman*, September 1969.
————. "Miracle Mission." *Airman*, August 1973.
Szulc, Tad. "Behind the Vietnam Cease-Fire Agreement." *Foreign Affairs* (Summer 1974).

Tillman, Barrett. *Mig Master: The Story of the F-8 Crusader*. Nautical and Aviation Publishing, 1980.
Thompson, Leroy. *Uniforms of the Indo-China and Vietnam Wars*. Blanford Pr., 1984.
"Tragedy of Linebacker II: The USAF Response." *Armed Forces Journal*, August 1977.
Tran Mai Nam. *The Narrow Strip of Land*. Foreign Languages Publishing House, 1969.

Ulsamer, Edgar. "Right from Hanoi's Own Backyard." *Air Force*, October 1972.
————. "TAC Air's Responsiveness." *Air Force*, December 1972.

Van Dyke, Jon M. *North Vietnam's Strategy for Survival*. Pacific Bks., 1972.
Van Vleet, Clarke. "Year of Action: 1972." *Naval Aviation News*, February 1973.
Vo Nguyen Giap. *People's War Against the U.S.: Aero-Naval War*. Foreign Languages Publishing House, 1975.

Volkman, Ernest. "Ex–Pilot Describes B–52 Mutiny." *Newsday*, June 27, 1977.

"Way Stations Over SEA." *Airman*, November 1969.
Weisberger, Lt. Joseph H. "Mig Killers All." *Naval Aviation News*, September 1972.
Wilson, L. I. "Thanks, Tank. . . ." *Aerospace Historian* (Summer 1976).
Wolff, Capt. Robert E. "Linebacker II: A Pilot's Perspective." *Air Force*, September 1979.

Yudkin, Maj. Gen. Richard A. "Vietnam: Policy, Strategy and Airpower." *Air Force*, February 1972.

II. Government and Military Publications

Air Power and Warfare. Proceedings of the 8th Military History Symposium, USAF Academy. Office of Air Force History, 1978.

Ballard, Jack L. *Development and Employment of Fixed–Wing Gunships, 1967–1972.* Office of Air Force History, 1982.
BDM Corporation. *A Study of Strategic Lessons Learned in Vietnam.* Vols. 1–8. National Technical Information Service, 1980.
Berger, Carl, ed. *The United States Air Force in Southeast Asia, 1961–1973.* Office of Air Force History, 1977.
Burbage, Maj. Paul, et al. *The Battle for the Skies Over North Vietnam, 1964–1972.* Vol. 1, Monograph 2, USAF Southeast Asia Monograph Series. Office of Air Force History, 1976.

Corum, Col. Delbert, et al. *The Tale of Two Bridges.* Vol. 1, Monograph 1, USAF Southeast Asia Monograph Series. Office of Air Force History, 1976.

Doglione, Col. John A., et al. *Airpower and the Spring Invasion.* Vol. 2, Monograph 3, USAF Southeast Asia Monograph Series. Office of Air Force History, 1976.

Fox, Roger P. *Air Base Defense in the Republic of Vietnam, 1961–1973.* Office of Air Force History, 1979.
Futrell, R. Frank, et al. *Aces and Aerial Victories.* Office of Air Force History, 1976.

Hopkins, Charles K. *SAC Tanker Operations in the Southeast Asia War.* Office of the Historian, Headquarters, Strategic Air Command, 1979.

Lane, Lt. Col. John J., Jr. *Command and Control and Communications Structures in Southeast Asia.* Airpower Research Institute, Air University, Air War College, Maxwell AFB, Alabama, 1981.
Langer, P. F. and J. J. Zasloff. *Revolution in Laos: The North Vietnamese and the Pathet Lao.* Rand Corporation, RM–5935–ARPA, September 1969.
Le Gro, Col. William E. *Vietnam From Cease–Fire to Capitulation.* U.S. Army Center of Military History, 1981.

McCarthy, Brig. Gen. James R., and Lt. Col. George B. Allison. *Linebacker II: A View From the Rock.* Vol. 6, Monograph 8, USAF Southeast Asia Monograph Series. Airpower Research Institute, Air War College, Maxwell AFB, Alabama, 1979.
Momyer, Gen. William W. (Ret.). *Airpower in Three Wars.* United States Air Force.
_____. *The Vietnamese Air Force, 1951–1975.* Vol. 3, Monograph 4, USAF Southeast Asia Monograph Series. Office of Air Force History, 1975.

Nguyen Duy Hinh, Maj. Gen. *Lam Son 719.* Indochina Monographs, U.S. Army Center of Military History, 1977.

Schneider, Maj. Donald K. *Air Force Heroes in Vietnam.* Vol. 7, Monograph 9, USAF Southeast Asia Monograph Series. Office of Air Force History, 1979.

Tilford, Earl H., Jr. *Search and Rescue in Southeast Asia, 1961–1975.* Office of Air Force History, 1980.
Tobin, Lt. Col. Thomas G. *Last Flight From Saigon.* Vol. 4, Monograph 6, USAF Southeast Asia Monograph Series, Office of Air Force History, 1978.
Tolson, Lt. Gen. John J. *Airmobility, 1961–1971.* Department of the Army, Vietnam Studies Series, 1973.
Tran Dinh Tho, Brig. Gen. *The Cambodian Incursion.* Indochina Monographs, U.S. Army Center of Military History, 1979.

U.S. Congress. House. Committee on Armed Services. *Full Committee Consideration of . . . House Resolution 1078 and House Resolution 1079 (Various Military Operations in North Vietnam).* 92d Congress, 2d sess., 1972.
_____. *Full Committee Hearing and Consideration of H. Res. 918, A Resolution of Inquiry Regarding the Bombing in Vietnam. . . .* 92d Congress, 2d sess., 1972.
_____. *Unauthorized Bombing of Military Targets in North Vietnam.* 92d Congress, 2d sess., 1972.
U.S. Congress. Senate. Committee on Armed Services. *Bombing in Cambodia.* 93d Congress, 1st sess., 1972.
_____. *Nomination of John D. Lavelle, Gen. Creighton W. Abrams, and Adm. John S. McCain.* 92d Congress, 2d sess., 1972.
U.S. Congress. Senate. Committee on Foreign Relations. *Cambodia: December 1970.* Staff Report. 91st Congress, 2d sess., 1970.
_____. *Laos: April 1971.* Staff Report. 92d Congress, 1st sess., 1971.
_____. *U.S. Air Operations in Cambodia: April 1973.* Staff Report. 93d Congress, 1st sess., 1973.
_____. *U.S. Security Agreements and Commitments Abroad. Kingdom of Laos.* 91st Congress, 1st sess., 1969.

U.S. Department of Commerce. Joint Publications Research Service. *Translations on North Vietnam, 1968–1973.*
U.S. Department of Defense. *United States–Vietnam Relations, 1945–1967 (Pentagon Papers).* 1971.

III. Unpublished Government and Military Sources
Airlift to Besieged Areas, 7 April–31 August 1972. Project CHECO Report, U.S. Air Force, HQ Pacific, Hickham AFB, Hawaii, December 7, 1973.
Allen, Capt. Ben H., Jr. (Ret.). Personal Diary, August–September 1965.
Alpsberger, Maj. E. J. *Unclassified Southeast Asia Glossary, 1961–1971.* Project CHECO Report, U.S. Air Force, HQ Pacific, Directorate of Operational Analysis, CHECO CORONA HARVEST Division, February 1, 1971.

The Battle for An Loc. Project CHECO Report, U.S. Air Force, HQ Pacific, Hickham AFB, Hawaii, January 31, 1973.

Center for Naval Analysis. *Documentation and Analysis of U.S. Marine Corps Activity in Southeast Asia, 1 April–31 July 1972.* Study 1016. 1973.

Kontum: The Battle for the Central Highlands. Project CHECO Report, U.S. Air Force, HQ Pacific, Hickham AFB, Hawaii, October 27, 1972.

Miller, Rear Adm. Henry L. Daily Diary, U.S.S. *Enterprise*, October 18, 1965–February 16, 1966.
Moody, Lt. Col. Ralph F., et al. "Backing Up the Troops." Pt. 7 of *U.S. Marines in Vietnam.* Historical Division, Headquarters, U.S. Marine Corps, April 10, 1970.
Moorer, Adm. Thomas H. "Procedures for the Conduct of Linebacker II Operations." Memo, CJCS to Secretary of Defense, December 26, 1972. Carrollton Pr.

National Security Study Memoranda–1.
The NVA 1972 Invasion of Military Region I: Fall of Quang Tri and Defense of Hue. Project CHECO Report, U.S. Air Force, HQ 7th Air Force, Saigon, January 22, 1973.

Tilford, Earl H., Jr., and William A. Buckingham, Jr., "The Limits of Superiority: Air Power in Vietnam." Unpublished paper, no date.

U.S. Department of Defense. Office of the Assistant Secretary of Defense (Systems Analysis). Southeast Asia Analysis Reports, 1968–1972.
U.S. Marine Corps. *A History of the First Marine Aircraft Wing, 1 November 1970–14 April 1971. Republic of Vietnam.* 1971.
_____. Fleet Marine Force, Pacific Command. Monthly Histories, 1968–1972.
_____. Fleet Marine Force, Pacific Command. *Operations of U.S. Marine Forces, Southeast Asia, 1 July 1971 thru 31 March 1973.*

Vogt, Gen. John W., Jr. "Implications of Modern Air Power in a Limited War." Office of PACAF History, HQ Hickham AFB, Hawaii, November 29, 1973.

Wheeler, Gen. Earle G. "Authority for B–52 Strikes Against Targets in Cambodia." CM–4003–69, Memo to the Secretary of Defense, March 13, 1969. Carrollton Pr.
_____. "Cambodia." JSCM–207–69, Memo to the Secretary of Defense, April 9, 1969. Carrollton Pr.

Youngblood, Lt. Col. Russell W. "Observations: Airpower Strategy in North Vietnam." U.S. Army War College, May 12, 1973.

IV. Newspapers and Periodicals
The author consulted the following newspapers and periodicals:

Bangkok Post, New York Times, Newsweek, Time, U.S. News & World Report, Wall Street Journal, Washington Post.

V. Archival Sources
U.S. Air Force, Albert Simpson Historical Research Center, Maxwell AFB, Alabama. Oral History Program:
Belli, Lt. Col. Robert E.—F–105 pilot, 6010th Wild Weasel Squadron, Korat AFB, Thailand, 1971–1972.
Brown, Col. Royal A.—JJ–53 pilot and commander, 37th Rescue Squadron, Da Nang, South Vietnam.
Costin, Maj. James L.—A–1 pilot, Special Operations Force, Nakhon Phanom AFB, Thailand, 1969–1970.
Erickson, Lt. Col. Robert A.—Advisory Team, Tan Son Nhut AFB, South Vietnam, 1970–1971.
Griffin, Maj. Richard L.—Forward air controller, 21st Tactical Air Support Squadron, Pleiku Province, South Vietnam, 1967–1969.
Hartman, Lt. Col. William B.—AC–130 fire control officer and navigator, 16th Special Operations Squadron, Ubon AFB, Thailand, 1971–1972.
Humphrey, M–Sgt. Arthur W.—AC–130 illuminator operator, 1972.
Kittinger, Col. Joseph W., Jr.—F–4 pilot and commander, 555th Tactical Fighter Squadron, Udorn AFB, Thailand, 1971–1972. (Former POW.)
King, Lt. Col. Loyd J.—AC–130 pilot, Ubon AFB, Thailand, 1971–1972.
Lanman, Maj. Ronald T.—Advisory Team, Tan Son Nhut AFB, South Vietnam, 1970–1971.
Manor, Brig. Gen. Leroy J.—Commander, Special Operations Force, Elgin AFB, Florida, 1970.
Opitz, Lt. Col. Stephen J.—AC–130 navigator, 1971–1972.
Ryan, Gen. John D.—Air Force Chief of Staff, 1969–1973.

Vogt, Gen. John W.—Commander, 7th Air Force, 1972–1973.
Webb, Lt. Col. William B.—Advisory Team, Tan Son Nhut AFB, South Vietnam, 1970–1971.

U.S. Air Force, Office of Air Force History, Bolling AFB, Washington, D.C.
U.S. Marine Corps, Headquarters, History and Museums Division, Washington, D.C.
U.S. Navy, Naval Historical Center, Washington, D.C.

VI. Interviews

Bates, Maj. Rick—Former F–4 weapons systems officer, 433d Tactical Fighter Squadron, 8th Tactical Fighter Wing, Ubon AFB, Thailand, 1972. (Former POW.)
Bricker, Maj. Steve—Former F–4 pilot, 421st Tactical Fighter Squadron, 3066th Tactical Fighter Wing, Da Nang AFB, South Vietnam, and Takhli AFB, Thailand, 1972.

Cooper, Vice Adm. Damon W. (Ret.)—Former commander of Task Force 77, 1972.
Connelly, Robert—Former flight commander, 432d Tactical Fighter Squadron, 13th Tactical Fighter Wing, Udorn AFB, Thailand, 1972.
Craw, Paul—Former commander, 4th Tactical Fighter Wing, Da Nang AFB, South Vietnam, 1972.
Curtin, Richard B.—Former U.S. Army UH–1 pilot and assistant operations officer, 118th Assault Helicopter Company, 145th Aviation Battalion, 1970.

Dunn, Maj. Peter M.—Former F–111 pilot, 374th Tactical Fighter Wing, Takhli AFB, Thailand. Intelligence staff, 7th Air Force, Saigon, South Vietnam, 1971–1972.

Guilmartin, Lt. Col. John F., Jr. (Ret.)—HH–53C pilot and chief of standardization/evaluation, 40th Aerospace Rescue and Recovery Squadron, Nakhon Phanom, 1975.

Hilton, Mark—Former U.S. Army OH–5A pilot, C Troop, 1st Squadron, 9th Regiment, 1st Cavalry Division (Airmobile), 1970–1971.

Kilgus, Col. Don—Former F–105G pilot, 6010th Wild Weasel Squadron, Takhli and Korat AFBs, Thailand, 1970, 1972.
Krisch, Al—Former F–111 pilot and assistant flight commander, 429th Tactical Fighter Squadron, 474th Tactical Fighter Wing, Takhli AFB, Thailand, 1972.

Mack, Vice Adm. William P.—Former commander of 7th Fleet, 1972.
McDonald, Adm. Wesley L.—Former commander, Air Wing 15, U.S.S. *Coral Sea*, 1965, and commander, Carrier Division Three, 1972.

Sheets, Capt. Roger (Ret.)—Former commander, Air Wing 15, U.S.S. *Coral Sea*, 1972.

Vogt, Gen. John W.—Former commander, 7th Air Force, 1972–1973.

Picture Credits

All illustrations by John Batchelor unless otherwise indicated.

Cover Photograph:
U.S. Air Force

Chapter One
p. 7, UPI/The Bettmann Archive. pp. 8–9, Co Rentmeester—LIFE Magazine, ©1965, Time Inc. pp. 12–13, 16, AP/Wide World. pp. 16–17, Dan McCoy—Black Star. pp. 18–19, AP/Wide World. p. 21, Bell Helicopter, courtesy Life Picture Service. p. 22, UPI/The Bettmann Archive. p. 23, U.S. Air Force.

Chapter Two
p. 25, Than Truong Hue—TIME Magazine. pp. 28–29, Loren Fessler—TIME Magazine. p. 30, Ken Regan—Camera Five. p. 31, Dick Swanson—LIFE Magazine, ©Time Inc. p. 32, AP/Wide World. pp. 34–35, 38, Ngo Vinh Long Collection. p. 39, U.S. Navy. p. 41, TOPHAM. pp. 44–45, UPI/The Bettmann Archive. pp. 48–49, Sergent—Gamma/Liaison.

U.S. in Laos
p. 50, top, Asia Resource Center Collection; bottom, Walt Haney Collection. pp. 50–51, U.S. Air Force. pp. 52–53, Earl Young. p. 53, top right, Earl Young; top left, John Guilmartin, Jr. pp. 54–55, Dick Swanson—LIFE Magazine, ©1970, Time Inc. pp. 55–57, Dick Swanson—LIFE Magazine, ©Time Inc.

Chapter Three
p. 59, U.S. Navy. p. 61, Charles Moore—LIFE Magazine, ©1965, Time Inc. pp. 62–63, ©1984 David Burnett/CONTACT. pp. 66–67, U.S. Air Force. p. 68, Howard Sochurek. pp. 70–71, U.S. Navy. p. 73, Rodney L. Dykhouse.

Search and Rescue
pp. 74–75, U.S. Air Force. p. 76, Howard Sochurek. p. 77, top, U.S. Air Force; bottom, Howard Sochurek. pp. 78–79, Howard Sochurek.

Chapter Four
p. 81, Mark Godfrey—LIFE Magazine, ©Time Inc. p. 83, UPI/The Bettmann Archive. p. 86, top, Ian Berry—Magnum; bottom, Mark Godfrey—Archive Pictures Inc. pp. 90–91, UPI/The Bettmann Archive. p. 92, Matt Franjola—Multimedia Agency, courtesy Black Star. pp. 95, 97, U.S. Air Force.

Chapter Five
p. 99, UPI/The Bettmann Archive. p. 101, U.S. Air Force. pp. 102–3, Ngo Vinh Long Collection. p. 105, U.S. Air Force. p. 106, UPI/The Bettmann Archive. pp. 108–9, David Terry—Black Star. pp. 110–11, Agence France-Presse. p. 112, UPI/The Bettmann Archive. p. 113, Bruno Barbey—Magnum. pp. 114–15, U.S. Army. p. 116, bottom, Bruno Barbey—Magnum. pp. 116–17, 117, right, ©1984 David Burnett/CONTACT. pp. 118–19, Rick Merron—Black Star.

An Evolution in Air Power
p. 124, Louis Kraar—TIME Magazine.

Chapter Six
p. 129, UPI/The Bettmann Archive. pp. 132–33, Ngo Vinh Long Collection. pp. 134–35, ©Mark and Matthew Waki. p. 137, top, UPI/The Bettmann Archive; bottom, Ngo Vinh Long Collection. p. 138, Ngo Vinh Long Collection. p. 139, AP/Wide World. p. 142, top, Ngo Vinh Long Collection. pp. 142–43, 143, top, Nihon Denpa News, Ltd. p. 145, U.S. Air Force.

Chapter Seven
p. 147, U.S. Air Force. p. 149, Gamma/Liaison. p. 151, top, Gamma/Liaison; bottom, U.S. Air Force. pp. 155–56, U.S. Air Force. p. 158, top, U.S. Air Force; bottom, UPI/The Bettmann Archive. pp. 159–61, Roger Pic—Gamma/Liaison.

POW
pp. 162–63, Zefa, courtesy Life Picture Service. p. 163, inset, Gamma/Liaison. pp. 164, right inset, Gamma/Liaison; left inset, Nihon Denpa News, Ltd. pp. 164–65, Gamma/Liaison. pp. 166–67, Camera Press Ltd. p. 167, top, Sovfoto/Eastfoto; bottom, Lee Lockwood—Black Star. pp. 168–69, illustrations by John M. McGrath, *POW*, ©1975, U.S. Naval Institute Press, Annapolis, MD.

Chapter Eight
p. 171, Dennis Brack—Black Star. pp. 173, 176, UPI/The Bettmann Archive. p. 177, Dieter Ludwig—Gamma/Liaison. p. 179–81, UPI/The Bettmann Archive. p. 182, Ngo Vinh Long Collection. pp. 184–85, Mourot—Gamma/Liaison.

Acknowledgements

Boston Publishing Company and the author would like to acknowledge the kind assistance of the following people: Dana Bell, National Air and Space Museum; Dr. William Hammond, U.S. Army Center of Military History, who read parts of the manuscript; Mrs. Judy Endicott, Chief of Circulation, Albert F. Simpson Historical Research Center, Maxwell AFB, Alabama; William Heimdahl and Capt. Sue Cober, Office of Air Force History; Kim Ketchell; Edward Marolda, Naval Historical Center; Patti Sheridan, Executive Secretary, and Frank Street, Secretary-At-Large, and the other officers and members of the Red River Valley Fighter Pilots' Association; Jack Shulimson and the archives staff, Marine Corps Historical Center; Major Earl H. Tilford, Associate Editor, *Air University Review*; and Anna Urband, U.S. Navy Media Services. The author would like to thank his wife, Megan, who assisted with interviews and proofread the manuscript. The author would also like to thank the following people who provided accounts of their experiences in Vietnam: Larry Kavouras; Tim Nash; Col. George W. Norwood, USAF; Bob Pardo; Brig. Gen. Ted Rees, USAF; Frosty Sheridan; Bob Wayne; and numerous veterans of the Vietnam War who wish to remain anonymous.

Index

U.S. Air Force Units

*The 7th Air Force, which superseded the 2d Air Division in early 1966, controlled all tactical aircraft based in South Vietnam and exercised operational control of all tactical air operations in Southeast Asia.

**The 7th/13th was a joint command established to control all tactical air units based in Thailand which were under the administrative control of the 13th Air Force and the operational control of the 7th Air Force.

Names, Acronyms, Terms

AA—antiaircraft.

AAA—antiaircraft artillery.

AFB—air force base.

AID—Agency for International Development. Responsible for administering American economic aid to many countries around the world, including South Vietnam.

Arc Light—code name for a B-52 combat mission in South Vietnam. First Arc Light mission took place in June 1965.

ARVN—Army of the Republic of Vietnam (South Vietnam).

Barrel Roll—code name for bombing missions in Laos beginning on December 14, 1964.

BDA—bomb damage assessment.

CBUs—cluster bomb units.

chaff—strips of metal foil or metalized Fiberglas used to mask incoming U.S. bombers from enemy radar.

CIA—Central Intelligence Agency.

CINCPAC—Commander-in-chief, Pacific. Commander of American forces in the Pacific region, which includes Southeast Asia.

Constant Guard—emergency deployment of aircraft from U.S. Air Force bases in response to North Vietnam's March 30, 1972, invasion across the DMZ into South Vietnam.

COSVN—Central office for South Vietnam. Communist party headquarters in South Vietnam, overseen by Hanoi.

DMZ—demilitarized zone. Area dividing North Vietnam from South Vietnam along seventeenth parallel.

Duck Hook—original code name for operation, conceived in July 1970, that included mining the major ports and harbors, including Haiphong, of North Vietnam. Executed in May 1972 under the code name Pocket Money.

ECM—electronic countermeasures. Equipment employed to identify and nullify enemy radar and radar-directed weapons systems.

EOGB—electro-optically guided bomb.

FAC—forward air controller. Pilot who controls strike aircraft engaged in close air support of ground troops or flying against other targets.

free fire zones—areas designated by the GVN to be completely under enemy control, thus permitting unlimited use of firepower against anyone in the zone.

Freedom Train—code name for spring 1972 limited bombing offensive against North Vietnamese supply lines and staging areas below the twentieth parallel. Begun in response to North Vietnam's March 30, 1972, invasion across the DMZ into South Vietnam.

Frequent Wind—code name for final U.S. evacuation from South Vietnam in April 1975.

FSB—fire support base.

Geneva accords—signed by the French and Vietminh on July 21, 1954, the Geneva accords marked the end of the French Indochina War. They established a provisional boundary at the seventeenth parallel between the Democratic Republic of Vietnam (DRV) and the new Republic of Vietnam.

IO—illuminator operator.

JCS—Joint Chiefs of Staff. Consists of the chairman, army chief of staff, chief of naval operations, air force chief of staff, and marine commandant. Created in 1949 to advise the president on military policy.

LGB—laser-guided bomb.

Linebacker I—code name for U.S. bombing of North Vietnam resumed under President Nixon in April 1972.

Linebacker II—code name for Christmas 1972 full-scale bombing of North Vietnam.

LORAN—long-range airborne navigation.

LZ—landing zone

MAC—Military Airlift Command. Responsible for maintaining a continuous strategic and tactical airlift of personnel and materiel from the U.S. to Southeast Asia and within the combat theater.

MACV—Military Assistance Command, Vietnam. U.S. command over all military activities in Vietnam.

Menu—collective code name for series (Breakfast, Lunch, Dinner, Snack, Supper, and Dessert) of covert bombings of Cambodia between March 1969 and May 1970.

MiG—Russian-built fighter aircraft developed by designers Mikoyan and Gurevich.

napalm—incendiary used in Vietnam by the French and the Americans as both a defoliant and antipersonnel weapon.

NSC—National Security Council.

NVA—North Vietnamese Army. Also called the People's Army of Vietnam (PAVN).

Pathet Lao—Laotian Communist guerillas who came to power in 1974 under the leadership of Prince Souphanouvang, the half-brother of Souvanna Phouma.

POL—petroleum, oil, and lubricants.

POW—prisoner of war.

Proud Deep—code name for 1,025 bombing sorties against North Vietnam for five days beginning December 26, 1971.

RLAF—Royal Laotian Air Force.

Rolling Thunder—code name for U.S. air campaign against North Vietnam conducted from March 2, 1965, to October 31, 1968.

Rules of engagement—issued from 1965 on to all Vietnam-bound soldiers, the rules of engagement dictated procedures for the control of air power and artillery in order to minimize civilian casualties.

SAC—Strategic Air Command. Branch of the USAF designed for sustained long-range air operations against vital target systems to destroy an enemy's ability or will to wage war.

SAM—surface-to-air missile.

"smart" bombs—laser-guided bombs (LGBs) and electro-optically guided bombs (EOGBs), as opposed to "dumb" (conventional) bombs.

sortie—a single aircraft flying a single mission.

Steel Tiger—code name for campaign of aerial interdiction of Communist infiltration routes in southern panhandle of Laos, begun April 3, 1965.

TACAIR—Tactical Air Command. Branch of the USAF designed for air operations in conjunction with ground forces against enemy combatants.

TFS—Tactical Fighter Squadron.

TFW—Tactical Fighter Wing.

Tiger Hound—Code name used to designate that portion of Operation Steel Tiger separated by CINCPAC from air force control and placed under control of MACV in 1965.

USAF—United States Air Force.

Vietcong—common reference to the National Liberation Front, a contraction of Vietnam Cong San (Vietnamese Communist).

Vietnamization—term given to President Nixon's phased withdrawal of U.S. troops and transfer of their responsibilities to South Vietnamese.

Vietminh—coalition founded by Ho Chi Minh in May 1941 and ruled by the DRV. Absorbed by the Lao Dong party in 1951.

VNAF—Vietnamese Air Force.